THROUGH THE LOOKING GLASS

*Women and Borderline
Personality Disorder*

Dana Becker

D0222040

Westview Press
A Member of the Perseus Books Group

New Directions in Theory and Psychology

Copyright © 1997 by **Westview Press, A Member of the Perseus Books Group**

Published in 1997 in the United States of America by Westview Press, 5500 Central Avenue, Boulder, Colorado, 80301-2877, and in the United Kingdom by Westview Press, 12 Hid's Copse Road, Cumnor Hill, Oxford OX2 9JJ

Library of Congress Cataloging-in-Publication Data
Becker, Dana.
    Through the looking glass: women and borderline personality
disorder / Dana Becker.
        p.   cm—(New directions in theory and psychology)
    Includes bibliographical references and index.
    ISBN 0-8133-3309-1.—ISBN 0-8133-3310-5 (pbk.)
    1. Borderline personality disorder.   2. Women—Mental health—
Sociological aspects.   3. Women—Socialization.   4. Sex role—
Psychological aspects.   I. Title.   II. Series.
RC569.5.B67B43   1997
616.85′852′0082—dc21   97-8091
                                                                            CIP

The paper used in this publication meets the requirements of the American National Standard for Permanence of Paper for Printed Library Materials Z39.48-1984.

10   9   8   7   6   5   4   3   2

Through the Looking Glass

New Directions in Theory and Psychology

Series Editors
Rachel T. Hare-Mustin and Jeanne Marecek

Focusing on emerging theory in psychology and related fields, this scholarly/trade series examines contemporary ideas broadly associated with postmodernism, social constructionism, feminist theory, and other critical reformulations of psychology. We seek manuscripts that propose or exemplify new ways of doing psychology, that reconsider foundational assumptions of psychological inquiry and practice, and that offer new approaches to therapy theory and practice. Among the topics considered are the social construction of such categories of difference/hierarchy as gender, race and ethnicity, class, and sexuality; and the politics of knowledge. Of interest as well are works that examine ways in which psychology—as a body of knowledge and a cultural institution—replicates or challenges arrangements of power and privilege in society.

Rachel T. Hare-Mustin, Villanova University, and **Jeanne Marecek,** Swarthmore College, coauthored *Making a Difference: Psychology and the Construction of Gender.*

Books in This Series

*Through the Looking Glass: Women and Borderline
Personality Disorder,* Dana Becker

Men's Ways of Being, edited by Christopher McLean,
Maggie Carey, and Cheryl White

Sex Is Not a Natural Act and Other Essays, Leonore Tiefer

FORTHCOMING

*Latina Realities: Essays on Healing, Migration,
and Sexuality,* Oliva M. Espín

To my mother and father,
Betty and Marvin Becker

Contents

Acknowledgments

This book would not exist were it not for the belief, handed down to me by my parents, that what one chooses for work must be something one cares deeply about. Conversations over many years with my father, Marvin Becker, have been encouraging and enlightening. He is a scholar whose methods of disciplined study, whose intellectual fearlessness, and whose passion for ideas have always inspired me.

I have become a better thinker about women's problems because I have worked hard to understand my own journey, and because my clients have permitted me to understand theirs. My clients, supervisees, and students continue to be instrumental in my learning.

Many others have contributed to this project in ways direct and indirect. Sharon Lamb is a mentor and friend who has encouraged, cajoled, and advised me at every turn, and who has provided important criticism of the manuscript. The interest that Rachel Hare-Mustin has shown in my work has been a source of great satisfaction, given my tremendous admiration for her. Jeanne Marecek gave valuable time to go over the entire manuscript with me, and her suggestions were right on the mark. These are just a few of the feminist thinkers whose work has influenced me profoundly.

I have been lucky to have had wonderful mentor-friends who have helped me to learn to take myself and my ideas seriously. Sally Russo, as a person, a therapist, and a teacher, has had an enormous impact on my way of feeling and thinking. Rose Schneiderman has always been helpful, interested, and interesting; so has John Steidl.

Howard Liddle has helped me become both a better therapist and a more careful thinker about the process of therapy. The agility of his mind, his confidence in me, and his generosity in providing me with fascinating work over the past five years are greatly appreciated. I have also learned much from my colleagues at the Center for Research on Adolescent Drug Abuse at Temple University.

I would like to acknowledge these institutions for their contributions: the Bryn Mawr College Graduate School of Social Work and Social Research, for teaching me how to look at context; the Philadelphia Child Guidance Clinic, where I began to think like a family therapist; the Institute of Pennsylvania Hospital, where I first started to think about "borderline" psychopathology and met the young women whose problems puzzled me; and the Women's Therapy Center, whose therapists have a deep commitment to working well with women.

When I began work on my doctorate in the Department of Human Development (now called Psychology) at Bryn Mawr, I did not realize that developmental theory would provide such an important basis for my thinking about women's distress. I am grateful to Robert Wozniak and my other professors for their rigorous teaching of developmental principles. As a single parent and a full-time psychotherapist, I could not have completed my doctorate part-time without the financial support of the college and the department.

Several people have occupied unique positions in my life day to day and year to year. Lee Kunkel has been a great friend and a constant source of humor and wisdom. My grandmother, Florence Becker, was, until her death, a much loved friend. The understanding and friendship of my sister, Wendy Cranfield, has been precious to me.

First in my life is my husband, Stan Tischler, who means everything to me and who has given unstinting love, nurturance, and uncritical encouragement. He has helped to create the happiest context for the writing of this book, as have Oliver, Nicholas, and Jesse.

Dana Becker

Prologue: "Borderline" Women Among the Mentally Ill

The *DSM-IV* (1994) describes the borderline personality disorder thus: "A pervasive pattern of instability of interpersonal relationships, self-image, and affects, and marked impulsivity beginning by early adulthood and present in a variety of contexts, as indicated by five (or more) of the following (p. 654):

1. frantic efforts to avoid real or imagined abandonment. Note: Do not include suicidal or self-mutilating behavior covered in Criterion 5.
2. a pattern of unstable and intense interpersonal relationships characterized by alternating between extremes of idealization and devaluation
3. identity disturbance: markedly and persistently unstable self-image or sense of self
4. impulsivity in at least two areas that are potentially self-damaging (e.g., spending, sex, substance abuse, reckless driving, binge eating). Note: Do not include suicidal or self-mutilating behavior covered in Criterion 5.
5. recurrent suicidal behavior, gestures, or threats, or self-mutilating behavior
6. affective instability due to a marked reactivity of mood (e.g., intense episodic dysphoria, irritability, or anxiety usually lasting a few hours and only rarely more than a few days)
7. chronic feelings of emptiness
8. inappropriate intense anger or difficulty controlling anger (e.g., frequent displays of temper, constant anger, recurrent physical fights)

9. transient, stress-related paranoid ideation or severe dissociative
   symptoms

Women who receive a diagnosis of borderline personality disorder find themselves "at the border" in several ways. First, they display behaviors that society deems inexplicably mad, and they frequently do so in a way that puts them at variance with the feminine stereotype—that is, on the border between so-called masculine and feminine behavior. In this way, they teeter precipitously on the edge of social acceptability. Some of them have repeated experiences of feeling they are crossing the border between sanity and insanity; some find themselves regularly on the verge of self-destruction.

Many of these so-called borderline women alternate living in the world outside and the world inside the psychiatric hospital. Inside the hospital they are, on the one hand, welcome patients because they often require a good deal of expensive treatment; on the other hand, however, they are often feared, disliked, and/or derogated by those who treat them. They are at once needed and unwanted. Their lives seem full of paradox. They desperately want to form intimate attachments, and at the same time they often cannot sustain them. Although they themselves feel powerless and unentitled to love and care, those around them—family and professionals alike—frequently perceive their behavior as controlling, manipulative, and entitled.

Borderline personality disorder (BPD) is certainly among the most theoretically complex and clinically challenging of the personality disorders. It has been researched, written about, debated, and fretted over a good deal within the past two and a half decades or so. When I first came to learn of it during an introductory class in psychopathology, I was fascinated by it. A good deal of this fascination sprang from the seeming difficulty I and my classmates had in understanding the theories that purported to explain it. As we waded through Kernberg's theories and thumbed through the then-current *DSM-III* (1980), we had difficulty imagining who this creature could be whose moods seemed to shift in the blink of an eye, who might in one moment idealize the therapist and, in the next, turn upon him/her in an unholy rage. That classroom discussion of the borderline disorder, I now understand, contained the seeds of many of the confusions with which we are grappling today.

To begin with, we students were led from an explanation of "borderline" in the historical sense as the true border between neurosis and psychosis straight into discussions of *borderline personality organization* and then on to the *DSM-III*'s criteria set for the diagnosis of borderline personality disorder.

We believed we were the only ones who were confused; we were unaware that we had been exposed to confusions that still permeate the field regarding what we are talking about when we use the term *borderline*. We would not have dared to consider that these thickets into which we ventured were adumbrated by problems that, at the time, had not been resolved even by those theorists who were seeking to make clear the etiology of the disorder. The more theoretically sticky the explanations, the more in awe I remained and the more I read and puzzled. From where we sat, my classmates and I could only feel confirmed that the mothering that individuals received during the first year or two of life, as many of us had been told, had enormous power to predict later development. After all, we had only to see how damaged these individuals called borderline were in relating to others and in functioning in the world to know what bad mothering could do. The borderline patient seemed even more frightening than the schizophrenics whom we had been studying just weeks before. What would I do if I needed to treat such a person? In class, as we attempted to get our instructor to give us a more concrete description of this unusual creature, I looked forward to having my anxieties quelled and my cognitive uncertainties vanquished. All the professor could muster, however, was a statement that the borderline client was hard to describe, but that if he/she were sitting in one of our offices, we would instantly *know*. I was not soothed. Thus began a many-year-long quest to master the challenges of understanding the borderline disorder.

In my first agency job, a colleague—like me, new to the profession—came to me and described a client who, embroiled in one crisis after another, was alternately skipping appointments, denigrating my friend, and calling to say that my friend was the only human standing between her and suicidal disaster. My friend felt panicky; how was she to deal with the situation? Might her graceless attempts to deal with her client result in her client's suicide? I had no advice to offer her. Instead, I replied, "She probably has borderline personality disorder"—as if it were some sort of virus—and went on to describe some of the criteria for diagnosis. My friend looked at me with an expression of undeserved gratitude as I went on to shave slivers of bone from the skeletons of the several theoretical explanations with which I was familiar. By the end of our talk, my colleague looked less worshipful and distinctly more confused. I felt sorely the limitations of my own understanding, and we parted with a mutual admission of our appalling ignorance.

Not too many years after this encounter, I found myself, a newly hired staff member, sitting in a morning conference on a unit of a private psychiatric hospital. I heard the nurses referring to a group of what appeared to be rather intractable patients as "cutters." The nurses were struggling to help one another deal with this difficult group. Thus began my enculturation into the ongoing treatment dialectic between the psychiatric hospital and the borderline inpatient. "They" did not respond well to limits, I was told. It seemed that "they" were manipulative. Some of the nurses, concerned with building a relationship, it appeared, spent a good deal of time with these patients; others were more content to talk bitterly about the patients' seemingly bizarre and manipulative behavior in the nursing station. The fact that most of the borderline patients were women did not seem noteworthy at the time.

Many of the "borderlines" in the hospital were being treated by psychiatrists who were either psychoanalysts or psychoanalytically oriented in their treatment approaches. The individual psychoanalytic psychotherapy practiced by the psychiatrists and the more behavioral approach required on the unit seemed to be strange bedfellows. In some cases, a reasonable treatment plan was made possible by the inclusion of the treating psychiatrist in team meetings with involved staff. I am not suggesting that treatment was never helpful or that many of the borderline patients were not difficult to treat, especially for hardworking staff members who had to consider the overall atmosphere of the unit and look out for the interests of the other patients. I *am* suggesting that my being a participant-observer who had a prior interest in the borderline diagnosis and continued exposure to the inpatient experience of the "borderlines" as well as knowledge of their personal, family, and treatment histories, fueled questions that I had not heard others asking or answering. Why were most of the borderline patients women? Was some of the limit-setting thought necessary by staff, in fact, essential? Why did some staff members have stronger countertransference reactions to these patients than others?

It is my impression that although empirical research on borderline personality disorder, using actual patients or case records for the collection of data, employs some rigor in ensuring that those studied fulfill criteria for the borderline diagnosis,[1] many practitioners are looser in their use of *borderline* as a descriptive term and, probably, looser in their adherence to strict diagnostic accuracy. In an outpatient or private practice setting, a woman who is angry or at all demanding or difficult for the therapist to treat may bring upon herself a borderline diagnosis. In saying that the client may bring the diagnosis upon herself I do not mean that she purposefully seeks such a diagnosis (and certainly would not if she were aware of what it implies), but that women who are "difficult" can unfortunately bring blame to themselves from some clinicians who are unable or unwilling to charge themselves with learning how better to treat them. There is no other diagnosis currently in use that has the intense pejorative connotations that have been attached to the borderline personality disorder diagnosis.

Recent research demonstrating connections between borderline personality disorder (BPD) and childhood sexual abuse has begun to illuminate the connection between gender and the borderline diagnosis. However, it would appear that for some theorists the establishment of this important relationship has been sufficient to explain the overwhelmingly greater application of the diagnosis to women than to men, given the fact of the higher incidence of sexual abuse histories among women. Nonetheless, there are a considerable number of borderline clients who do not have abuse histories. If BPD cannot be specifically linked only to sexual abuse, then we must develop a broader framework for understanding how women come to be the majority of those diagnosed "borderline." There has been much impressive work that has helped us to conceptualize how a sexually abused woman could develop features of borderline personality disorder, but there has been less work aimed specifically at addressing the "woman question" in the borderline diagnosis. How does the fact of the preponderance of women in this diagnostic category relate to the vagueness of the diagnostic criteria? How does it relate to the tailoring of the criteria to fit women? Why do more women than men display so-called borderline symptoms? Many books written about treatment of BPD do not, despite using women primarily as case examples, discuss gender in relation to the borderline diagnosis.[2]

Scull (1989) raises an issue critical to this inquiry when he questions how feminist theorists can assert that women are victims of a double standard of mental health that unfairly assigns to them the stigma of "psychiatric patient"—particularly when they defy male stereotypes for feminine behavior—and at the same time maintain that women are driven mad in disproportionate numbers by the stressful oppression imposed on them by a patriarchal society. He calls for more attention to "the crucial issue of the degree to which women's presence among the ranks of the mentally disturbed can be attributed to each of these processes" (p. 268). I hope, in this book, to present a balanced view of these processes.

Elaine Showalter (1985) predicted that "if 'depression' is soon viewed as a meaningless catchall category, another female malady will appear to take its place for another generation" (p. 249). I believe that BPD is fast becoming that female malady. This does not by any means imply that women who are diagnosed with BPD do not suffer acute distress; it does, however, suggest, that we need to broaden our understanding of how women are affected both by the diagnosis and by the disorder.

Mental Illness as Representation

If by personality we mean . . . "distinctive personal character" we are obliged to recognize that we can only conceive of such an entity in terms of contrasting it with other personal characters.

—Anthony Storr, *The Integrity of the Personality*

It is difficult to know "when society should be labeled as *unjust* and when the individual should be labeled as *crazy*" (Kaplan, 1983, p. 789). One certainly need not embrace without reservation, à la Thomas Szasz (1961), the view that mental illness is no more than a cultural artifact in order to be impressed by the impact of culture upon our notions of what constitutes mental illness; to survey the history of psychiatry is to be deluged with examples (Ellenberger, 1970; Showalter, 1985). The most significant of the cultural constructions that contribute to our conceptions of madness is that of gender. There is a good deal of evidence that in the nineteenth century madness became the "female malady" (Showalter, 1985), and that women today continue to be regulated by the "discourse of madness," although some of us are more likely to be positioned within that discourse than others (Ussher, 1992, p. 166).

Notwithstanding the influence of gender in all that we as a society have come to know and believe about madness, psychiatry has been late in coming to the recognition that gender has significance in the diagnosis and treatment of disorder, and "traditionally, when gender has been considered at all, it has usually been treated as a genetic or endogenous factor" (Waites, 1993). Little empirical research finds its way into theoretical formulations of psychopathology, and the result is the failure to explain sex differences in the development of many emotional problems or to explain the timing of changes in the developmental course of individuals after the period of infancy (Rutter & Garmezy, 1983). None of this should surprise us at all when we consider—as we will shortly—the history of the psychiatric profession and its relationship to the female sex.

Any discussion of women and mental illness must be guided by a will toward theoretical comprehensiveness and must eschew reliance upon any single theoretical premise. As Ussher (1992) has so compellingly pointed out, in discussing women and madness it is not sufficient to take account only of the psychiatric or psychological perspective, for that perspective is "rarely critical, offering individualized solutions to complex problems, buttressed by the institutional frameworks within which these professions operate . . . [where] science is still the God, and gender is rarely acknowledged" (p. 283). Neither can the views of the antipsychiatry movement or of feminists of varying theoretical persuasions stand alone; nor can we look to sociology, history, anthropology, or other individual disciplines for answers. Any discourse about women and mental illness that speaks to the real pain of real women must deny the prerogatives of ownership of the issue to any single discipline, for no single analysis will suffice (Ussher, 1992).

Since the meanings ascribed to masculinity and femininity undergird all theories of women's madness, and since the concepts of masculinity and femininity are socially constructed, it is clear why all such theories reflect (if not amplify) prevailing cultural narratives of gender (Hare-Mustin & Marecek, 1988; Ussher, 1992). Walkerdine maintains that these theories are "linked to fantasies deeply embedded in the social world which can take on the status of fact when inscribed with the powerful practices . . . through which we [women] are regulated" (1990).[3] So, since "the discourses which regulate 'femininity,' 'women,' and 'the mad' are irrevocably linked . . . madness can thus be viewed as a *fiction linked to a fantasy, seen as a fact,* and *experienced as 'real'* by individual women; and located within a material world in which both 'madness' and 'woman' act as important signifiers" (Ussher, 1992, p. 13, italics mine). Social representations are accepted by women as fact-based reality, then, and it is by this means that the representation "madness" acts as a signifier that identifies women as pathological, as ill, as outside—as the second-rate second sex. A woman who is in distress experiences that very real distress "in a way which is defined by the particular discourse associated with madness. She is positioned within the discourse in a way which determines her experience" (p. 12). She accepts the representation of her experience, having no access to another, and having few alternate means for expressing her suffering, she is "mentally ill."

We all are defined by representations, and we define ourselves by them. Throughout history, images both pictorial and verbal have summoned women up, but although the images may have altered over time, the message that women are weak, dangerous, and needful of control by virtue of their threatening sexuality has remained the same (Ussher, 1992). Every day we put on makeup—that is, we *make ourselves up*—for the world of men. We look in the mirror, but the reflected image has been filtered through the gaze of others. These encounters with mirrors are endlessly unsatisfying. Not only diagnosis as a mode of representation but also other means of representation of female experience—other images of ourselves with which women are presented or *re*presented—will be discussed in the next chapters. In the discussion of female adolescence, we will explore further the relationship between representation, self-consciousness, devaluation, and sexualization. First, however, I will present the statistical evidence for the link between women and madness.

The Statistical Story of Women's Madness

Since the publication of Phyllis Chesler's *Women and Madness* in 1972, a variety of hypotheses advanced to account for the seeming overrepresentation of women among those individuals seeking treatment for mental illness have been countered with well-documented, equally vigorous assertions that no such overrepresentation exists. Even where epidemiological evidence clearly demonstrates sex differences in the prevalence of a disorder, as in the case of depression (Weissman, Bruce, Leaf, Florio, & Holser, 1991; Weissman & Klerman, 1977), there is disagreement as to the cause of such differences.[4] Explanations range from the biological to the psychosocial. During the 1980s, criticism was leveled against psychotherapists for failing to give sufficient attention to psychological problems that are more prevalent among women (Hare-Mustin, 1983). Researchers became more aware that most of the research and theoretical work on psychopathology had focused on men, and that the research that concerned itself with factors related to gender differences had been uneven, with some areas of psychopathology well researched, and others substantially lacking in data (Franks & Rothblum, 1983; Rutter & Garmezy, 1983; Zigler & Glick, 1986).

Epidemiological Survey Research

The main sources of information available to help us in answering the question of which groups of men and women are viewed as mentally ill are data on admissions to mental hospitals and intakes at mental health facilities as well as data collected from epidemiological surveys. One of the underlying problems with utilization data, such as that from the National Institute of Mental Health (NIMH), is that they indicate the extent of, but not the need for, treatment (Russo & Sobel, 1981). However, evidence from responses to epidemiological survey questionnaires—surveys that, by randomly sampling nonclinical populations, do purport to demonstrate the true prevalence of mental illness—has been inconsistent at best (Goldman & Ravid, 1980).

The wide variations in the results of epidemiological survey research undertaken over the years may be explained by variations in methodology from study to study, differences in data-gathering techniques, and evaluator bias. Even more significant than these explanations, however, is the fact that different definitions of mental illness were used by different researchers (Goldman & Ravid, 1980). In 1973, Gove and Tudor, for example, included only neurotic disorders and functional psychoses in their definition. Since the 1950s the trend has been to employ broader and broader definitions of mental illness, but as yet no stability has been achieved (Dohrenwend & Dohrenwend, 1976). Sex differences in prevalence rates of mental illness are in the eye of the researcher, depending upon how mental illness is defined.

The Epidemiologic Catchment Area (ECA) Study, begun in 1977 and completed in 1989 (Robins & Regier, 1991), is the largest such survey yet undertaken. With its collection of data from 20,000 subjects at five sites, it presents the most current and best estimates of the prevalence of psychiatric disorder in the United States. The survey shows men to have a higher rate of disorder over their lifetimes than women. There is a catch here, however. Not only were men highly represented in *fewer* specific disorder categories than were women, but also the high overall rate of disorder for men is accounted for by the large numbers of men who reported alcohol abuse/dependence, which is now categorized in *DSM* terms as mental illness. The ECA study found that the most common disorders, in order of prevalence, were phobia, alcoholism, and generalized anxiety disorder. Depression and drug abuse shared the next position. Phobia (Eaton, Dryman, & Weissman, 1991) and generalized anxiety disorder (Blazer, Hughes, George, Swartz, & Boyer, 1991) were more common among women, and more than twice as many women as men were found to suffer from major depression and dysthymia (Weissman et al., 1991).

ECA study researchers point out that according to studies of outpatient settings, depression and anxiety are the disorders most commonly treated, whereas in their survey of the general population, phobia and alcoholism are the disorders most frequently reported.[5] Their results show how this difference can occur: "Depression and panic disorder are much more likely to be brought to the attention of clinicians than are alcoholism and phobia, probably in part because they are more limited to women, who seek care more readily, and partly because they are more widely recognized by the public as a mental health problem" (Robins, Locke, & Regier, 1991, p. 362).

Because it is socially sanctioned for women to discuss personal problems to an extent that it is not sanctioned for men, women may find it easier, when they are surveyed, to admit to such difficulties (Phillips & Segal, 1969). Estimates of the prevalence of mental illness among women may be confounded not only by gender differences in help-seeking behavior but also by the greater social support for help seeking that women enjoy in our society (Kessler, Brown, & Broman, 1981). Social approval for help seeking among women is a mixed blessing, however, for just as there is a relationship between help-seeking behavior and gender, there is a relationship between help-seeking behavior and low self-esteem:

> Individuals with high self-esteem appear to seek less help than others with low self-esteem. Sex-related differences, then, may both lead to and derive from circular processes involving differential attributions and expectations about the need for help, and "real" differences in willingness to ask for help. . . . These, then, both lead to and produce sex-related differences in self-appraisal, which lead to further differences in help-seeking behavior, thereby fulfilling initial social expectations. (Piliavin & Unger, 1985, p. 178)

Who Is Being Treated?

As difficult as it is to answer the question of whether more women than men are mad in our society, there may be a more important question to ask and to answer—that is, *which* women are more at risk for mental illness, since the group "women" is not homogeneous, and since it is *particular* women who are more at risk of being diagnosed and treated (Ussher, 1992). Although men predominate as patients in state and county psychiatric hospitals and in intensive community treatment settings (Mowbray, Herman, & Hazel, 1992), of those in community outpatient treatment, adult females constitute the largest number (Mowbray et al., 1992; Russo & Sobel, 1981). The ECA study showed that women who reported difficulties in their day-to-day lives obtained more treatment than men who reported similar problems—23 percent as contrasted with 14 percent (Robins et al., 1991). Even data from studies that have shown approximately equal rates of utilization of mental health facilities by men and women have revealed quite different patterns of use by each sex. In Michigan's community and state psychiatric hospitals, for example, women patients were, on average, found to be older than men, more likely than the men to be voluntary patients, and functioning at significantly higher levels than the men at time of admission (Mowbray &

Chamberlain, 1986). If women have a greater readiness than men to label themselves "crazy," the authors of this study suggest, we might question the value of some of these voluntary hospital admissions.

Of the women in treatment, those who are separated, divorced, and/or those who head single-parent families make up the majority (Belle, 1980). White women have longer stays in state and city mental hospitals than do other populations (Carmen, Russo, & Miller, 1981). As outpatients, women are also more likely to be referred for individual psychotherapy than for other forms of psychiatric treatment and to remain in therapy longer than men (Abramowitz, Abramowitz, Roback, Corney, & McKee, 1976; Geller & Munetz, 1988; Zeldow, 1978). Physicians prescribe more prescription medications, including psychotropic medications, for women than for men (Fidell, 1981; Mowbray & Chamberlain, 1986). Fidell (1981) believes this difference has to do with the tendency of physicians to attribute women's symptoms to psychological and (internal) psychosomatic causes and to view men's symptoms as of (external) organic origin. Thus, there may exist a "congruence between physician expectations, based on sex stereotypes, and reports by female patients of more numerous mental health symptoms" (Fidell, 1981, p. 159). Because twice as many women as men are prescribed psychotropic medications by physicians, it is not surprising that suicide attempts by overdose are more common among women than among men (Jack, 1992).

Sex Differences and Personality Disorders

Study of the relationship between sex differences and the symptoms of personality disorder has been quite recent, and some definitions of mental illness—such as that of Gove (1980)—excluded the personality disorders altogether. Although a review of the literature by Goldman and Ravid (1980) failed to uncover a single study on the subject, there did exist one 1976 study of the epidemiology of personality disorders showing the overall prevalence of personality disorders among men to be significantly higher than among women (Dohrenwend & Dohrenwend, 1976). Given this finding, it is no wonder that the personality disorders did not initially attract a great deal of attention in the burgeoning debate over gender differences in psychopathology.

Interest in the relationship of gender to the personality disorders *was* sparked by the 1987 publication of the *Diagnostic and Statistical Manual of Mental Disorders (DSM-III-R)*, whose new and proposed categories of personality disorders raised both the consciousness and the hackles of many. The manual indicated that the new category "Dependent Personality Disorder" was more frequently diagnosed in women than in men, as was the proposed "Self-Defeating Personality Disorder."[6] The creators of the "Dependent" and "Self-Defeating" categories were roundly accused of "blaming the victim"—that is, blaming women for adopting roles that society has traditionally endorsed for them and for which they have been well and truly socialized (Rosewater, 1988).

Sex Differences and the Borderline Personality Disorder

Of all the personality disorders, borderline personality disorder is probably the most frequently applied, both to inpatients and outpatients (Frances & Widiger, 1987; Kroll, 1988). It is more commonly diagnosed in women than in men, at a rate of anywhere from 2:1 to 9:1, depending upon the sample under investigation (Akhtar, Byrne, & Doghramji, 1986; Castaneda & Franco, 1985; Frances & Widiger, 1987; Gilbertson, McGraw, & Brown, 1986; Henry & Cohen, 1983; Kirshner & Johnston, 1983; Sheehy, Goldsmith, & Charles, 1980). Preliminary estimates are available for the prevalence of BPD in the general population from the second wave of the NIMH Epidemiologic Catchment Area study of the general population (Swartz, Blazer, George, & Winfield, 1990). Among 2,993 subjects aged 19 to 55 from the Piedmont area of North Carolina, the prevalence of BPD was 1.8 percent. This is roughly equivalent to the incidence of depression in this population. It must be noted that 73.2 percent of those identified as "borderline" were women. The highest rates of disorder were found among those in the 19–34 age range. The larger number of these individuals was non-white, single or widowed,[7] and of lower socioeconomic status. Nearly 50 percent of the BPD group reported one or more visits to mental health facilities in the past six months.

Women with BPD symptoms are overrepresented not only in the general population but in treatment settings as well. BPD patients who appear in treatment settings are 70 to 77 percent female (Widiger & Frances, 1989); moreover, individuals diagnosed with BPD seem to be overrepresented generally in treatment settings, an overrepresentation equaled only by schizophrenics (Swartz et al., 1990). On the subject of the overrepresentation of borderline females in outpatient facilities, Swartz and his colleagues suggest that men with BPD "may be . . . found preferentially in treatment settings for comorbid conditions such as substance and alcohol abuse" (p. 258).

Women, they imply, are treated for a personality disorder; men for an addiction or, perhaps, for antisocial behaviors. If that is true, however, what are we to make of the ECA statistics? Would a tendency on the part of women to have an easier time reporting psychological problems than men—this fact alone—account for so gross a sex difference in the prevalence of BPD in an anonymous questionnaire survey of the general population? It seems highly unlikely. I will say much more in this book about why women are diagnosed with BPD in such large numbers.

A 1988 Danish study (Mors, cited in Swartz et al., 1990) showed an increase in the number of BPD patients admitted to inpatient and day treatment settings between the years 1970 and 1985. Individuals in metropolitan Copenhagen were five times as likely to receive the BPD diagnosis as their cohorts in three less urban counties surveyed. Changes in the way clinicians diagnose the disorder may well account for the rising prevalence of the BPD diagnosis. As we shall explore further in Chapter 3, over the years the "borderline" concept has undergone transformations that have feminized the diagnosis. Indeed, the originator of the term would likely not recognize it in its present form.

Conclusion

What we call normal and pathological behaviors have their origins not only in the biological and psychological but also in the sociocultural experiences of individuals. To ignore the effects of gender socialization, pressures toward conformity via stereotyping, and the impact of the differential evaluation of masculine and feminine characteristics and behavior upon the development of personality disorder—or, more accurately, upon the process that eventuates in the labeling of an individual as having a personality disorder—is to seal off the possibility of developing a more complete understanding of how so-called disorder develops.

Some individuals, following Chesler's (1972) lead, see the "madness" of women as sheer societal invention. Others say we would do well to stop quibbling over person/environment distinctions, accept the fact of gender-linked psychopathology, and get on with the business of ascertaining what aspects of women's experience render it so maladaptive (Dohrenwend & Dohrenwend, 1976; Franks, 1986; Gove & Tudor, 1973). Theory building in the present can ill afford to neglect the contribution of either point of view. Socialization of the young is informed by social definitions of what constitutes appropriate behavior for each sex. The experience of men and women is culture bound. Notions about the psychological nature of each sex, whether or not we choose to accept them, as well as notions about what constitutes positive mental health, have a powerful effect on perception and behavior.

Notions of what is deviant are quite variable from society to society, and in a given society, what is not socially approved can be deemed mad, criminal, or both. It is essential to understand the history of society's—and, more particularly, the medical profession's—judgment of and treatment for women who have suffered psychological distress if we are to understand current practices of diagnosis in general and the relationship between gender and the borderline personality disorder in particular. It is equally important, however, to study the socialization of girls and the psychology of women in order to understand how some women have come to experience forms of distress that the medical profession currently calls "borderline."

1

From Witchcraft to Hysteria to BPD: A Brief History of Female Insanity

The stage conventions of the role have always emphasized the feminine nature of Ophelia's insanity contrasted with Hamlet's metaphysical distress.

—Elaine Showalter, *The Female Malady*

Women and Madness: A Historical View

The complex story of borderline personality disorder cannot be told without reference to the historical association between women and madness. By the nineteenth century, women had become the most frequent consumers of treatment for "nervous complaints" and had entered into a relationship with male physicians that was to have pervasive and enduring implications for the representation—through diagnosis—of women to themselves and to others. In the nineteenth century, as today, women absorbed a view of themselves that was strongly shaped by societal notions of what constitutes madness. The history of the association between women and madness, however, has its origins in the more primitive association made between women and evil.

1

Witches, Evil, and Madness

For centuries, witches carried the burden of the opprobrium for women's evil. As early as the sixteenth century, however, a physician, Johann Meyer, had come to view witches as mad rather than evil or possessed (Ussher, 1992). Although many present-day historians share Meyer's equation of madness and witchery,[1] such a perspective, although intuitively appealing, is reductionistic:

> One explanation cannot completely explain the myriad reasons for their [the witches'] persecution or their supposed deviancy. The 'witch' may have been a healer, a deviant worshipper of Diana, a lonely spinster, a hated rival, a random woman picked by the picker for his own gratification. She *may* have been evil, or have practised strange sexual rituals. She may have been 'mad' or 'melancholic,' was possibly depressed, anxious, and unhappy. (p. 61)

The notion of witchcraft as "undiagnosed madness" does not help us understand why communities singled out certain women for extrusion; it merely passes the locus of blame from the persecutors of these women, who are deemed innocent by virtue of their ignorance of the "true" cause of the women's distress, to the women themselves, whose behavior is seen to have occasioned the "diagnosis" of witchery and, thereby, brought on their own destruction (Ussher, 1992).

There is no doubt that the persecution of witches *did* provide an important vehicle for expunging the collective fears and uncertainties of the communities in which they lived. However, one need not subscribe to the witch-as-madwoman theory in order to explain the phenomenon of witch-hunting. In some cases, for example, the persecution of witches may have been attempts to expel from the social order women whose skills in various healing arts as well as in midwifery and abortion were threatening to the medical orthodoxy. The fact that a witch/healer was often successful in her ministrations "was seen as corroboration of her guilt, for if she could effect a cure after . . . male physicians had failed, she must be employing magic" (Ussher, 1992, p. 56).

As the tenets of science superseded those of theology and philosophy, replacing the notion of "evil" with that of "illness" (Ussher, 1992), control of women through allegations of witchcraft came gradually to be replaced by another potent means of social control—psychiatric diagnosis. Whereas in the eighteenth century during the Romantic period, madness had been defined as "loss of reason" and mad individuals, thought to be primitive beasts, were treated accordingly in a bestial fashion—locked up in primitive madhouses, sometimes chained, and otherwise maltreated—in the Victorian era the definition of madness as loss of reason was replaced by the idea that madness was actually "moral insanity," or deviance from socially sanctioned behavior.[2] The raving lunatics of the Romantic period were pushed aside to make room for their more decorous Victorian counterparts by means of a transformation in thinking about madness that made it possible to identify nearly any deviant or disruptive behavior as "morally insane." In England, this Victorian domestication of insanity coincided with the gradual increase in the proportion of women in asylums, until by the 1890s the predominance of women among the institutionalized was universal. Paradoxically, however, as the numbers of women patients increased, the proportion of caretakers who were women declined.

Foucault (1965) outlines the transformation in the common understanding of so-called nervous complaints, which had once been seen to be

> associated with the organic movements of the lower parts of the body . . . , they were located within a certain ethic of desire; they represented the revenge of a crude body; it had been as the result of an excessive violence that one became ill. From now on one fell ill from *too much feeling;* one suffered from an excessive solidarity with all the beings around one. One was no longer compelled by one's secret nature; one was the victim of everything which, on the surface of the world, solicited the body and the soul. (pp. 156–157)

What Foucault does not mention, however, is that to render an excess of feeling as the defining attribute of "nervous complaints" (i.e., madness) is to feminize those same complaints, for it is women who were (and are still) thought to be the more keenly "feeling" of the sexes. There was a steady movement during the nineteenth century from the perception of nervous complaints as bodily illnesses toward the perception of those same complaints as mental disorders: "As long as vapors were convulsions or strange sympathetic communications throughout the body, even when they led to fainting and loss of consciousness, they were not madness. But once the mind becomes blind through the very excess of sensibility—then madness appears" (Foucault, 1965, p. 157). The association between the "excess of sensibility," madness, and women had been sturdily forged.

The Medicalization of Madness: A Confidence Game

In 1817 John Haslam expressed the view of the medical profession with respect to insanity in women as follows:

In females who become insane the disease is often connected with the peculiarities of their sex. . . . It ought to be fully understood that the education, character, and established habits of medical men, entitle them to confidence of their patients: the most virtuous women unreservedly communicate to them their feelings and complaints, when they would shudder at imparting their disorders to a male of any other profession; or even to their own husbands. Medical science, associated with decorous manners, has generated this confidence, and rendered the practitioner the friend of the afflicted, and the depository of their secrets. (Haslam, as cited in Skultans, 1975)

In a patriarchal society such as ours where women have not classically been accorded a status equal to that of men, women's uneasy relationship to psychiatry may be conceptualized in terms of male-female differences along the dimensions of status, power, and sex roles (Piliavin & Unger, 1985). We can trace this relationship to the emerging prepotence of medicine over other healing arts as the favored treatment for ill women at the turn of the century:

It was the combination of upper class and male superiority that gave medicine its essential authority. . . . Now at last the medical profession had arrived at a method of faith-healing potent enough to compare with women's traditional healing but one which was decisively masculine. It did not require a nurturant attitude, nor long hours by the patient's bedside. In fact, with the new style of healing, the less time a doctor spends with the patient, and the fewer questions he permits, the greater his powers would seem to be. (Eherenreich & English, 1978, p. 83)

Neurology had emerged from general medicine and psychiatry as a separate discipline in the period between the 1850s and 1870s, and it was this new discipline that addressed itself to the treatment of disorders of the nervous system—particularly those that seemed to occupy the borderline between normality and madness:

These disorders, neurologists argued, had been ignored or misunderstood. Alienists[3] mistook them for types of madness. General physicians regarded them as gross physical diseases, as purely imaginary or as malingering. Only the most scientific diagnosis could establish their existence and lay the basis for sound treatment. By explaining all of them as somatic in origin, neurologists drew them within the medical model of involuntary sickness. (Hale, 1971, p. 49)

Women lost the place they had occupied over the centuries as healers and midwives. The alleged rationality and objectivity of science was used by the experts then, as it is today, "to neutralize criticism and dissent" (Ussher,

1992, p. 66), as medicine claimed for itself the exclusive right to deal with madness by insisting that it was the *brain* of the mad person and not his or her *mind* that was afflicted. Madness was bodily disease, and women were, by nature, "weak, dependent and diseased" (p. 92). Adolescence was considered to be a period particularly fraught with peril for women, as adolescent girls were especially susceptible to nervous excitability, it was thought. Women's sickness was innate and had its origins in the fact of women's possession of ovaries and uteruses.

Hysteria

"Diseased" women were to become, in increasing numbers, the primary candidates for study and treatment by members of the newly burgeoning group of specialists in "nerve medicine." These physicians ministered to large numbers of Victorian women who, bound over to idleness by the strictures of an emotionally repressive society, succumbed to a variety of "nervous" diseases. The early equation of female nervous problems with illness, however, carried with it a dilemma for the male physician: If female sickness were innate and had its origins in the fact of possession of ovaries and uteruses, could the physician not be easily made a fool of by his failure to cure the nervous invalids in his care (Eherenreich & English, 1978)? How could he explain the refractory nature of some of these nervous illnesses? The means out of this clinical dilemma were close at hand.

Hysteria, for some twenty-five centuries before it began to be studied systematically, had been looked upon as a mystifying disease (Ellenberger, 1970). In the view of the ancient Greeks, if a woman remained childless too long, the uterus wandered around in the body, causing extreme pain and a multiplicity of diseases. Hysteria (the meaning of the Greek word is "wandering uterus") was thought by the Greeks to afflict only those women with unsatisfactory sex lives. By the Middle Ages, however, the tables had turned, and what was thought to predispose women to hysteria was "wanton sexuality, precisely the opposite of the enforced sexual abstinence that was the responsible factor of the ancient world" (Chodoff, 1982, p. 547). Beginning in the sixteenth century, some physicians began to locate the cause of hysteria in the brain, and in 1859 Paul Briquet, in his *Traité de l'Hysterie,* presented the first systematic study of the disease (Ellenberger, 1970). Although Briquet himself did not subscribe to the sexual theory of hysteria, the notion that hysteria derived from sexual frustration was never completely given up either in the public mind or by gynecologists and neurologists. Jean-Martin

Charcot, having studied 430 hysterical patients, found a 20:1 ratio of female to male hysterics, and concluded that hysteria was "caused by the effect of violent emotions, protracted sorrows, family conflicts, and frustrated love, upon predisposed and hypersensitive persons" (Charcot, quoted on p. 142).

It was the artifact of hysteria that finally broke "the gynecologists' monopoly of the female psyche" (Eherenreich & English, 1978, p. 124). American health books and medical manuals published between 1840 and 1900 commonly refer to the vast numbers of middle-class women stricken by illness, and even commentators of the time remarked upon how fashionable illness had become among this group. In the previous century, women had not referred to themselves as weak, delicate, or sick, nor were they defined through illness. Their nineteenth-century sisters, however, did appear to succumb to nervous ailments at an appalling rate. This is not to say that men were not afflicted with similar symptoms, but that, to an extent, diagnosis and treatment of the sexes differed because of the focus upon—and some might say, the obsession with—the female uterus (Wood, 1973). Physicians of more than one school of thought were swayed not only by their view that women were dominated by their sexual organs; they also held "even less carefully scrutinized beliefs about the social and psychological nature of femininity and its role and responsibilities in their society, beliefs which colored their attitude toward the illness of their female patients" (p. 34).

The history of the treatment of hysteria, neurasthenia, and other so-called nervous diseases in the United States is the history of a movement from the practice of somatic medicine by neurologists in the second half of the nineteenth century toward the professionalization of psychiatry and the enthusiastic endorsement of psychoanalysis in the United States beginning in the second decade of the twentieth (Hale, 1971). It is a story in which women played—and still play—a prominent role, and it is a movement that profoundly affects them.

A "Chattering, Canting Age"

The whole generation is womanized, the masculine tone is passing out of the world; it's a feminine, a nervous, hysterical, chattering, canting age, an age of hollow phrases and false delicacy and exaggerated solicitudes and coddled sensibilities, which, if we don't soon look out, will usher in the reign of mediocrity, of the feeblest and flattest and the most pretentious that has ever been.

—Basil Ransom in Henry James, *The Bostonians*

> *Loss of power or will is a characteristic symptom of hysteria in all its Protean forms, and with the perverted sensations and disordered movements there is always some degree of moral perversion. This increases until it swallows up the other symptoms: the patient loses more and more of her energy and self-control, becoming capriciously fanciful about her health, imagining or feigning strange diseases, and keeping up the delusion or the imposture with a pertinacity that might seem incredible, getting more and more impatient of the advice and interference of others, and indifferent to the interests and duties of her position.*

> —Henry Maudsley, *Body and Mind,* 1873

Hysteria, as diagnosed in the nineteenth century, embraced such disorders as hypochondriasis, depression, conversion reaction, and ambulatory schizophrenia (Smith-Rosenberg, 1972). Typically, those said to suffer from hysteria manifested symptoms such as trances, convulsive fits, tearing of the hair, choking, and rapid shifts in mood (Sicherman, 1977). Neurasthenia encompassed a large group of symptoms and conditions as well, ranging from depressive, phobic, and obsessive states to moderately psychotic and borderline states, physical illnesses that were not otherwise diagnosable at the time, and a host of psychophysiological symptoms. George M. Beard, the prominent neurologist who coined the term *neurasthenia,* once listed forty-eight illnesses with which neurasthenia could be confounded (Sicherman, 1977). Hysteria was thought to be more a female and neurasthenia more a male disease, even though the differences between the two afflictions were often less than distinct (Strouse, 1980). Alice James, as we shall soon see, received both these diagnoses and more in her long career as a patient. Beard considered hysteria to be characterized by "acuteness, violence, activity, and severity" (Beard, *Nervous Exhaustion,* quoted in Sicherman, p. 41) and neurasthenia by languor. Decisions to diagnose one as against the other were profoundly affected by moral considerations, however:

Where neurasthenics seemed deeply concerned about their condition and eager to cooperate, hysterics were accused of evasiveness—*la belle indifférence*—and even intentional deception. Physicians sometimes contrasted the hysteric's lack of moral sense with the neurasthenic's refined and unselfish nature. "The sense of moral obligations [in the hysteric] is so generally defective as to render it difficult to determine whether the patient is mad or simply bad." By contrast, patients suffering from "impaired vitality" were "of good position in society . . . just the kind of women one likes to meet with—sensible, not over sensitive or emotional, exhibiting a proper amount of illness . . . and a willingness to perform their share of work quietly and to the best of their ability." (first quote, S. Weir Mitchell's *Rest in Nervous Disease*; second, Beard's *Nervous Exhaustion*;

third, A. S. Myrtle's *On a Common Form of Impaired Vitality,* Sicherman, 1977, p. 41)

Records from Massachusetts General Hospital (1880–1900) show that patients described as stupid, morally weak, or deceitful were more frequently diagnosed hysterical than neurasthenic. (Sicherman, 1977). Neurasthenia was, in fact, the preferred diagnosis "for those men and women whose diffuse symptoms might otherwise have been dismissed as hypochondria or hysteria." "As a new diagnosis, neurasthenia escaped the pejorative connotations associated with its nearest alternatives" (p. 42). "Class considerations, the tolerance of physicians for particular symptoms, and the ability of family members to care for patients undoubtedly influenced diagnostic decisions, then as now" (p. 43) and may, in many cases, have led the physician to diagnose neurasthenia over insanity, then thought to be incurable, even though neurasthenics suffered many symptoms shared by the "insane."

The new labels for nervous maladies implied an optimistic therapeutic precision that inspired confidence on the part of patients. At the same time the new labels permitted some physicians who had hitherto felt comfortable treating only disorders of clearly organic origin to "address themselves to less tangible clinical issues and to provide an essentially psychological therapy under a somatic label" (Sicherman, 1977, p. 39).

As neurologist Silas Weir Mitchell described it, hysteria was "the nosological limbo of all unnamed female maladies. It were as well called mysteria" (Mitchell, *Rest in Nervous Disease,* quoted in Strouse, 1980, p. 112). A disease with such a wide array of symptoms could not easily be vanquished, and women who suffered from hysterical symptoms swelled the practice of many a physician. However, although treatment of hysterical women may have brought financial gain, it was not an unalloyed privilege, for

> when the hysterical woman became sick, she no longer played the role of the self-sacrificing daughter or wife, as did the anorexic. Instead, she demanded service and attention from others. The families of hysterics found themselves reorganized around the patient, who had to be constantly nursed, indulged with special delicacies, and excused from ordinary duties. . . . Despite a certain sympathy for women's restricted lives, . . . doctors found their hysterical patients personally and morally repulsive, idle, intractable, and manipulative. (Showalter, 1985, p. 133)

"The more women became hysterical, the more doctors became punitive toward the disease; and at the same time, they began to see the disease everywhere . . . until they were diagnosing every independent act by a woman as 'hysterical.'" Hysteria became a rampant epidemic, with women accepting their "illness" while at the same time "finding a way to rebel against an intolerable social role." Sickness became not only a way of life but also a means of rebellion, and "medical treatment, which had always had strong overtones of coercion, revealed itself as frankly and brutally repressive" (Showalter, 1985, p. 125). Although some feminists have celebrated Freud's "Dora" and other hysterical patients of the nineteenth century as "champions of defiant womanhood, whose opposition, expressed in physical symptoms and coded speech, subverted the linear logic of male science," to romanticize or endorse madness as a form of admirable rebellion is to fail to see it for what it is— "the desperate communication of the powerless"—and to commit an error just as grievous as that of equating femininity and insanity (p. 5).

Two Women's Histories:
Charlotte Perkins Gilman and Alice James

The lives of two nineteenth-century women—one a very public figure of her time, and one virtually unknown until the publication of her *Diaries* after her death—serve to illuminate a number of issues that surface in any history of women and mental illness as well as to adumbrate the forthcoming discussion of the connection between the borderline personality disorder and the nineteenth-century notion of hysteria. Through these lives we can trace the origins of pain acutely suffered, the family context of that distress, the social conditions that influenced the nature and interpretation of that suffering, and the relationship of female patients to it.

Both women throughout their lives were prey to the symptoms of what were considered, in their time, "nervous" ailments. Their odysseys—their efforts not only to be "cured" of their illnesses but also to make meaning of what was happening to them—offer a personal view of the struggles of two intelligent and strong-minded women at a period in history when women's intelligence and their strong-mindedness were far from valued or encouraged. Each woman found different means for confronting the strictures of her life and for dealing with the "medical" treatments offered to her.

When we examine the lives of Alice James and Charlotte Perkins Gilman, we can see a surprising number of continuities between their psychological dilemmas and those of women of our own time. Although social conventions for female behavior and methods of child rearing have changed substantially since the mid- to late nineteenth century, many of the confusions about anger and dependency with which Alice and Charlotte grappled and which played themselves out in their relationships with others have a distinctly contemporary flavor and manifested themselves in ways that currently might be seen as "borderline."

Charlotte Perkins Gilman

Although Charlotte Perkins Gilman is best known today for her utopian novel *Herland* and her short story "The Yellow Wallpaper," her seminal work, *Women and Economics: The Economic Relations Between Men and Women as a Factor in Social Evolution*, was the cornerstone upon which her reputation was built.[4] Throughout her life, she fought numerous episodes of debilitating depression and succeeded in becoming a writer and lecturer of unflagging energy and prodigious output. Born in 1860, the youngest child of Frederick Beecher Perkins—grandson of the famous Lyman Beecher—and Mary Ann Fitch Westkott Perkins, Charlotte endured a family life that was neither happy nor stable. Her father, a man who never succeeded in establishing himself solidly in the world, left the family following her birth and returned only sporadically. Even as an adult, Charlotte had little contact with him. Left with two children and little money, Charlotte's mother, sorrowful and abandoned, often had to depend on relatives for lodging, and mother and children moved constantly from one house to another. Mary Perkins finally divorced her husband after thirteen years of marriage. A rigid disciplinarian, she gave little physical affection to her children. Charlotte's brother, Thomas, teased Charlotte cruelly, vindictively, and mercilessly. The world of fantasy became Charlotte's frequent childhood refuge from the realities of this bleak emotional landscape.

As she entered adolescence, however, fantasy could no longer hold her anxieties in abeyance. Ann J. Lane (1990), in her excellent biography of Gilman, discusses the strains felt by Charlotte at this time in her life. In the late nineteenth century, puberty was considered a dangerous time, especially for young women. The delicate balance between mind and body was conceived of as more precarious in adolescent girls than in boys, since women were considered more fragile, and therefore more vulnerable to mental excitation. Beyond these considerations, however, Charlotte had to contend with particular coming-of-age difficulties that emerged out of her unique history of childhood deprivation:

> The risk in adolescence, the risk of taking one's love and one's need to love
> into the world outside, undoubtedly frightened Charlotte's contemporaries, as

it continues to frighten young people today, but it probably aroused extreme apprehension in Charlotte. The ability to struggle for and achieve independence must rest upon a sense of trust in others, which ordinarily has its roots in deep attachment. (p. 50)

Charlotte, strong-willed and somewhat rebellious at fifteen, yet still unable to express her anger to her mother directly, resolved to be the obedient daughter until such time as she left home, which she had determined to do at twenty-one. By her own account, for eight years—from the age of sixteen to the age of twenty-four when she married—she held herself to a rigorous program of self-improvement that included discipline and denial from the physical sphere to the emotional realm. At the same time, she attempted to discover what her life's work would be: "'female' or 'male,' mothering or career" (Lane, 1990, p. 57). The "emotional cost to Charlotte," however, of "this driven and conflicted adolescence was high":

> She said of herself that during these years she learned self-control and discipline. Someone else might say that during this period of emerging womanhood she learned to deny her emotions and her sexuality. At age seventeen she wrote in her diary: "Am going to try hard this winter to see if I cannot enjoy myself like other people." She was truly very hard on herself at that young age, trying desperately to force herself into a mold of perfection. She later . . . said that inside there was much "earnest living" going on. It seems more valid to call what was going on inside denial rather than earnest living. It is not surprising, given her herculean efforts at self-suppression, that from age seventeen on Charlotte spoke in terms of great weariness and depression. (pp. 59–60)

It was not, however, until after her marriage to (Charles) Walter Stetson in 1884 and the birth of her daughter Katharine in 1885 that Charlotte first experienced the debilitating depression that was to revisit her throughout her life. She became clingingly dependent on Walter, who, for all his patience, was not able to help her. Lane (1990) suggests that the birth of a child had opened up for Charlotte the "old, never-healed wounds of neediness in herself, setting off her sense of herself as a child in need of mothering" (p. 100). Charlotte blamed herself for a lack of maternal feeling. Marriage had not brought her the security she longed for; rather, it seemed to point up a sense of unworthiness, of being unlovable. Lane suggests that, in order to ensure her own undeservedness, she "provoked the inevitable response. Making herself unable to take care of her child and her husband, demonstrating how incompetent a woman she was, she illustrated how undeserving she remained. She punished herself, but at the same time she punished her family, forced them to respond to her incapacities by taking over" (p. 135). A winter in California did much to improve her health; however, when she returned home to her wifely and motherly duties, she was again beset with "hysteria, incompetence, impatience, lethargy, paralysis" (p. 101).

With one hundred dollars borrowed from a friend of her mother's, Charlotte set off to Philadelphia to seek help from Dr. Silas Weir Mitchell, one of the most prominent neurologists of the day. He had had extensive experience treating "nerve wounds" and diseases during the Civil War, and his popularity as a physician to hysterical and/or neurasthenic women was unparalleled in the country at the time Charlotte met him. Mitchell's own childhood had been difficult, shaped as it had been by an overbearing father whom he held in awe and a mother whom he passionately adored. Mitchell himself had had two nervous breakdowns after the war—one occasioned by the loss of his wife and his father, the other by the loss of his mother. "As a doctor," he "sought groups to minister to who helped him define his own maleness. By controlling women patients who were weak and helpless, perhaps he could purge himself of those remaining fears of female weakness that had tied him to his revered mother" (Lane, 1990, p. 116).

Prior to her visit, Charlotte had sent Mitchell a lengthy letter giving a detailed history of her symptoms. He found the letter useless, and considered her assumption that he might find it helpful an indicator of her "self conceit" (Lane, 1990, p. 113). He diagnosed her as suffering from "neurasthenia," or exhaustion of the nerves. He told Charlotte that she was sick—not "lazy" or lacking in character or will, as she (and her intimates) had adduced. For this condition he prescribed the "rest cure," a treatment that included separation from the family, overfeeding on rich foods, and massage or electricity to stimulate the muscles in an otherwise inert body. For many of Mitchell's patients, "the psychological value of receiving attention and acknowledgment that the ailment was legitimate in an environment that encouraged self-confidence was sufficient to restore some semblance of normal functioning" (p. 119). But for Charlotte, it was not the treatment itself but the flight from treatment that proved the cure.

Although we do not know what treatment Mitchell actually gave her, the prescription he gave Charlotte to take home with her is known from her autobiography: "Live as domestic a life as possible. Have your child with you all the time. . . . Lie down an hour after each meal. Have but two hours' intellectual life a day. And never touch pen, brush or pencil as long as you live" (*The Living of Charlotte Perkins Gilman: An Autobiography*, quoted in Lane, 1990, p. 121). After following these injunctions to the letter for many months, Charlotte found herself sliding further and further into insanity.

She later recalled that during this period she made a rag doll that she hung on the doorknob and played with, and that she found herself crawling under beds and into closets, trying in vain to escape mounting dejection. Finally, however, in her first act of true defiance, Charlotte determined not only to do away with Dr. Mitchell's advice but to leave her husband of only two years as well. The voices both of Dr. Mitchell and of her patient and devoted husband echoed the cultural commands of an age: "that she abide by a Victorian morality that denied her, as it had denied her mother, avenues to express feelings of rage and hostility; that she achieve mastery of self and womanly restraint but without being permitted to develop the tools of adulthood" (Lane, 1990, p. 128). Charlotte's "'hand-made character,' so carefully constructed, had collapsed immediately after she and Walter were wed" (p. 136).

Charlotte had difficulty for years in defining for herself an intimate relationship that was not determined by her early fears of abandonment or her later fears of engulfment. At twenty-one, prior to her marriage to Walter, she had developed an intense love for her friend Martha Luther. Lane's descriptions of this relationship, reconstructed through Gilman's letters, show a Charlotte who depended utterly upon Martha for a sense of worth and who was devastated when she heard that Martha was to marry. For Charlotte, at this time in her life, independence and the desire to be nurtured by Martha "like a half-fed amiable kitten" (letter from Charlotte to Martha, quoted in Lane, 1990, p. 73) seemed incompatible. Some years after her divorce, she struck up an extremely sudden and intense intimacy with a reporter, Adeline "Delle" Knapp, and the subsequent relationship between the two needy women turned highly destructive. Initially, Charlotte relied on Delle for assistance with everything, from emotional support to financial help in caring for Charlotte's ailing mother. Eventually, however, it was Delle's excessive clinging and the public scenes that ensued when Delle's needs were not met that led to Charlotte's breaking off the relationship. There was to be a long period of self-enforced abstinence from all relationships before Charlotte was able to achieve the partnership of true mutuality that she was to find in her marriage with Houghton Gilman.

Even during the courtship with Houghton, or Ho, as she called him, however, Charlotte struggled to see herself as worthy of love, to identify her needs, and to ask that they be met. In a letter to Ho, she attempted to explain the derivation of the neediness that had marred many of her former relationships:

> You see all my life I haven't had what I wanted in the way of being loved. . . . From mother up. The whole way is lined with—not all gravestones, but some, and some kind of trap-door-stones that keep things down. When the

will-strength or brain-strength, or whatever it is that keeps me happy and steady and brave, gives out, up hop all these buried things, dead and alive.

I want everything I haven't had—all at once—It isn't as if I'd had 'em and lost 'em, you understand. I have never had—save in one girl friend—a satisfied love. The others have all gone wrong somehow. (letter from Charlotte to Houghton, quoted by Lane, 1990, pp. 201–202)

Charlotte was able to identify her hunger for affection and to take responsibility for finding new, less destructive ways to assuage it. Unlike Alice James, whose story is to follow, Charlotte's life was eventually to bring her great satisfactions in both love and work.

Alice James

Alice was born in 1848, the youngest of five children and the only girl. Two of her brothers went on to achieve great prestige in their chosen fields—Henry James Jr. as a novelist and William James as a psychologist. Their father, Henry James Sr., devoted his life to elaborating a system of ideas—called Divine Natural Humanity—concerning the relationship between humankind and God. The James family provided the most intimate laboratory for the explication of Henry Sr.'s ideas, many of which were, in their abstraction, confusing and contradictory:

> Though he based his entire philosophy on the personal confrontation of evil, he did his loving best to protect his offspring from all knowledge of sin, to prolong their innocence and develop their spontaneous natural goodness. Evil, acknowledged in the abstract, had no place at the family hearth. That basic contradiction, between what their father espoused (man finds God only after directly experiencing the evil in his own nature) and what he practiced (evil does not exist), fostered in each of the children a preoccupation with morality and a tendency to dichotomize. To be innocent and good meant *not to know* the darker sides of one's own nature. To love and be loved, then, required the renunciation of certain kinds of knowledge and feeling.
>
> In their relative freedom from parental tyranny, the only right the James children did not have . . . was the right to be unhappy. . . . For all his avowals of altruism, . . . [Alice's] father steadfastly refused to acknowledge the reality of his children's pain. (Strouse, 1980, p. 18)

Although Alice's mother, Mary James, did not hold much with her husband's liberal notions of child rearing, she kept her views to herself. Not unlike other women of her time, she had learned that she could accomplish more by selflessness than she could through assertion, and her self-sacrificing nature was appreciated and frequently idealized by her husband and children.[5]

Despite the care taken with the educational plans for her brothers, Alice's education was a rather hit-or-miss affair.[6] The family moved frequently, and Alice spent a portion of her childhood living in hotels in Europe. In her early adolescence, the family settled in Newport, Rhode Island. Later in life she commented on this manner of peripatetic childhood to her brother William: "What enrichment of mind and memory can children have without continuity and if they are torn up by the roots every little while as we were! Of all things don't make the mistake which brought about our rootless and accidental childhood" (A. J. to W. J., November 4, 1888, in James, 1981, p. 148).

Throughout her childhood, Alice was favorite prey for the teasing of her brothers—all except Henry. When she was young, her brothers Wilky (Garth Wilkinson) and Bob (Robertson) meted out corporal punishment; from a young age well into adulthood she was also exposed to the seductive teasing and dominating behavior of her brother William, who was five years her senior.[7] Although the James children certainly enjoyed a less constrained atmosphere than many of their contemporaries, some subjects were clearly taboo in the James household—sex among them. William's attentions were, on the one hand, flattering; on the other hand, his flirtatious behavior toward her and his letters, which frequently referred to her physical attributes, were often confusing and disturbing to Alice:

> Alice was inevitably an object of fraternal curiosity, and yet William's playful references to her body were probably the only kind that could be made. She grew up like a rare, fragile tropical plant . . . fed on special preparations of solicitude and indifference. The overstimulations of this heated atmosphere had no natural means of release. Alice . . . shared in the family amusement at William's carryings-on, watching herself as object and learning to detach from the flushed confusions involved in also being the subject of the diversion. (Strouse, 1980, pp. 57–58)

Mores of the time dictated that Alice not respond overtly to any of the covert, sexualized behavior directed toward her. A pressure equally burdensome, however, was the requirement to join in the competitive, witty intellectualism of the James household even while she was denied access to the same types of educational and vocational opportunities available to her brothers. It is little wonder that as her adolescence progressed, this highly intelligent young woman began showing symptoms of "nervous" disease.

Although Alice was by no means the only one in her family to suffer from such symptoms (at twenty-five, as a medical student, William had experi-

enced an extended "crisis" of nerves), she was the only family member to enter into an unremitting, lifelong battle with her illness. Alice's condition was
called, at different times in her life, hysteria, neurasthenia, suppressed gout,
rheumatic gout, cardiac complication, nervous hyperesthesia, spinal neurosis, and spiritual crisis (Strouse, 1980, p. xi). She underwent many of the somatic therapies of her day and endured the examinations and ministrations
of legions of medical "experts" with forbearance, if not always with good
grace, as these letters to William suggest:

> It requires the strength of a horse to survive the fatigue of waiting hour after
> hour for the great man and then the fierce struggle to recover one's self-respect
> after having been reduced to the mental level of Charlie Moring [a dim-witted
> acquaintance]. I think the difficulty is my inability to assume the receptive atti-
> tude, that cardinal virtue in women, the absence of which has always made me
> so uncharming to and uncharmed by the male sex. (A. J. to W. J., 1886 [?], in
> James, 1981, p. 107)
>
> My doctor came last week and examined me for an hour with a conscien-
> tiousness that my diaphragm has not hitherto been used to. When he came to
> the end he was as inscrutable as they always are and the little he told me I was
> too tired to understand. . . . I was much disappointed by his lack of remedial
> suggestions, all great doctors are chiefly interested in the diagnosis and don't
> care for anything interesting. They ought to have a lot of lesser men . . . to do
> their dirty work for them, curing their patients, etc. (A. J. to W. J., 1884, in
> James, 1981, p. 100)

Despite her frequent irritation with the "great men," Alice did not express
her anger and frustration to the physicians who treated her; to them she was
the model of a genteel neurasthenic. She had few outlets for her strong emotions, and, if these outlets had been available to her, the idea of "goodness" to
which she and her family subscribed would not have permitted use of them.
The internal pressures were enormous: As Alice wrote to her aunt, Catherine
"Kate" Walsh in 1885, "To have a tornado going on within one whilst one is
chained to a sofa, is no joke, I can assure you." In the same letter, Alice,
whom William took to calling "bottled lightning" (W. J. to A. J., June 3,
1888, in James, 1981, p. 28), observed that "as my physical strength increases my nervous distress and susceptibility grows with it, so that from an
inside view it is somewhat of an exchange of evils" (p. 104). Her somatic
complaints, then, were observed by Alice to be, if not expressive of her internal distress, at least in some way linked to it.

Consider, for a moment, the extraordinary description that Alice gave to
William twenty years later of her first complete "breakdown" from hysteria
in 1868, when she was nineteen:

In looking back now I see how it began in my childhood, altho' I wasn't conscious of the necessity until '67 or '68 when I broke down first, acutely, and violent turns of hysteria. As I lay prostrate after the storm with my mind luminous and active and susceptible of the clearest, strongest impressions, I saw so distinctly that it was a fight simply between my body and my will, a battle in wh. the former was to be triumphant to the end. Owing to some physical weakness, excess of nervous susceptibility, the moral power pauses, as it were for a moment and refuses to maintain muscular sanity worn out with the strain of its constabulary functions. As I used to sit immovable reading in the library with waves of violent inclination suddenly invading my muscles taking some one of their myriad forms such as throwing myself out of the window or knocking off the head of the benignant pater as he sat with his silver locks, writing at his table, it used to seem to me that the only difference between me and the insane was that I had not only all the horror and suffering of insanity but the duties of doctor and nurse and strait-jacket imposed upon me too. Conceive of never being without the sense that if you let yr. self go for a moment your mechanism will fall into pie and that at some given moment you must abandon it all, let the dykes break and the flood sweep in acknowledging yourself abjectly impotent before the immutable laws. When all one's moral and natural stock in trade is a temperament forbidding the abandonment of an inch or the relaxation of a muscle 'tis a never ending fight. When the fancy took me of a morning at school to study my lessons by way of variety instead of shirking or wiggling thro' the most impossible sensations of upheaval violent revolt overtook me so that I had to "abandon" my brain as it were. So it has always been, anything that sticks of itself is free to do so, but conscious and continuous cerebration is an impossible exercise and from just behind the eyes my head feels like a dense jungle into wh. no ray of light has ever penetrated. So with the rest, you abandon the pit of yr. stomach the palms of yr. hands the soles of yr. feet and refuse to keep them sane when you find in turn one moral impression after another producing despair in the one, terror in the other anxiety in the third and so on until life becomes one long flight from remote suggestion and complicated eluding of the multifold traps set for your undoing. (A. J. to W. J., October 26, 1890, in Strouse, 1980, pp. 128–129)

In the torment of her first breakdown, Alice had briefly considered two violent alternatives—that of killing herself or that of killing her father ("knocking off the head of the benignant pater"). The roiling emotion of her rage and despair caused her to fear that she would lose control of herself, while at the same time the effort to restrain it caused her to assume the burden of being "doctor and nurse and strait-jacket" to herself.

In letters of that period written to Robertson, his youngest son, Henry Sr. describes how, amidst Alice's "violent turns of hysteria," she was "half the time, indeed much more than half, on the verge of insanity and suicide" (James, 1963, p. 6). Alice required her father to be at her bedside night and day. Not infrequently she spoke to him of her wish to commit suicide, and he did, indeed, give her permission to end her life. In later conversations with her father, Alice realized that her more profound purpose in attempting to gain this permission had been that of asserting her autonomy. She told him at that time that "now [that] she could perceive it to be her *right* to dispose of her own body when life had become intolerable, she could never do it" (p. 7). Since Alice had few—if any—means available through which to express her autonomous strivings, perhaps it is not surprising that she considered the only one at her disposal: the decision whether to choose life or death. Throughout her life she returned "again and again . . . to the idea that only in death could the self achieve definition" (James [Yeazell], 1981, p. 78).

Alice maintained one of her longest periods of good health during a time when she had a clear mission that required a high level of organization, energy, and attention. This was the several-year period directly following her mother's death in 1882, when she ran the James household, first for her father prior to his death and then, more briefly, for her brother Henry. It was during this period that she strengthened her relationship with Katharine Peabody Loring, a woman who was very involved in social and charitable works and whom Alice described to a friend as having "all the mere brute superiority which distinguishes man from woman, combined with all the distinctively feminine virtues. There is nothing she cannot do from heaving wood and drawing water to driving runaway horses and educating all the women in North America" (James [Edel], 1964, p. 10). Alice's attachment to Katharine was an intense one, and one predicated on Katharine's strength and ability to care for her in a variety of ways. When, in 1884, Katharine decided to take her own sister Louisa, an invalid, to Europe, Alice, who by then was living alone in the family home, determined to leave for Europe as well. Edel (author of the introduction to *The Diary of Alice James*) interprets Alice's abrupt departure as an indication of her panic at being left behind. Henry James made frequent note of Alice's jealousy of Katharine's ministrations to Louisa. It appeared to him that whenever Louisa called Katharine away, Alice's illness became more acute and Katharine had to be summoned. Strouse (1980) refers to Alice's "tenacious dependence" (p. 266) on Katharine, which took the form of "tyrannical helplessness" (267). Eventually, Alice had Katharine all to herself. Alice never returned to America, nor did she ever regain the robust health she had displayed in the early 1880s. Katharine was with her until her death on March 6, 1892.

When Alice was told by her doctors in 1890 that she had a terminal illness, she embraced her fate with a high energy and good spirits that seemed natural to one who had finally been permitted to take up, with legitimate cause, her true and lifelong vocation—the preparation for death. It was only in the two years before she died that Alice was able to unleash her intellectual and creative energies in the service of a sustained labor—the keeping of her remarkable *Diary,* which was published after her death.

Hysteria and Borderline Personality Disorder

Alice and Charlotte lived at a time when manifold problems were labeled "hysterical." They likewise lived at a time when physicians' descriptions of the most common nervous disorders emphasized conflicts within the individual. Many of those who suffered were, on the one hand, unable to meet social norms and, on the other, unable to release themselves from the force of these norms, since the norms had been internalized. Hysteria undermined the norm of female refinement in two ways: first, in direct violation, through the "fits," or unseemly emotional outbursts to which hysterical individuals were prone, and second, through debilitating physical symptoms that rendered the individual helpless, in a caricature of feminine delicacy (Hale, 1971).

Alice's and Charlotte's afflictions did not reflect only a response to cultural conditions, however. They were equally a response to the unique familial contexts in which they found themselves. Charlotte had lost a father through desertion; her mother's affection was equally lost to her, as it never was expressed, either verbally or physically. Both Charlotte and Alice were subjected as children to geographical dislocation and relocations; likewise, each was exposed to harsh teasing from brothers, teasing that today might be termed abusive. The attempts of each to be "good" in her own repressive environment resulted in harsh self-blame. Each had an intense need for the exclusive attention and care of another, and this craving dictated important life decisions. At different times, these women's illnesses dominated their relationships and achieved important ends. In Charlotte's case, illness led to a separation from domesticity and opened up the possibility of an autonomous existence; for Alice, illness kept her loved one safely with her.

There is a malignant kinship between hysteria, as it was conceived of and treated during the latter part of the nineteenth century, and current conceptualizations and treatment of borderline personality disorder. This sisterhood is rooted in similarities in the way these two "women's diseases" and the women who suffered from them are viewed.

Both hysteria and BPD have primarily affected women from adolescence to early middle age. In the case of each, criteria for diagnosis transformed and expanded over time until an increasingly large number of women bore these labels. Each "disease" had a symptom or symptoms that had early on been considered central to its diagnosis but that over time diminished in importance. In the case of hysteria, it was the seizure that was originally considered the symptom most characteristic of the "disease" (Smith-Rosenberg, 1972); in the case of BPD, transient psychotic symptoms and cognitive distortions were thought to be essential for diagnosis.[8] In addition to a shift in core symptomatology, in both cases the diagnoses—BPD and hysteria—came to be signifiers for a heterogeneous group of symptoms that could not easily be said to describe a unitary diagnostic entity. As time went on, more and more women came to be given a diagnosis whose criteria became more and more difficult to specify. As is true in the case of "borderline" women, many of the women diagnosed "hysterical" looked very different from other women carrying the identical diagnosis.

The way in which physicians responded to hysteria in general and to their hysterical patients in particular mirrors the present-day struggles of psychiatrists and other nonmedical psychotherapists to understand borderline personality disorder and to work with the "borderline" patient. Many nineteenth-century physicians viewed their patients as willful, selfish, and manipulative in the use of their symptoms. At the same time, these hysterical women were thought to be emotionally indulgent, morally weak, and lacking in power or will; they were "in effect, children, and ill-behaved, difficult children at that." One physician wrote of his hysterical patients, "They have in fact all the instability of childhood, joined to the vices and passions of adult age" (Smith-Rosenberg, 1972, p. 668). In describing their patients, nineteenth-century physicians felt no compunction to mince their words. Silas Weir Mitchell, who had built a reputation for his effective treatment of hysterics, wrote in 1877: "There is often no success possible until we have broken up the whole daily drama of the sick-room, with its selfishness and its craving for sympathy and indulgence. . . . A hysterical girl is . . . a vampire who sucks the blood of the healthy people around her" (Mitchell, *Fat and Blood: And How to Make Them,* quoted in Ussher, 1992, p. 76). As Smith-Rosenberg (1972) tells us, "The hysteric's exploitive dependency often functioned to cue a corresponding hostility in the men who cared for her or lived with her. Whether father, husband, or physician, they reacted with ambivalence and in many cases with hostility to her aggressive and never-ending demands" (p. 671). She speculates that the physicians' resentment of their hysterical patients stemmed first from the baffling and elusive nature of hysteria itself, and second, the relations which existed in the physicians' minds between their categorizing of hysteria as a disease and the role women were expected to play in society. These patients did not function as women were expected to function, and . . . the physician who treated them felt threatened both as professional and as a rejected male. He was the therapist thwarted, the child untended, the husband denied nurturance and sex. (p. 663)[9]

As currently with respect to BPD patients, physicians were not anxious to treat hysterical women. Often the treatment relationship resembled nothing so much as a battleground over which the physician was determined to have supremacy, even if this meant threatening, ridiculing, and frightening his patients, or applying physical force of varying kinds (Smith-Rosenberg, 1972). Alice James wrote in her diary in 1890: "I suppose one has a greater sense of intellectual degradation after an interview with a doctor than from any human experience" (quoted in Showalter, 1985, p. 144).

In 1990, Michael Stone, a psychiatrist and one of the most prolific contributors to the literature on borderline personality disorder, listed the traits that he believed best describe the individual diagnosed with BPD:

Impulsive: chaotic, fickle, desultory, flighty, inconstant, reckless, unpredictable
Moody: mercurial, volatile
Extreme: unreasonable, alternately adoring and contemptuous, childish, vehement, outrageous, unstable, creating "scenes"
Irritable: cranky, hostile, irascible
Manipulative: demanding, importunate, possessive, seductive
Dependent: clingy
Lacking depth: without abiding interests, shallow
Vulnerable: fragile

As we shall later discuss, much that is wrong with our thinking about women diagnosed with BPD today is embedded in such descriptions, as well as in much of the current literature exploring the "management" of these clients and the management of countertransference reactions toward them. BPD, like hysteria, has been considered to be a disorder with a refractory nature, but unlike "hysterics" who often tried a variety of recommended *treatments*, many clients given the BPD diagnosis move on to a succession of *therapists*.[10]

From the Somatic Style to Psychoanalytic Psychiatry

Just as the movement toward the somatic style of the neurologists in the latter part of the nineteenth century had implications for the treatment of American women, so did the movement away from it in the early twentieth, when adherence to the somatic form of treatment for the "nervous" diseases was gradually supplanted by an enthusiasm for the psychoanalytic method.[11] American practitioners found psychoanalysis particularly attractive for a variety of reasons. For one, somatic medicine had failed over the years to provide effective treatments for and theories about the causes of nervous disease, and psychoanalysis was the most highly developed model yet juxtaposed to it. For another, psychoanalysts claimed to be scientists with a rigorous and systematic method, and psychoanalytic treatment brought to the physician treating nervous disorder a scientific-medical aura with all its attendant authority.

Psychoanalytic theory became the prevailing medical psychology in America, and the effectiveness of the psychoanalytic method was widely touted. The American incarnation of psychoanalysis was a version of the Freudian model modified and simplified to fit the demand characteristics of the culture (Hale, 1971). For American psychiatry, turning toward psychoanalysis represented the acceptance of a psychodynamic model of illness in which psychological and social factors were seen to cause strain or anxiety, resulting in a wide range of disturbances from ulcers to schizophrenia (Hale, 1995, chap. 9). The roles of sexuality and aggression were muted in the American version; *this* psychoanalytic model had a more moralistic and optimistic tone than Freud had intended, and it may be that the experience many of the practicing psychoanalysts of the day had undergone as immigrants to America contributed to their strong emphasis on social conformity or "adaptation" (Hale, 1971). In the main, psychoanalysis in the United States developed into an ethical system:

> Its first commandment was to face "reality," to know one's own inner desires the better to control and sublimate them. This new code absorbed most of the equations of the old one. What had once been "good" was now "adapted," "conscious," "civilized," and "mature." What had been "bad" was "unconscious," "primitive," "childish," "emotional," "unadapted." Mere pleasure, sexual indulgence, passivity, laziness, and selfishness were "immature." Rationality, unselfishness, control of instinct, independence, were "evolved," "scientific," and "progressive." (p. 346)

Most popularizations of psychoanalysis in its early days included some description of how neuroses "prevented the successful fulfillment of a social role, be it the characteristics of the ideal male or female, or a man's career or a woman's marriage" (Hale, 1971, p. 413). In the American case histories, "patients seemed untroubled about what standards to follow. . . . But they had failed in their own eyes to fulfill the conditions of a clearly outlined morality, internalized in a strong, scrutinizing conscience. They were assailed by intense guilt, shame, and fear of punishment. They seemed to take over in their feelings about themselves the sharp moral judgments of the period" (p. 466).

The era of overdiagnosis of hysteria came to an end only when women's desires for self-gratification began clashing more strongly with the Victorian notions of the home as a true "haven in a heartless world" (Lasch, 1977) and the "experts' ideal of maternal self-sacrifice . . . became unbearable. To bridge the contradiction, psychomedical theory would become ever more tortured and bizarre—until once again femininity could only be explained as a kind of disease—'masochism'" (Eherenreich & English, 1978, p. 244). With the advent of psychoanalysis, new, psychological, explanations were found for women's madness. In women's desire for greater control over their own lives gynecologists and psychiatrists found an unhealthy "rejection of femininity" (Eherenreich & English, 1978). If femininity was masochistic and a rejection of femininity pathological, women were subjected to a psychological double bind tighter than the corsets and stays they had been so relieved to cast off.

Fashionable Disease: Past and Present

Even shortly after the turn of the century, it was recognized that hysteria and neurasthenia had become the fashionable and overused diagnoses of their day. In 1904 James Jackson Putnam wrote in the *Boston Medical and Surgical Journal*, "Imitation and fashion play a large part even in scientific investigation" (Quoted in Hale, 1971, p. 92). In 1905 Clarence B. Farrar wrote in the *American Journal of Insanity*:

> It is a conspicuous fact that at certain intervals of time new nosographic entities appear on the psychiatric horizon, which have the misfortune to become popular. . . . In their passage they increase in bulk at the expense of less well defined pathological conditions, especially by the absorption of numerous cases from that important category in all classifications—the undiagnosed group, which are often found to fit the new pattern with singular convenience. (Quoted in Hale, 1971, p. 85)

However, the "scientific" and "medical" practice of psychiatry in the twentieth century failed to eliminate such large and ill-defined categories. In 1906, a hospital superintendent, G. Alder Blumer, argued that Emil Kraepelin had defined dementia with so much ambiguity that such conditions as senile dementia, in which memory and perception were impaired, and dementia praecox, in which they were unaffected, were included in the same category (Hale, 1971). The diagnosis of dementia was likewise attacked at the time on the basis that dementia cases were considered hopeless and, therefore received less treatment than other cases. A "gloomy prognosis" was considered harmful in such situations, according to J.T.W. Rowe (*American Journal of Insanity,* 1907, quoted in Hale, 1971, p. 86). Compare this warning with the contemporary advice to psychiatric residents by Reiser and Levenson: For the psychiatrist to view patients as "borderlines" and not as individuals is to compromise the quality of treatment by yielding to "an unwarranted sense of therapeutic cynicism and prognostic despair" (1984, p. 255).

During the early part of the twentieth century, practitioners were divided in their views on the etiology of nervous disorder. At that time, one group leaned more toward purely organic explanations, and the other was not inclined to view such a large group of disorders as having an organic basis (Hale, 1971). Among the many controversies today surrounding the borderline personality disorder, one of the most fierce has been the debate over the biological etiology of the disorder. So significant is this question for those studying the disorder that it was given prominence at the 1990 meeting of the American Psychiatric Association.[12]

Five years before that conference, Showalter, Cassandra-like, stated that "medical management has replaced moral management as a way of containing women's suffering without confronting its causes. We can predict that if 'depression' is soon viewed as a meaningless catchall category, another female malady will appear to take its place for another generation" (1985, p. 249). I believe that this has now occurred, and that this new American female malady is borderline personality disorder. Following in the tradition of hysteria and neurasthenia, BPD has become the fashionable diagnosis of our time.

Medicalization and Representation

Medicalization is a form of representation, and insofar as it has affected society's interpretation of women's experience, it has affected women's own interpretation of their experience as well. The link between women and disease is based on social devaluation; both women and disease are "marginalized elements which constantly threaten to infiltrate and contaminate that which is more central, health or masculinity" (Doane, 1986, p. 152). Diagnosis of women

> is likely to reflect not only theories about disease as such, but implicit views about woman's normal place and function. Such views in turn are colored by the nearly universal experiences of scientists, medicine men, technocrats, and priests. Almost everybody remembers mother as being somehow at the origin of things, a mysterious power to be reckoned with. And almost everybody feels ambivalent about that.
>
> One response to this ambivalence has been the social control of women, the careful, institutionalized, legally codified limiting of women's feared power. Another response has been the assumption that such controls are normal as well as normative and that if physical, psychological, and institutional constraints lead to symptoms in women, that too is normal. Female complaints, then, are inherently paradoxical. Yes, she is sick, but all women are delicate. Yes, she is dissatisfied, but all women complain.
>
> In modern times, as psychological theories became increasingly influential in social life, explanations of female complaints became more complicated, but many of them still reflected primitive myths about the sexes as well as biases of particular theories. (Waites, 1993, p. 158)

The dominance of scientific philosophy in the nineteenth century gave legitimacy to men with scientific expertise, and "with it the power to define reality," a power from which women were excluded as "science itself emerged as a singularly male enterprise" (Ussher, 1992, p. 66). In nineteenth-century America, the relationship between women, who had no other means to escape the constraints of their "feminine" roles, and an emerging professional class of physicians became a symbiotic one in which

> medicine thrived on the perceived physical and psychological woes of middle-class women, and women exploited the legitimation that doctors provided to deviate in sickly ways.
>
> What this historical example suggests, of course, is that the expansion of the health-care system is also the expansion of a system that helps to define for women the nature of the stresses they confront. Stresses are refracted through an ideology which encourages women to search within their psyches and bodies for the sources of their problems. Moreover the health-care industry also provides the resources for acting on the understanding of stress which it generates; it provides . . . an elaborate paraphernalia whose utilization only reinforces the

ideology of stress as sickness, encouraging women to search all the more inten-
sively in their private selves for the sources of the problems they experience.

Finally, the utilization of these resources helps set women on the path toward
. . . privatized and self-destructive forms of deviance. (Cloward & Piven, 1979,
p. 668)

As "the establishment of syndromes and the classification of madness
within discrete categories marked the reification of the medical approach by
the god of taxonomy" (Ussher, 1992, p. 98), it in no way loosened the association between madness and femininity. Medicalization merely gave legitimacy to the discourse and allowed "a wider spectrum of experts to pro-
nounce on causes and cures, fortified by the new taxonomies adopted as
official classifications of 'madness'" (p. 99). The medicalization of "madness"
as "mental illness" sanctified the profession of psychiatry by cloaking it in the
mantle of physical medicine. Borderline personality disorder is one of the
newer taxonomic inventions, and in order to examine how this diagnosis
serves the medical community well while it serves women ill, we must explore further the devices of our present system of psychiatric classification.

2

Taxonomy as Destiny? The Birth of Labels

Individuals are types of themselves and enslavement to conventional names and their association is only too apt to blind the student to the facts before him.

—William James, *1896 Lowell Lectures*

In our present state of knowledge . . . we are quite unable to make a specific correlation between the physical findings and the mental symptoms, while . . . it is quite possible to express the symptomatology of the disease, to describe it, so to speak, purely in psychological terms.

—Smith & Jelliffe, *Diseases of the Nervous System: A Textbook of Neurology and Psychiatry* (1915)

The impetus from the psychiatric community to devise a comprehensive classificatory system of mental disorders has been a relatively recent phenomenon (Loring & Powell, 1988), and one not without its detractors (Zigler & Phillips, 1961). The theories of Szasz (1961) and others in the antipsychiatry movement who believe that criteria employed in making judgments about mental health and mental illness are closely related to the status ideal of our time (Scheff, 1984) are difficult to test experimentally, since no operational criterion of mental illness exists independent of psychiatric diagnosis. After all, mental illness is a "mentalistic" concept—that is, one that is never directly observable, but only able to be inferred from symptomatic behaviors

(Temerlin, 1968). Diagnosis is "an *interpretation* of an individual's experience" (Kleinman, 1988, p. 7), which "implies a tacit categorization of some forms of human misery as medical problems" (p. 8), and psychopathology, in its broadest definition, represents "the tendency of people to do the same painful things, feel the same unpleasant feelings, [and] establish the same self-destructive relationships, over and over and over" (Mitchell, 1988, p. 26).

From a cultural anthropological perspective, only specific psychiatric diagnoses—schizophrenia, bipolar disorder, organic brain disorders, certain anxiety disorders, and, perhaps, major depression—have cross-cultural validity, and other popular Western diagnoses such as dysthymia, agoraphobia, anorexia nervosa, and personality disorders probably do not: "Cultural norms reciprocally interact with biological processes to pattern . . . body/self experiences so that different archetypes are predominant in different social groups [societies or countries]" (Kleinman, 1988, p. 60). Definitions of what constitutes psychopathological conditions "mirror the deep preoccupations of a society" (Brumberg, 1992, p. 147). Neither of the responses to the traditional psychoanalytic models of mental illness after World War II—the antipsychiatry movement and the more recent biologically oriented psychiatry—would appear to have taken into account that it is the "*idea* of mental illness [that] structures both the perception of disease and its form" (Gilman, 1988).

The deconstruction of madness undertaken by the antipsychiatrists and dissenters, and the generalizations that accompanied it, did little to advance our understanding of the etiology and treatment of mental illness (Ussher, 1992). To insist that madness is merely a fiction or a social construction is to embrace too simplistic a view, since "even if oppression *is* part of madness, and if labelling *is* tyranny in practice, we cannot claim that all the different experiences of those positioned mad are a result of a common chain of events, or that they can be ameliorated in an homogeneous way" (p. 222). We must look at the social elements of madness from within a perspective that does not deny its reality. "If one considers the ideas of disease—all disease, including mental illness—as realities mirrored in and conceptualized through the pressures of social forces and psychological models, then the question becomes much more complex and, indeed, much more interesting" (Gilman, 1988, p. 9).

To medicalize psychological problems is to exert a form of social control that may deny or diminish the importance of social problems:

> Those who benefit most from the existing social order are for obvious reasons attracted by an explanatory schema which locates the source of the pathology in in-

tra-individual forces, and which allows the redefinition of all protest and deviation from the dominant social order in such individualistic and pathological terms. Not least, psychiatry is appealing because it masks the necessarily evaluative dimension of its activities behind a screen of scientific objectivity and neutrality. It was and is, therefore, of great potential value in legitimizing and depoliticizing efforts to regulate social life and to keep the recalcitrant and socially disruptive in line. (Scull, 1993, p. 392)

Positivistic premises assume that values, beliefs, and politics never sully the purity of scientific observation and that "concepts and questions can be defined operationally, and investigated in an *exact* and *replicable* fashion" (Ussher, 1992, p. 143). The *DSM-III-R* (1987) represented the decrement over time of the influence of social and psychological theories of the etiology of mental illness and the entrenchment and enlargement of the biomedical view (Conrad & Schneider, 1992), and the *DSM-IV* (1994) does little better, paying only lip service to social and psychological theories. The replacement of the term *mental illness* with the term *mental disorder* in the transition between *DSM-II* and *DSM-III* may have reflected "the long-standing failure of psychiatry to answer the conceptual challenge posed by the anti-psychiatrists or . . . a broadening of the conceptual formulation in order to incorporate more phenomena under the domain of psychiatry" (Russell, 1985, p. 299).

"Mad" Women and "Bad" Men

In Chapter 1, we discussed how witches came to be considered "mad" rather than "bad." In our society, a behavior that is considered "mad" when engaged in by women is considered "bad" when engaged in by men. Courts are more likely to assign women to psychiatric treatment and men to prison for criminal activity. Women who *do* go to prison are more likely to be given treatment and prescribed psychotropic medication than are men (Ussher, 1992). Women who commit crimes, then, are thought to be out of their senses; men who do the same, to be "bad":

The ascription of the label of criminality to men is less stigmatizing, as well as somehow more "natural." We know that men commit crimes, that they are sometimes *bad*, and thus we merely punish them for their antisocial actions, without looking any deeper for an explanation of their behavior. The man who stabs his lover is merely acting like a man. He must be punished, but his behavior causes no particular surprise. Whereas the woman who stabs her lover must be mad. (Ussher, 1992, p. 172)

Just as criminalization has its dark side, so too does the medicalization of deviance, for, among its other effects, medicalization divorces deviance from responsibility, individualizes social problems, and depoliticizes deviant behavior (Conrad & Schneider, 1992).

Mental Illness and Labeling Theory: Are We Blaming the Victim?

To designate is also to create and to enforce. By devising and allocating words, which are names, people create entities and modes of experience and enforce specific subjective experiences. Names render events, situations, and relationships available or unavailable for psychological life that might otherwise remain cognitively indeterminate. Consequently, whether or not something will be an instance of masculinity or femininity, activity or passivity, aggression or masochism, dominance or submission, or something else altogether, or nothing at all, will depend on whether or not we consistently call it this or that or consistently do not name it at all, hence do not constitute and authorize its being. Similarly, to the extent that we link or equate such names as, for example, femininity and passivity, we exert a profound and lasting formative influence on what it is said to be like to be feminine or passive. Logically, there is no right answer to the questions, what is masculine and what is feminine and what is active and what is passive. There are no preconceptual facts to be discovered and arrayed. There are only loose conventions governing the uses and groupings of the words in question. And these conventions, like all others, must manifest values. (Schafer, 1974, p. 478)

The labeling approach to deviance when applied to mental illness considers psychiatric symptoms to be "labeled violations of social norms and stable mental illness to be a social role" (Scheff, 1984, p. 13). This approach also concerns itself with what contingencies may lead to status demotions for some norm violators and not for others:

The labeling theory of mental illness is founded on the idea that what are called "symptoms of mental illness" can also be conceptualized as a certain kind of non-conformity: the violation of residual rules. . . . When a person's behavior is disruptive or upsetting and we cannot find a conventional label of deviance (crime, drunkenness, etc.), we may resort to a miscellaneous or residual category. In earlier societies, witchcraft or spirit or demonic possession were used. In our society, our residual category is mental illness. (Scheff, 1984, p. 188)

The designation of some individuals as "mad" helps us to "affirm our own normality, or even ascertain what it is" and, as Foucault has pointed out, helps keep those parts of ourselves that we fear the most at a remove. "The 'Other' is needed to define the 'One'" (Ussher, 1992, p. 140).

Has the prevailing psychology become "unwittingly the agent of the privileged" (Kegan, 1982, p. 213), so that status demotions are more likely to be inflicted on a lower than a higher status group? The action taken to remedy social problems—and mental health problems are among these—depends, in large part, upon whether the causes of the problem are found to be within individuals or in the environment (Caplan & Nelson, 1973). Definitions of a problem, once arrived at—"once legitimated and acted upon, tend to define the problem indefinitely, irrespective of their validity. Once in effect, they resist replacement by other definitions" (p. 201). Those performing psychotherapy focus primarily upon person-centered variables, which they prefer to see as independent variables having causal relationships to other behavior, and in so doing, they frequently overlook situational determinants of behavior in favor of more person-blaming definitions (Caplan & Nelson, 1973). This bias may be particularly disadvantageous to women, since personal, rather than environmental, factors have been more often used to explain female behavior, whereas for males, the opposite has been the case (Wallston & Grady, 1985). Gender itself, which is a personal factor, is often used as an "explanatory variable, although it may frequently have been confounded with situational factors, such as status and power" (p. 10). Because of the strong correlation between status and gender (Unger, 1978), and because of women's generally lower status in our society, women may be at greater risk for being labeled mentally ill.

Gender Roles, Mental Illness, and the Price of Deviance

"There have always been those who argued that women's high rate of mental disorder is a product of their social situation, both their confining roles as daughters, wives, and mothers and their mistreatment by a male-dominated and possibly misogynistic psychiatric profession" (Showalter, 1985, p. 3). Many have argued that women's lower status increases their exposure to stressful life events (Dohrenwend, 1973; Unger, 1978) or that the female social role (Gove & Tudor, 1973; Lipshitz, 1978) and/or competing role demands (Gomberg, 1981) are responsible for their higher rates of mental illness. They neglect, however, to say exactly how gender-role expectations and gender differences in distress are related. Many of these explanations lack empirical validation (Kaplan, 1983), and most fail to examine mechanisms that intervene "between sex role and distress for different types of psychological disturbances" (Horwitz, 1982, p. 621). A major limitation of models that define madness merely as deviation from a social role is that they deny the reality of the distress experienced by those who are labeled "mad" (Ussher, 1992).

There is clearly a need for more careful consideration of two aspects of gender roles: (1) whether an individual conforms to or deviates from gender-role expectations, and (2) how the degree of power inherent in a given role relates to psychological distress (Horwitz, 1982). In general, the likelihood that an individual will be labeled mentally ill increases with his/her deviance from expected role behavior, as does the probability that person-centered explanations will be found to account for that behavior (Coie, Pennington, & Buckley, 1974). For women, a particular problem arises by virtue of the fact that those who conform to traditional role expectations occupy powerless roles. Horwitz (1982) claims that when women deviate from such expectations and still fail to occupy powerful roles, the highest rates of psychological distress will likely be found; when they deviate from traditional role expectations but *do* occupy powerful roles, the benefits of dominance may be offset by the pull of the deviation. Combining this theory with the labeling theory model, we might hypothesize that women in powerless roles who deviate from traditional role expectations are at the highest risk for being *labeled* mentally ill.

There is some evidence that socially valued masculine qualities and socially undesirable feminine characteristics are polar opposites, as are socially valued feminine attributes and socially undesirable masculine characteristics (Huston, 1983). Social penalties are levied upon women for violating the female norm of passive dependency and upon men for violating the norm of masculine aggression or self-assertion (Costrich, Feinstein, Kidder, Marecek, & Pascale, 1975; Israel, Raskin, Libow, & Pravder, 1978). A woman who steps out of place may be treated much as a stigmatized individual is treated (Unger, 1978). However, although women whose behavior is seen to be more masculine than feminine are still frequently labeled "deviant" or "castrating" or are said to be having "identity problems," women are equally at risk for being labeled deviant if they show extreme manifestations of sex-typed characteristics—too much dependency or passivity, for example (Franks, 1986). Such a psychological Catch-22 in itself "could drive a woman crazy" (Kaplan, 1983, p. 788). Although there is no doubt that men suffer for their failures to conform to the norm of masculinity, Chesler (1972) believes that men can reject more of their stereotype than can women without perceiving themselves as "sick" or without being psychiatrically hospitalized.

Newer research focuses on "situation-specific norms that tend to be gender-related" (Macaulay, 1985, p. 218) rather than on a single "role" for each sex. Nonetheless, almost a century's worth of research efforts have failed to yield any absolute empirical evidence of relationships between any particular source of stress and any particular form of deviation.[1] Perhaps theories of stress have been made to explain too much, and *social context*, rather than stress, is the key determinant of what form(s) deviance will take:

> If the study of social life has taught us anything, . . . it is that social behavior is socially regulated. How people think about their circumstances and act upon them is influenced by powerful and pervasive forces by which world views are transmitted to them; by which social, economic and political structures enmesh them; and by which elements of age, sex, social class and religious socialization are imposed upon them. Taken together, these regulatory influences define the parameters of possibilities.
>
> Given the large influence of these regulatory processes, why would people cease being subject to them as they gravitate toward deviant behavior? After all, deviant behavior is still *social* behavior. Is it imaginable that people would cease being subject to their particular world view? Or to the modes of social organization that variously link and divide them? Or the myriad socializing influences that regularly impinge upon them? The classical paradigm is based on the assumption that, in the evolution of deviant adaptations, people are suddenly freed from the historically specific context that has already determined what they are or can be. In the most fundamental sense, then, the classical paradigm is probably wrong. Social context cannot be ignored. Stress ought to be understood as indeterminant, as a generalized condition in which any of various rule-violating behaviors may potentially result. In turn, it is features of social context which determine the forms of deviation. (Cloward & Piven, 1979, p. 654)

The problem is one of ascertaining which features of the social context influence some individuals to violate certain societal norms. Women's deviance differs from men's in quantity—frequency—and in quality, in that it is "typically individualistic and self-destructive" (Cloward & Piven, 1979, p. 652), if we take into account women's rates of suicide, prostitution, substance abuse, mental illness, and physical illness. By virtue of their socialization, women "are constrained from acting in violent ways" (p. 656). When women *are* violent, it is generally in ways that are "consistent with their socially defined responsibility for the care and feeding of families" (p. 657). Not only is there a dearth of what Cloward and Piven call "rule-violating options" available to women, but women are constrained by a social ideology that encourages female preoccupation with illness. As a result, "the only models of female deviance which our society encourages or permits women to imagine, emulate, and act out are essentially privatized modes of self-destruction" (p. 660). How can stress be the culprit for women's deviance when women, in many cases, choose to endure a great deal of stress rather than to submit to the self-destructive options for deviance available to them?

   Cloward and Piven (1979) take issue with the conventional wisdom that as gender role distinctions continue to blur, male and female deviance will come to look alike. That will not happen, they hold, not only because of the enduring force of sex norms, but principally because of the enormous institutional power that the health care industry exerts. They state: "We suspect that the proportion of women being drawn into the health system, including the mental health system, is enlarging, and that the proportion will continue to enlarge. More and more women are being led to think of the tensions they experience as rooted in their health or mental health" (p. 666). Once labeled, individuals enter a deviant group that has its own behavior and perceptions that, in turn, can adversely affect self-esteem (Ussher, 1992). The sick role "acts both to legitimate the doctor-patient relationship, and to prescribe behaviour for the individual designated as 'ill'" (p. 132).

Psychiatry's Family Bible: *DSM*

Some critics have directed their fire, not at the notion of diagnostic classification per se, but toward the "prematurity and rarifications of many . . . conceptual schemata" and at the "slavish adherence" of psychiatrists to them (Zigler & Phillips, 1961, p. 607). Despite the fact that diagnostic schemes have become ever more inclusive over the past two decades and the methodology used to test them increasingly sophisticated (Loring & Powell, 1988), the system of psychiatric classification remains, in the thinking of some, still a primitive one (Goodwin & Guze, 1989). Nonetheless, diagnoses presented in the latest version of the *Diagnostic and Statistical Manual of Mental Disorders (DSM-IV,* 1994) are utilized throughout the mental health system as well as by systems outside it, such as the criminal justice system; they are required for managed care reimbursement or, in fact, any third-party payment.

   In the opinion of many, it was the publication in 1980 of a much transformed and expanded system of classification of mental disorders—*DSM-III*

(1980)—that snatched psychiatry from the jaws of professional extinction. By divorcing psychiatry from psychoanalysis and medicalizing the profession anew, the *DSM-III* helped establish the primacy of the psychiatric profession at a time in its history when psychiatry had been having great difficulty establishing its own legitimacy and differentiating itself from psychology and social work.[2] The well of research funding had almost run dry. Although a good deal of research *has* been undertaken in the wake of the conservative *DSM* revolution, much of it has been supported by pharmaceutical companies intent on testing and developing their own psychotropic medications (Wylie, 1995). Moreover, the fact that medication is less expensive than psychotherapy has not escaped the notice of the managers of managed care, whose devotion to the bottom line is legendary. The stakes in a biological model of mental and emotional disorder are high, and a psychiatric establishment that has only recently emerged from its embattled position is unlikely to retreat any time soon from the system of classification—*DSM*—that has become the codified justification for its own existence.

DSM-III, *DSM-III-R*, and *DSM-IV* take a phenomenological approach to the classification of disorder that can hardly be said to be atheoretical, even though this theory-free status has been claimed for them. It has been argued that an approach that consigns the attitudes of psychotherapy clients, the meanings that these clients give to their symptoms, and the social and historical context of their pain to the status of epiphenomena that are peripheral to diagnosis is hardly an approach undetermined by theory (Frank & Frank, 1991). In fact, as soon as one assumes that motivation is unconscious, one must "make inferences about the motives behind the patient's behavior, and the moment one makes an inference, one abandons an atheoretical stance" (Caplan, 1988, p. 196). Observations can be consistent in their overall reliability without necessarily being valid, so that diagnosticians can be "consistent but wrong" (Kleinman, 1988, p. 11). The "medicalized" *DSM-IV*, for all its efforts to devise a way of including psychosocial factors in the diagnostic process through its multi-axial format, remains acontextual and ahistorical in a fashion that denies the very real social problems women face and the substantial contributions of those problems in the development of their psychological difficulties. The *DSM-IV*'s instruction to the clinician is first to rule out the possibility of a general medical or physiological condition as well as any physical condition caused by medication or substance abuse. When it only "*then* moves to the individual psychological level, and only *then* to the social and family level, the prime cause of the disorder is implicitly understood to be biological, and that understanding makes every other factor peripheral" (William Doherty, professor of family social science, University of Minnesota, quoted by Wylie, 1995, p. 27).

The Clinical Realities of Naming and Diagnosis

Since it is not possible for an individual to process more than a small part of the information available in any situation, labels can provide a handy means not only for organizing the input but also for determining what further information the individual will find salient (Langer & Abelson, 1974). There are inherent dangers in the practice of labeling, however. What clinicians attend to when making diagnoses may be organized, in the first place, by "confirmatory bias," or a prompting "to seek information that confirms their category hypothesis" (Murdock, 1988, p. 341). Thus, clinicians may be influenced by one salient symptom to find others that will confirm a given diagnosis and, by so doing, fail to gather information that may be equally or more relevant in the formulation of treatment decisions. They likewise may be influenced to such an extent by a descriptor that happens to be a diagnostic category that they might overlook information not consistent with such a diagnosis. Personality disorders frequently provide more handy labels than do some other categories, since most personality disorders carry such descriptors as titles: "Dependent," "histrionic," and "passive-aggressive" are examples of these. Regardless of the "tyranny" that labels can exert, however, we must guard against embracing label-changing alone as a panacea for what ails our mental health system, since the removal of labels fails to remove an individual's pain, misery, and distress, and "the new label . . . soon takes on the old associations" (Ussher, 1992, p. 222).

Male-Female Differences

It was long thought that femininity and masculinity existed as traits at opposite ends of a single, bipolar continuum, so that the more "feminine" the individual, the less "masculine" she was thought to be, and vice versa. More recent theory would have it that masculine and feminine traits are present in all individuals to greater or lesser degrees (Constantinople, 1973; Spence, Helmreich, & Stapp, 1975). The question then arises as to how much difference actually constitutes a difference between the sexes (Hare-Mustin & Marecek, 1988).

Since degree of aggression appears to be the sole biologically based, prominent personality difference between males and females, most male-female differences owe their origins to culture (Deaux, 1984; Newson, Newson, Richardson, & Scaife, 1978). It has been alleged that we really know next to nothing about gender-related differences in behavior (Sherif, 1979), and that about all that can be said with any authority on the subject, given the conflicting research evidence, is that men and women can be "reliably differentiated on the basis of their perceptions of their own masculinity and femininity" (Spence & Sawin, 1985, p. 4). I hold with the constructivist perspective that assumes we cannot determine the "real" nature of what constitutes male-ness and female-ness (Hare-Mustin & Marecek, 1988), and that we must, therefore, carefully examine the cultural expectations that result in stereotypical notions of what it means to be male or female.

What's in a Stereotype?

In 1954, Allport defined a stereotype as "an exaggerated belief associated with a category. Its function is to justify (rationalize) our conduct in relation to that category" (p. 191). Gender-role stereotypes have traditionally been defined in terms of the personality traits of men and women. Work of the late 1960s and early 1970s on male-female personality traits (Broverman, Broverman, Clarkson, Rosenkrantz, & Vogel, 1972; Rosenkrantz, Vogel, Bee, Broverman, & Broverman, 1968; Spence et al., 1975) showed that there was broad acceptance of the distinction that Parsons and Bales had drawn earlier (1955) between *expressive* behaviors as more characteristic of females and *instrumental* behaviors as more characteristic of males, and Bakan's (1966) distinction between "female" *communion* and "male" *agency*. However, in addition to personality traits that cluster around these dimensions, popular stereotypes surround physical appearance, role behaviors, and occupations (Ashmore & Del Boca, 1979).

Gender-role stereotypes appear to be learned early—prior to the attainment of gender constancy and most other sex-typed behaviors (Reis & Wright, 1982). These stereotypes show a remarkable stability in the face of changing social conditions.[3] As one might imagine, the majority of men are masculine sex-typed and the majority of women feminine sex-typed (Bem, 1974). There is a good deal of evidence, as well, that sex itself is a social category that influences judgments, explanations for performance, and expectations for behavior (Deaux & Major, 1987; Deaux, 1984; Maccoby, 1988). One individual's stereotyped belief about another may constrain the possibilities for action (Gilbert, 1981) by generating in that other person behavior that confirms the stereotype, thus operating as a self-fulfilling prophecy and accounting, at least in part, for differences in behavior between men and women (Skrypnek & Snyder, 1982; Zanna & Pack, 1975).

Parents seem to perceive "boy" and "girl" differences in infants from the first moments of life. In a study by Rubin, Provenzano, and Luria (1976), infants matched on every salient dimension except sex were described differently by adults, the girls being seen as "softer," "finer," and "littler," and the boys perceived as "firmer," "more alert," and "stronger." In yet another study, controlling every aspect of the experimental situation and varying only the label "boy" or "girl" led adults observably to change their emotional responses to the infants (Condry & Condry, 1976). Early labeling of behavior by parents and early responses to such labeled behavior may strongly influence the development of sex-stereotyped attitudes and behavior in children. In those family and social situations that encourage socially approved behavior, acting according to stereotype is both a cooperative response as well as a means of avoiding anxiety that may result when a child anticipates disapproval from adults or peers (Block, 1983).

In our society, behaving in a socially approved manner for men can mean showing greater aggression, self-confidence, dominance (Franks & Rothblum, 1983), forcefulness, independence, and, possibly, more stubbornness and recklessness than women (Werner & La Russa, 1985). For women, social expectations may center around emotional empathy, dependence or passivity, politeness in speech (Kemper, 1984), submissiveness, emotionality, and self-deprecation (Franks & Rothblum, 1983; Piliavin & Unger, 1985; Werner & La Russa, 1985). These expectations have a significant impact upon socialization practices, practices that, in turn, affect the individual's view of him- or herself as a worthwhile person capable of functioning adequately in the world, and it can be anticipated that such expectations affect the diagnosis and treatment of those seeking psychotherapy.

Women more often than men carry diagnoses that are congruent with idealized, stereotyped notions of femininity, and the women who carry such diagnoses are frequent users of mental health services. The "feminine" disorders include depression (Al-Issa, 1980; Dohrenwend & Dohrenwend, 1976; Franks, 1986; Robins et al., 1984; Rothblum, 1983; Russo & Sobel, 1981; Weissman & Klerman, 1977; Williams & Spitzer, 1983; Zigler & Glick, 1986) agoraphobia (Brehony, 1983; Franks, 1986; Hare-Mustin, 1983; Williams & Spitzer, 1983), disorders of sexual dysfunction (Al-Issa, 1980; Hare-Mustin, 1983; Tevlin & Leiblum, 1983; Wakefield, 1987), hysteria, or histrionic personality disorder (Al-Issa, 1980; Gilbertson et al., 1986; Reich, 1987; Warner, 1978), dependent personality disorder (Bornstein, 1995; Gilberston et al., 1986), marital conflicts (Hare-Mustin, 1983), and somatization disorder (Fernbach, Winstead, & Derlega, 1989; Williams & Spitzer, 1983). For disorders that are at variance with feminine stereotypes—such as alcoholism—women more often may go mistreated or misdiagnosed than men (Gomberg, 1981; Russo & Sobel, 1981). Although data on rates of prevalence of mental "disorder" and on rates of utilization of mental health services are frequently collected, less attention has been paid to collecting data about rape, wife-battering, and incest—all problems that relate to the societal devaluation of women (Russo & Sobel, 1981).

Men appear to be more often diagnosed as having disorders that reflect aggressive, antisocial behavior (Dohrenwend & Dohrenwend, 1976; Franks, 1986). Antisocial personality disorder is one of these (Fernbach et al., 1989; Gilbertson et al., 1986; Reich, 1987; Williams & Spitzer, 1983). Substance abuse (Lipshitz, 1978, Robins et al., 1984; Williams & Spitzer, 1983), criminality (Lipshitz, 1978), and certain personality disorders such as antisocial personality disorder (Fernbach et al., 1989; Gilbertson et al., 1986; Reich, 1987; Williams & Spitzer, 1983) are less likely to involve depressive symptomatology than those disorders said to afflict women more frequently (Dohrenwend & Dohrenwend, 1976).

The Personality Disorders: Prevalence and Politics

According to the *DSM-III-R* (1987), *personality disorders* develop "only when *personality traits* are inflexible and maladaptive and cause either significant functional impairment or subjective distress" (p. 335). Some suggest that these disorders, as they are currently categorized, are not discontinuous, real types, but, rather, represent arbitrary classifications (Tellegen & Lubinski, 1983); others believe that they constitute, not mental illness, but behavior that does not conform to social norms (Gove & Tudor, 1973).

It is not surprising that among the disorders that have been examined for possible sex bias, personality disorders are those most frequently represented, for "despite the many similarities between medical and psychiatric conditions, the personality disorders seem to resemble medical diseases least of all and to be dependent upon social conventions most of all" (Kroll, 1988, p. 9). Kaplan (1983) is convinced that the personality disorders[4] offer the most complete showcase for male biased assumptions about what constitutes mental health and mental illness.

The idea that the Axis II personality disorders represent mutually exclusive categories has been repeatedly challenged by members of the psychiatric community itself (Lilienfeld, Van Valkenburg, Larntz, & Akiskal, 1986;

Oldham et al., 1992; Pope, Jonas, Hudson, Cohen, & Gunderson, 1983; Stangl, Pfohl, Zimmerman, Bowers, & Corenthal, 1985; Widiger & Rogers, 1989). Several members of the *DSM-III-R*'s own Advisory Committee on Personality Disorders have stated that "the 13 personality disorders described in *DSM-III-R* are not the final word. The extensive degree of overlap may suggest an overrepresentation of some domains of personality disorder pathology and an underrepresentation of others" (Widiger, Frances, Spitzer, & Williams, 1988, p. 787). It was difficult for the committee to assign weight to individual criteria and to reach consensus on the criteria because of the unavailability of supporting research (Kroll, 1988). The "overlap" referred to consists in similarities among criteria that are said to differentiate one personality disorder from another (Kroll, 1988; Livesley, 1986; Widiger et al., 1988), and the committee made an attempt to reduce the extent of such overlap by simply dropping from the *DSM-III-R* some of the offending diagnostic criteria that had been used in *DSM-III*. This action seems akin to Henry VIII's resolving his conceptual differences with the Church over divorce by eliminating overlapping wives through decapitation: The action appears at once too extreme and, at the same time, insufficiently radical. As a result of the many difficulties encountered in the attempt to define and categorize the personality disorders, the process has been particularly susceptible to economic, historical, ideological, and political considerations (Kroll, 1988).

"Male" Versus "Female" Personality Disorders

Of the thirteen personality disorders named in *DSM-III-R,* only six were able to be compared by sex ratio. One must assume that information on the sex ratios of the remaining seven was too scanty to warrant inclusion in the volume. In the *DSM-III-R,* the paranoid, antisocial, and obsessive-compulsive personality disorders are said to be more commonly diagnosed in men than in women, and the dependent, histrionic, and borderline disorders are said to be more regularly diagnosed in women.

Criteria for the histrionic and borderline disorders have been widely assumed to overlap (Aronson, 1985; *DSM-III-R*, 1987; Livesley, 1986; Widiger et al., 1988), and the dependent personality disorder is not generally included along with these other two in the so-called impulsive or dramatic cluster—a group that may include the antisocial and narcissistic personality disorders as well (Livesley, 1986). However, Widiger et al. (1988) trace the sole change in criteria necessary for diagnosis of the borderline personality disorder (BPD) from *DSM-III* to *DSM-III-R* (a change in one of the criteria, "intolerance of being alone," to "frantic efforts to avoid real or imagined abandonment") to the need to prevent overlap between BPD and the *dependent* personality category.

Are gender roles "masquerading as madness" (Landrine, 1989, p. 332)? Widiger and his colleagues (1988) themselves raise the possibility of gender bias in the diagnosis of the dependent and histrionic personality disorders. Some have called hysteria (the former label for histrionic personality disorder) a "caricature of femininity" (Chodoff, 1982; Easser & Lesser, 1965).[5] In comparing the *DSM-III* criteria for histrionic personality disorder with Broverman et al.'s (Broverman, Broverman, Clarkson, Rosenkrantz, & Vogel, 1970) female-valued, stereotypic items, Kaplan (1983) discovered close parallels among five of the Broverman items and ten of the *DSM-III* criteria, when only five diagnostic criteria need to be satisfied in order for a diagnosis of histrionic personality disorder to be made.

Landrine (1989) makes the case[6] that the gender distribution of the personality disorders "does not result from misogyny on the part of clinicians or within the taxonomy, but instead from the overlap between personality disorders and the role/role-stereotypes of both sexes" (p. 327). "Gender role categories and personality categories," she asserts, "are simply flip sides of the same stereotyped coin" (p. 332). On the other side, Kaplan (1983) insists that, whereas stereotypical feminine behavior alone can earn an individual a diagnosis of dependent or histrionic personality disorder, masculine stereotyped behavior alone does not justify a label of "personality-disordered." Although a number of the personality disorder classifications may be said to codify extremes of feminine stereotyped behavior, there are others, such as the borderline personality disorder, whose base rates of prevalence cannot be attributed directly to gender stereotypes and for whose high rate of diagnosis among women other explanations must be found.

Gender Bias in Diagnosis

Different sets of diagnostic expectations for men and women may eventuate in "1) differential diagnoses of men and of women even when they exhibit the same problems and behavior; 2) variation in treatment of males and females by those in the mental health profession; and 3) codification of these expectations in the publicized reports on the mental health of men and of women" (Loring & Powell, 1988, p. 5). Research into gender bias in diagnosis and treatment has not kept pace with other areas of clinical research, perhaps because researchers have been susceptible to the prevailing ideology that psychotherapy is a scientific procedure. From this perspective, the role attributes of the therapists and clients—their orientations or diagnoses—appear most salient, whereas personal attributes such as gender appear only peripheral (Orlinsky & Howard, 1980).

Clinical biases in the treatment and diagnosis of women have always been difficult to measure. Questionnaires that purport to uncover clinicians' conceptions of mental health may not necessarily tap the ingrained attitudes and emotional reactions evoked in the course of the actual therapy situation (Abramowitz et al., 1976; Adinolfi, 1971; Maffeo, 1979). Arguably the best-known piece of research on clinical judgments of mental health was that performed by Broverman and her colleagues in 1970. In that study, the researchers gave seventy-nine clinicians a Stereotype Questionnaire composed of 122 bipolar items, each of which described a behavior trait or characteristic (e.g., very passive—very active). One group of clinicians was instructed to indicate the item that would most closely correspond to mature, healthy, socially competent male behavior, one group was instructed to make the same judgment about mature female behavior, and a third group was asked to describe a healthy, mature, socially competent *adult*. Results indicated that the clinicians' concept of a mature, competent man differed little from their concept of a healthy adult, whereas they were significantly less likely to perceive a mature competent woman as a healthy adult. Broverman and colleagues adduced from this that the influence of gender-role stereotypes upon the clinicians produced a double standard of mental health: A mature man is a mentally healthy person, whereas a mature woman is not.

A spate of surveys, adjective checklists, and analogue studies was performed on the heels of Broverman's research. They confirmed the existence of stereotyped attitudes and behaviors that might contribute to clinical bias in treatment (Haan & Livson, 1973; Israel et al., 1978; Nowacki & Poe, 1973; Williams & Bennett, 1975). Newer research, however (Brodsky & Hare-Mustin, 1980; Kaplan, Winget, & Free, 1990), including Broverman's own,[7] has indicated, with some exceptions (cf. Teri, 1982) a moderating on the part of psychotherapists of the sort of stereotyping that can result in a double standard of mental health. Even so, it remains unclear whether this more recent development is attributable to actual changes in clinicians' attitudes or whether it represents the fruit of unrepresentative sampling or socially desirable responding by clinicians sensitized to issues of gender bias (Maffeo, 1979; Phillips & Gilroy, 1985; Whitely, 1979).

If clinical competence is related to the ability to perceive another person with accuracy, "implicit or informal theories on the co-occurrence of certain traits in others can distort perception" (Adinolfi, 1971, p. 169). Accuracy in perception implies familiarity or similarity along some dimension, and since familiarity, similarity, and liking are interrelated and generally occur together (Newcomb, 1961), it might follow that psychotherapists will have the most inaccurate perceptions of those clients whose personalities and situations are at the farthest remove from their own, and that these clients may, therefore, receive less than optimal treatment. This may explain the findings of Orlinsky & Howard (1980), who discovered that only male therapists with many years of experience approached the level of competence of female therapists when it came to the treatment of women.

Studies of Gender Bias

The majority of studies that explore the possible influence of the sex of the patient upon diagnosis (and such studies are fairly few in number when compared to other areas of clinical research) are analogue studies in which at least two groups of therapist-subjects read case histories that are identical except for the sex of the client and are asked to select a diagnosis on the basis of the information given. This brief review of the conclusions reached in a number of these studies must be taken as preliminary, given the methodological weaknesses of many of the studies. Sex bias has thus far been found in the diagnoses of antisocial personality disorder (Fernbach et al., 1989; Ford & Widiger, 1989; Warner, 1978) and histrionic personality disorder (Ford & Widiger, 1989; Hamilton, Rothbart, & Dawes, 1986; Warner, 1978). Not surprisingly, men were found to be more often diagnosed "antisocial" and women "histrionic," regardless of whether the case history presented ambiguous criteria for diagnosis or whether criteria were clear-cut and prototypical of the disorders. Unreplicated studies have shown a lack of sex bias in the *DSM-III* diagnoses of masochistic personality disorder (Fuller & Blashfield, 1989), somatization disorder (Fernbach et al., 1989), and primary orgasmic dysfunction (Wakefield, 1987).

A heated argument in the literature on sex bias in diagnosis is whether what is called "sex bias" by some researchers is merely a reflection of actual sex differences in the true prevalence of a disorder. The thrust of the argument is that it is natural for a clinician to assign a diagnosis more frequently to the sex that is known to be more prone to a given disorder. However, what therapists know about prevalence and about sex stereotypes may not only lead to overdiagnosis of some disorders in women (or in men) but may actually bias the rates of prevalence of those disorders.[8] So, if histrionic personality disorder, for instance, is thought to be a "female" disorder both because it is more often diagnosed in women and because its criteria include many stereotypically feminine personality characteristics, therapists may overdiagnose that disorder in women and underdiagnose it in men, thereby further biasing the rates of prevalence for the disorder.

Gender bias in psychiatric diagnosis can take a number of forms.[9] These include: (1) *sampling sex bias* (Widiger & Spitzer, 1991), which occurs as a result of unrepresentative sampling of the patient population under study; (2) *diagnostic sex bias*, or a form of clinician bias in which the practitioner's own sex-role stereotypes influence judgments about what is pathological and what is "normal" in men and women; (3) *self-report bias*, which reflects differences in the willingness of men and women to acknowledge certain attitudes, traits, and behaviors, and (4) *criterion sex bias,* which exists when the criteria for a particular disorder are selected in such a way that the disorder, in its very nature, is either "male" or "female" (Bornstein, 1996). This fourth type—criterion sex bias—which Wakefield (1987) calls *logical* or *factual bias,* occurs "where the criteria for diagnosis, which are the same for men and women, include extreme versions of traits and behaviors that are considered stereotypically female and are normally emphasized in the socialization of women but not men" (p. 466).

Some researchers have tried to ascertain under what conditions gender bias is likely to occur. Bias may occur more often when diagnostic categories describe personality traits rather than behaviors (Hamilton et al., 1986). In a large and methodologically sophisticated study, Ford & Widiger (1989) asked clinicians to render diagnostic assessments on "histrionic" and "antisocial" cases designated either male, female, or of unspecified sex. Clinicians were asked both to rate the degree to which particular features extracted from the case histories met a variety of antisocial and histrionic criteria *and* to make Axis I and Axis II diagnoses. Sex biases were evident for the diagnoses but not for the ratings of diagnostic criteria. The researchers concluded that even when clinicians judge individual criteria for a diagnosis with relative objectivity, their final diagnosis may reflect gender bias that has been "generated by stereotypic expectations with respect to the diagnostic label" (p. 304).

There are other disagreements that pervade the literature on gender bias. Of particular significance is the disagreement over whether the elimination of bias in diagnosis *should* eventuate in the diagnostic equality of the sexes or whether it is reasonable to assume that some diagnoses will naturally include more "feminine" than "masculine" criteria. Although Kaplan (1983) and others believe that the existence of this sort of diagnostic double standard leads to the overpathologizing of women, some disagree, claiming that "within-gender standards . . . [are] more equitable and valid" (Fisher & Barak, 1989, p. 1081).

So-called gender-equal standards, however, may themselves lead to bias. When Warner performed a study of sex bias in the antisocial and hysterical diagnoses, he concluded that these disorders "refer to essentially the same condition which is shaped into different forms in the two sexes by the cultural forces which determine masculine and feminine identity and stereotypes" (1978, p. 841). He pointed out that, of the two diagnoses, antisocial personality disorder is considered the more difficult to treat. In this case, cleaving to separate but equal standards would not result in equality of treatment. In the period since Warner's study, diagnostic criteria have undergone a number of changes, and it is more widely suggested that borderline personality disorder, rather than hysterical personality disorder, may be the polar opposite of antisocial personality disorder in the manner Warner had suggested. If that were the case, we could again assume, because so many men who might be diagnosed as having antisocial personality disorder never enter the mental health system but, rather, are involved in the criminal justice system, that "borderline" men would be viewed as criminal and "borderline" women would be designated as mentally ill.

Studies of Sex Bias in the Diagnosis of BPD

The earliest study of possible sex bias in the diagnosis of borderline personality disorder was conducted in 1983 by Henry and Cohen. To test their first hypothesis—that, all things being equal symptomatically, women were more likely than men to be diagnosed borderline—the researchers, using *DSM-III* criteria, took case studies of BPD from the 1981 *DSM-III Casebook* and sent them to 242 attending and resident psychiatrists at two city hospitals, asking each subject to give a primary and a differential diagnosis. Half of the case studies were "female," in that they used female pronouns, and half were "male." They found no significant differences in the diagnosis given to the male and female case studies. To test their second hypothesis—that there are genuine sex-related differences in the prevalence of BPD characteristics within the general population, Henry and Cohen designed a questionnaire to elicit the presence of BPD characteristics and administered it to 277 graduate and undergraduate students. On twenty-two of the twenty-four questionnaire items, men exhibited more "borderline" features than women.[10] Interpreting their findings, the authors suggested that labeling processes may be determining the process of diagnosis in BPD cases, since the rate of diagnosis does not reflect the frequency with which borderline personality characteristics are reported by men. They speculated that clinicians may perceive these features as more congruent with male sex-role stereotypes and, therefore, may find them more tolerable in men than in women. Contradictory findings, as we discussed in the Prologue, however, have emerged from the ECA Survey's data on borderline characteristics in the general population—data derived from over two thousand subjects (Swartz et al., 1990). These data revealed that in the general population women make up over 70 percent of those with so-called "borderline" symptomatology. The list of symptoms upon which that questionnaire survey was based is similar enough to Henry and Cohen's list[11] to raise questions about the generalizability of Henry and Cohen's results and suggest that there may have been sampling bias in the selection of a student population.

An analogue study by Adler, Drake, and Teague (1990) attempted to assess *DSM-III* Axis II personality assessment by providing 46 clinicians with a case study in which the "patient" met the criteria for borderline personality disorder as well as the histrionic, narcissistic, and dependent personality disorders. Two versions of the case study differing only in sex of the patient were randomly assigned to participants in the study. Clinicians were asked to check "trait," "no trait," or "disorder" for each of eleven Axis II diagnoses. BPD and narcissistic personality disorder were the diagnoses most frequently used (by about half the clinicians); next in frequency was the histrionic personality disorder. The researchers found that the BPD diagnosis was not related to the sex of the case or to the sex of the clinician, although the narcissistic and histrionic diagnoses were clearly perceived as male and female, respectively.

The largest study of gender bias in the diagnosis of BPD to date is an analogue study that I undertook (Becker & Lamb, 1994). In that study, 1,080[12] experienced practicing clinicians—social workers, psychiatrists, and psychologists in equal numbers—were asked to read a case study in which the client showed symptoms of BPD and posttraumatic stress disorder (PTSD) in equal measure, but not in sufficient quantity to qualify him/her for a clear-cut diagnosis of either. Each clinician was randomly assigned either a male or female version of the case study,[13] identical apart from use of male or female pronouns, and was asked to rate on a seven-point scale the extent that the client described in the case history appeared to have symptoms of each of seven *DSM-III-R* Axis I[14] and seven Axis II[15] disorders. Therapists were free to provide multiple diagnoses for the case study, as is the case in actual practice. Likewise, clinicians were asked to rate their practical familiarity with each diagnosis and requested to formulate three questions that they would wish to ask the client if they were the therapist in the case. Subjects found the borderline personality disorder diagnosis more applicable to the case studies than any other Axis I or Axis II diagnosis. In contrast to Henry and Cohen's and Adler and associates' findings, in this large-scale study the female "client" was significantly more frequently seen as "borderline" than her male counterpart.

As in Ford and Widiger's (1989) study, when clients described in the cases were female, the cases were rated significantly higher than male cases for the presence of histrionic characteristics; when the identical clients were male, the cases were rated significantly higher for presence of antisocial characteristics. Interestingly, the three most popular diagnoses—BPD, dysthymia, and self-defeating personality disorder—showed no correlation with one another, despite a logical relationship supported in the literature and delineated in the case studies. The clinicians appeared to see the borderline category as more exclusive than might have been anticipated, especially given the many depressive (dysthymic) characteristics embedded in BPD criteria. The "borderline-ness" of the client seemed to be particularly salient and be immediately tagged. Younger psychologists and psychiatrists rated the case studies higher for the presence of BPD symptoms than did their older counterparts—testimony, perhaps, both to the increasing popularity of BPD over the past fifteen years and the transformations in its conceptualization that we will soon explore.

Just as Adler and associates and Becker and Lamb saw clinicians gravitating toward the borderline diagnosis even when plentiful symptomatic criteria of other disorders had been woven into the case studies, Fernbach and colleagues (1989) found BPD to be the most frequent *misdiagnosis* applied to case vignettes that had been specifically designed to highlight the symptomatology of antisocial personality disorder and somatization disorder, and this misdiagnosis was applied twice as often to the female case vignettes.

Diagnostic Accuracy and the Attractiveness of Labels

In the Becker and Lamb study, lesser familiarity with a specific diagnosis did not seem to inhibit practitioners from judging it applicable to the case study before them. This was particularly true in the case of the self-defeating personality disorder diagnosis, a classification that in both the *DSM-III-R* and *DSM-IV* is listed in the appendix as one of the "Proposed Diagnostic Categories Needing Further Study." Although the clinicians, overall, rated themselves unfamiliar with the categories, they rated self-defeating personality disorder the diagnosis *third* most applicable to the case study. This rating was higher than that for the PTSD diagnosis, criteria for which had been carefully and purposefully interwoven into the case history. The lack of logical relationship among several frequently applied diagnoses and the tendency of clinicians to indicate that clients in the case studies showed many symptoms of diagnoses with which they themselves said they were not familiar seem to call into question the capacity of our present system of classification to reflect accurately the diagnostic considerations of practitioners, the ability of the practitioners themselves to utilize the classificatory system adequately, or both. It appears that many clinicians often find what they expect to find, not necessarily what is "out there" to find.

What are we, then, to make of the borderline diagnosis? What are we to make of the fact that BPD would not even fit many conventional definitions of personality disorder? If individuals with personality disorders "do not experience personal discomfort, being neither anxious nor distressed, nor . . . suffering from any other form of psychotic disorganization" (Gove & Tudor, 1973, p. 813), how do we account for the immoderate "personal discomfort" experienced by "borderline" clients? We must distinguish between the distress and the diagnosis. The distress is real; the diagnosis is a fiction that has become a fact of psychiatric classification. If we follow the evolution of borderline concept to borderline diagnosis, the fictive nature of the diagnosis becomes yet more clear and the question of the origin and nature of the distress we now term *borderline* becomes more pressing.

3

The Rise and Fall of the Borderline Concept

Currently, conceptualizations of BPD can be assigned to one of three general categories: (1) psychodynamic theories that focus attention on developmental problems primarily attributable to separation/individuation struggles of early childhood; (2) views of the syndrome "as primarily an atypical affective disorder, with mood instability and rejection-sensitive dysphoria" responsible for a wide range of so-called borderline behaviors; and (3) theories that focus on the traumatic etiology of BPD as an understandable characterological development linked to childhood and adolescent physical and/or sexual abuse (Kroll, 1993, p. 31). This chapter will include a discussion of older, psychoanalytically based theories of the borderline *concept;* Chapter 4 will take us into current controversies surrounding attempts to define the causes of the borderline personality *disorder.*

The term *borderline* has seen wide variations in its definition since its first use approximately fifty years ago. It has referred, variously, to: (1) borderline personality disorder, (2) a borderline psychostructural organization, in a psychoanalytic sense, (3) borderline affective disorder, and (4) borderline schizophrenia. Each use of the term has had a unique historical development, and each is rife with "ambiguities, unresolved questions, inconsistencies, and limitations," and—despite the conceptual overlap among them—because these meanings lie on different planes of discourse reflecting different notions of illness and etiology, they are totally unreconcilable (Aronson, 1985, p. 209).

Psychodynamic theories are the oldest attempts to explain borderline phenomena. Although the term *borderline* was first employed in 1938 by Adolph Stern, it did not come into wide use until 1953, when Robert Knight wrote about the "borderline state."[1] Knight, with prescience, it would appear, warned his readers that the term *borderline* had more to say about diagnostic uncertainty than about patient psychopathology. He discussed how the borderline state could result from a combination of a number of constitutional factors, trauma-induced predispositions, disturbed relationships, and current stressors that could cause ego impairments of various kinds. The "borderline state" referred to a breakthrough psychotic episode in an otherwise nonpsychotic individual rather than to an invariant character structure.

In 1968, Grinker, Werble, and Drye attempted both to describe unifying characteristics of what they termed the "borderline syndrome" and to classify subtypes of the disorder ranging from the "psychotic border" to the "neurotic border." Their emphasis was upon the description and definition of what Knight (1953) had called the "borderline strip" between neurosis and psychosis. These researchers identified as core borderline features anger, dysfunctional relationships, identity problems, and "depressive loneliness." In 1975, Gunderson and Singer attempted further to isolate symptoms commonly experienced by borderline patients. These included intense affect, impulsivity, brief psychotic experiences, and vacillation in interpersonal relationships.

To revisit the object relations and developmental arrest conceptualizations of the borderline phenomenon that held sway in the 1960s and 1970s is to understand the current psychodynamic formulations that, like paintings that imperfectly cover other paintings, display the outlines of their predecessors and arrive at a sort of ghostly revisionism that causes the newer work to be shaped by the older one in ways the artist had not intended. If we understand the confusions inherent in the first set of theories, we can more easily comprehend the present state of psychodynamic theory.

Object Relations, Developmental Arrest, and the Borderline Syndrome

The older theory that explained the development of the borderline personality structure as a failure to negotiate successfully the early separation/individuation phase of childhood has to be abandoned as a unifying theory because it has not been supported by the evidence. It is, for some, a felicitous theory that assists the conduct of therapy (i.e., it gives the therapist confidence that he/she knows what is going on), but it is untested, improbable in its breadth, explains only a small portion of borderline psychopathology, and has limited applicability to the practical problems encountered in therapy. (Kroll, 1993, p. xvii)

Of the numerous theorists who have attempted over the years to develop comprehensive explanations of borderline phenomena, perhaps none has been more influential than Otto Kernberg. Meissner (1989) credits Kernberg with lessening the confusion brought on by earlier attempts to describe the borderline syndrome as both a psychotic and a neurotic condition. This he did by defining borderline conditions as stable forms of personality organization. Thus did a "state" yield to a "syndrome" and, eventually, to a "personality organization," and with this development emerged a common view of so-called borderline features as parts of an enduring character pathology. Because Kernberg's formulations "have a comprehensiveness and a sweep that makes them seem both formidable and definitive," they have gained a broad acceptance that may have discouraged the development of other competing explanations (p. 161). This is all the more remarkable when one considers that Kernberg has never truly committed himself to any one theory of borderline personality organization.

Kernberg

Kernberg (1967, 1975) maintained that borderline psychopathology stemmed from ego defects resulting from the predominance of intense, pathological pregenital aggressive impulses and their derivatives, which he conceived of as attributable either to constitutional factors or to early environmental frustrations. These ego defects, Kernberg argued, produced a stable personality organization neither wholly psychotic nor wholly neurotic, characterized by identity diffusion and maintained by the use of primitive defense mechanisms—splitting, in particular.

Pregenital—particularly oral—aggression is generally projected onto the mother and, to a lesser extent, the father. The mother becomes, by this means, a dangerous and potentially destructive object, and the father gradually also becomes a screen for aggressive projection. The individual attempts to deny oral-dependency needs and to avoid the fear and rage associated with them. The borderline individual, in Kernberg's scheme, remains developmentally arrested at the stage of early object relations where representations of self and other remain unintegrated. Kernberg defines splitting as the "active, defensive separation of contradictory ego states" (Kernberg, 1989, p. 133). The need to keep primitive aggression from contaminating the good self- and the good object-images leads to division (splitting) of the ego, a process that is essentially defensive. Splitting keeps contradictory all-bad and all-good self-representations and object-representations separate from each other. Splitting and other related primitive defenses such as primitive idealization, omnipotence, projection, and projective identification protect the ego from unendurable conflicts. However, because ego integration is sacrificed in this effort, "an integrated self-concept cannot develop, and chronic overdependence on external objects occurs in an effort to achieve some continuity in action, thought, and feeling in relating to them. Lack of integration of the self-concept determines the syndrome of identity diffusion" (p. 134).

In addition to identity diffusion, Kernberg goes on to explain, the development of "contradictory character traits" that represent the contradictory self- and object-representations hinders the development of sound interpersonal relationships. Likewise, lack of integration of self- and object-images affects the capacity for empathy with others as unique, separate individuals. Because of the lack of ego integration, *superego* integration does not fully occur, leading, among other things, to impairments in anxiety tolerance and impulse control.

Whereas Kernberg's theory purports to be a theory of pathological internal object relationships, it appears to concern itself more with the individual's inner *representations* of object relations than with her/his actual relationships with the objects—the people—themselves (Meissner, 1989). Kernberg's, then, is essentially a theory of object *representations* rather than one of object *relations*. In reading a passage from Kernberg such as the following, one can easily agree with Mitchell (1988) that Kernberg's theory, although starting out with a "relational matrix," somehow manages to arrive at "the traditional version of the Oedipus complex" (p. 142):

> In both sexes, the displacement of frustrated dependency needs from mother to father colors the positive oedipal relation of the girl and the negative oedipal relation of the boy. The displacement of oral-aggressive conflicts from mother onto father increases castration anxiety and oedipal rivalry in boys, and penis envy and related character distortions in girls. In girls, severe pregenital aggression toward the mother reinforces masochistic tendencies in their relation to men, severe superego prohibitions against genitality in general, and the nega-

tive oedipal relation to the mother as a defensive idealization and reaction formation against aggression. The projection of primitive conflicts around aggression onto the sexual relation between the parents increases distorting and frightening versions of the primal scene, which may become extended into hatred of all mutual love offered by others. (Kernberg, 1984)

Despite the claims to descriptive specificity and stability of the borderline personality organization (BPO), Kernberg's list of the diagnostic elements that characterize the BPO reads like the Acta Psychopathologica.[2] His list includes chronic anxiety, phobias, dissociation, obsessive-compulsive symptoms, hypochondrias, polymorphously perverse sexuality, impulsivity, and addiction. Borderline personality organization encompasses paranoid, schizoid, and hypomanic personality structures. It likewise includes other, presumably lower-level, character disorders—hysterical/infantile, narcissistic, depressive/masochistic. Far from specifying a "stable form of pathological ego structure" manifested by a specific constellation of symptoms, Kernberg's borderline personality organization is a generously proportioned umbrella in whose shade many symptoms and conditions can comfortably coexist and overlap (Calef & Wenshel, 1989). Kernberg could no more claim a unitary identity for borderline personality organization in 1975 than could S. Weir Mitchell for hysteria a century ago.

Splitting

The concept of splitting is central to Kernberg's conceptualization of borderline psychopathology. It is splitting as a defensive operation[3] that Kernberg believes differentiates borderline from neurotic conditions (Meissner, 1989).[4] Of all Kernberg's contributions, it is the concept of splitting that seems to have achieved a position of theoretical inviolability, retaining its clinical currency even among those who are quick to eschew the majority of Kernberg's ideas. The attachment to the notion of splitting stands, perhaps, as more of a testament to its heuristic value as a description of the apparently unintegrated shifts and contradictions in the borderline patient's behaviors and emotions (Meissner, 1989) than to its validity as a concept.

From the beginning of life infants "mainly experience reality" (Stern, 1985, p. 255).[5] The principal distortions in the experience of infants arise, not from defenses or wishes, but from cognitive or perceptual immaturity; the defensive distortions to which Kernberg refers depend upon greater cognitive maturity than infants possess (Stern, 1985; Meissner, 1989). There are several convincing developmental arguments to be made against Kernberg's conceptualization of defensive splitting. The first of these is that, in reality, the world of the infant is one of continuous affective gradation, not one in which "good" and "bad" experiences are strictly divided, as Kernberg believes (Stern, 1985). Research on infants does not support the precedence of affect over cognition—the sequence that would be necessary in order for the infant to categorize his/her experience—but rather demonstrates the simultaneity of development of these interpenetrating domains. Further, Kernberg's view that the self and the other cannot come together until the infant can cognitively process the separate good and bad selves seems to postulate the existence of a good self and a bad self prior to the development of such an entity as the "self." In addition, the equation of "good" with "pleasure" and "bad" with "unpleasure" assumes a capacity for intentionality on the part of the infant that presents a developmental impossibility. The developing child's ability eventually to locate her experience in the categories "good" and "bad" can be viewed, not as splitting, but as a higher order means of integrating her experience.

The concept of splitting retains a hallowed place in some current theoretical formulations. For example, Gunderson hedges his bets by splitting *splitting itself* into two types: One form he calls "intrapsychic splitting," and the other he terms "interactive splitting" (Cauwels, 1992, p. 200). According to Gunderson, rather than alternating between views of herself and others as either all good or all bad, the borderline's relationships with herself and others are distinctly ambivalent, and her view of herself does not necessarily reverse when she reverses her view of another. "Interactive splitting" refers to the borderline's fluctuation between three separate levels of functioning, depending on the degree of support available to her. Gunderson's description of the three levels of interactive splitting is an exercise in loyalty to Kernberg: He appears to be attempting to hold onto the concept while ridding himself of it at the same time. The result of such diplomatic maneuvering is little more than a description of borderline interpersonal behavior. While decrying the uselessness of making interpretations of splitting to the patient, Gunderson manages to describe the behavior variously as dependent, masochistic, sarcastic, belligerent, accusatory, and manipulative.[6]

Instead of trying to redefine splitting, it would seem more useful to consider how there exists in some individuals currently diagnosed borderline a cognitive rigidity that does not permit them to maintain two contradictory positions at the same time. The resolution of this conflict "requires first the recognition of the polarities and then the ability to rise above them, so to speak" (Linehan, 1993, p. 36). I would go a step further and suggest that a prevailing mistrust of her own judgment combined with extreme self-criticism (about which there will be much more said later) renders it very difficult for the "borderline" woman to take the perspective of the other.

Mahler, Masterson, and Developmental Arrest Theories

There is a good deal of overlap between object relations theories and developmental theories. Nonetheless, the centrality of Kernberg's focus upon constitutional factors—principally, upon oral aggression in the etiology of the borderline personality organization—distinguishes his formulation from that of Mahler, Masterson, and others who pay more attention to the mother-child interaction. The latter emphasize the mother's ability to provide emotional nurturing (her "libidinal availability," as they would put it) "in eliciting the development of the child's intrapsychic structure" (Meissner, 1989, p. 169). Using Mahler's developmental sequence (and extending her theory), Masterson (Masterson & Rinsley, 1975; Masterson, 1976) views the personality development of the borderline as having been arrested at the separation/individuation stage of development (between eighteen and thirty-six months)—more particularly, during the rapprochement subphase of separation/individuation. This is the period of toddlerhood when the child seeks opportunities for exploration, returning to her caretaker for refueling prior to making the kind of forays out into the world that are the core building blocks for development of his capacity for autonomy. According to Masterson (1972, 1976), the mother of the future borderline herself has borderline characteristics. Although she finds a great deal of gratification in the early symbiotic relationship with her child, she responds to the expression of the toddler's autonomous strivings by withdrawing nurturance and affection—that is, by withholding "libidinal" supplies, in Masterson's terms. Despite this abandonment, the child attempts to sustain an image of the good, nurturing mother by splitting it off from the image of the bad, rejecting mother. It is the child's defense against her feelings of abandonment that produces the inevitable developmental arrest (Masterson & Rinsley, 1975). The caretaker's continuing availability during the rapprochement crisis depends upon the child's regressive behavior. To the extent that the child clings, the mother is gratified.

Because of the magnetic pull exerted by the mother/caretaker, the child is unable to separate adequately. The borderline-to-be, then, carries forward this unresolved symbiotic attachment to her mother in ways that come to define future relationships (Masterson, 1976). Fear of losing herself or losing the object of her loving feelings results in clinging and/or distancing behaviors that interfere with the establishment of intimate relationships in adulthood because this intimacy threatens to strangle her with a symbiotic noose reminiscent of the one with which mother first restrained her. It is guilt over desiring separateness, Masterson claims, that leads to her defensive clinging and demandingness. When these behaviors fail to stave off feelings of abandonment, depression follows, with its constituent components of rage and anger, fear, guilt, helplessness, and emptiness. These feelings are further defended against by splitting, projection, acting out, and by other behaviors (obsessive-compulsive and schizoid, among others) that protect her against despair and thoughts of the abandonment: "In other words, the patient develops an abandonment depression; his ego structure remains orally fixated; his object relations transpire at an oral level; and his most basic fears are of engulfment or abandonment. His most basic problems have to do with the primitive sense of identity and separateness, as well as of mastery and control of impulses" (Masterson, 1976, p. 54).

According to this theoretical formulation, the child is particularly vulnerable just prior to puberty, since his/her need to separate further during this period reintroduces earlier conflicts. Certain life stresses to which individuals are exposed are seen as *individuation* stresses; others as *separation* stresses. Individuation stresses result from life changes such as graduation and leaving home. Separation stresses can be evoked even by minor fluctuations in the quality of connectedness in relationships. Yet even while Masterson is giving credence to developments beyond the separation/individuation phase that may have impact upon the individual, he views these developments primarily as events that stir up very early conflicts, not as events that may evoke later traumata or that may in and of themselves have a shaping force. It is as though he is pulling a single strand of the individual's experience through the life span, theoretically speaking, when what is required is a double helix, the strands of which, as we shall soon discuss, are interwoven in a continuous reciprocal interplay between earlier and later experience.

Critiques of Theoretical Formulations

Each of the approaches we have reviewed expands upon one particular aspect of the condition at the expense of other aspects, leading us to question "the extent to which specific theoretical formulations tend to mask an underlying diagnostic heterogeneity" (Meissner, 1989, p. 164). At the same time, a good portion of the difficulty that has plagued the attempts over the past two decades to explain BPO can be attributed to an insistence on combining two basically incompatible models—the Freudian "drive" model and the "developmental arrest" model (Mitchell, 1988). Freudian theory emphasizes the role of infantile aggression and infantile sexuality in borderline personality organization as sources of motivation throughout the life cycle—the mature as the infantile in disguise. Theories of developmental arrest, which derive from an object relations model, in contrast, promote the view that "environmental deficiencies result in highly specific developmental arrests, and . . . failures in maternal care in early infancy generate the etiological core of later psychopathology" (p. 149).

Developmental arrest theorists, by combining the drive and relational models in order to formulate basic object relations concepts, have produced what Mitchell (1988) calls "developmental tilt." They insist that object relations begin to operate prior to the separation and articulation of the id, ego, and superego. Thus, "the traditional [drive] model is jacked up, and new relational concepts are slid underneath" (p. 137).

> The developmental tilt has generated what at times seems to be an infinite regress in claims to developmental priority. A psychodynamic account which each author regards as more basic, more primary, than structural conflict, is presented as earlier, as leading to attribution to the newborn of extraordinary complex affective and cognitive capacities . . . , to assignment of great weight to prenatal and birth experiences. . . . "Deeper" is translated into "earlier," rather than into "more fundamental," as if dynamics attributable to the first months of life or to prenatal existence still occupy the most basic layers of experience, underlying and governing psychic events and processes of later origin. This mode of introducing theoretical innovation strains credulity; it also skews these innovations in a peculiar way, by collapsing relational issues into the interaction between mother and infant during the earliest months of life. (p. 140)

The developmental arrest baby is a product of early interactive experience. However, once early emotional growth is stunted, major aspects of personality are immured from other elements in the interpersonal environment to which the individual is exposed throughout the life cycle. The infant within the adult then projects old longings onto new situations in an attempt to restore what was lacking in early life. Thus do the developmental arrest theorists explain what they assume to be an "arrested" individual's unceasing search for what was never obtained in the early interpersonal relationship of infant and caretaker. Psychological processes "shaped in dyadic exchanges within an interpersonal field" become, by and large, monadic, as "the deepest, most significant psychological recesses of the personality become isolated, buffered from new elements in the interpersonal field" (Mitchell, 1988, p. 131).

Mahler (1971) herself expressed doubts about the existence of an unswerving developmental line leading from difficulties in the separation/individuation process during late infancy straight to borderline symptoms in childhood and adulthood:

> My intention, at first, was to establish, in this paper linking up, in neat detail, the described substantive issues with specific aspects of borderline phenomena shown by child and adult patients in the psychoanalytic situation. But I have come to be more and more convinced that there is no "direct line" from the deductive use of borderline phenomena to one or another substantive finding of observational research. (p. 181)

With its inclusion in the *DSM-III* (1980) list of Axis II personality disorders, the term *borderline* became part of the "official psychiatric nomenclature" and "heir to the viewpoint . . . that [it] . . . represents a truly independent clinical entity that can be differentiated by behavioral criteria" (Aronson, 1985, p. 213). In the *DSM-III-R*, published in 1987, the diagnosis was little changed. The only alteration was the substitution of "frantic efforts to avoid real or imagined abandonment" for the *DSM-III* criterion "intolerance of being alone, e.g., frantic efforts to avoid being alone, depressed when alone" (*DSM-III-R*, 1987, p. 323). The latest incarnation (*DSM-IV*, 1994),[7] differs from those that have gone before principally in the addition of one new criterion: "transient, stress-related paranoid ideation or severe dissociative symptoms" (p. 654).

BPD is a broad—in Aronson's terms, an *overinclusive*—classification, descriptions of which have been shrouded in conceptual confusion. Stone (1990) tallied up ninety-three ways in which the BPD diagnosis could be reached, using the *DSM-III-R* criteria (one hesitates to consider the increase in combinations possible with the addition of the new *DSM-IV* criterion). Even to those responsible for having included it in the *DSM-III-R*, "borderline" has not shown itself to be a particularly meaningful or useful construct, and to a number of those in the psychiatric community (cf. Akiskal et al., 1985; Frances & Widiger, 1987; Kroll et al., 1981; Lykowski & Tsuang, 1980), "it is not yet clear whether borderline personality disorder describes a distinct personality syndrome, a subaffective disorder, the overlap of affective and personality disorder pathology, or a heterogeneous hodgepodge" (Widiger et al., 1988, p. 790). There has been a dearth of systematic longitudinal studies performed. Data that exist have been gathered primarily from adult psychotherapy patients and generally yield interpretations and impressions rather than interrater reliability and statistical significance (Aronson, 1985). Methodological problems have also affected the quality of research outcomes—problems such as variations from study to study in evaluative instruments used in diagnosis of patients, in use of voluntarily versus involuntarily hospitalized patients as subjects, and in differences in the conditions under which patients are observed (Gunderson & Singer, 1975).

In a review of studies from 1984 to 1987 it was found that most patients with one personality disorder also met the criteria for at least one other personality disorder,[8] and that, for those that did, the diagnosis most often carried was that of borderline disorder (Widiger & Rogers, 1989). Almost half the BPD and histrionic patients met the criteria for the other disorder. The BPD diagnosis was also commonly given along with antisocial, schizotypal, dependent, and passive-aggressive personality disorder diagnoses.[9] It may be that the best use for the BPD diagnosis is "as an indicator of dysfunction severity rather than as a distinct personality disorder" (p. 134). It is not possible to determine as yet whether BPD provides unique, nonredundant information about a given individual beyond that which other personality disorder diagnoses provide (Gruenrich, 1992), and research efforts to ferret out which specific markers successfully discriminate BPD from other Axis II diorders have met with only mixed success.[10] Zanarini and her colleagues (1991) found the *DSM-III* and *DSM-III-R* criteria sets for BPD to be overinclusive and lacking in specificity "when compared with a rigorous but representative clinical standard" and stated that the results of studies using these criteria sets may prove misleading to researchers and clinicians because they seem to define a nonspecific type of serious character pathology" (p. 870).

In the Epidemiologic Catchment Area Study, those surveyed in the general population who, as a result of their responses, were diagnosed borderline[11] carried a significantly greater number of concurrent Axis I diagnoses than other respondents (Swartz, Blazer, George, & Winfield, 1990). Over half of them had a diagnosis of generalized anxiety disorder. The next most common diagnoses were, in order of frequency: simple phobia (41.1 percent), major depression (40.7 percent), agoraphobia (36.9 percent), social phobia (34.6 percent), and posttraumatic stress disorder (34.3 percent). Not surprisingly, in the ECA study, as was noted in the Prologue, phobia, generalized anxiety disorder, and depression were found to be more prevalent among women. That these diagnoses overlap will not surprise us once we fully understand how to relate the associated but diverse symptoms we now call "borderline personality disorder" with developmental theory in general and female development in particular.

4

Toward an Etiology of Borderline Symptomatology

Recent attempts to ascertain the etiology of borderline personality disorder have had mixed success. BPD has been swept along on the currents of recent research into the biological bases for mental disorders. In addition, sexual abuse, neglect, and early separation from caretakers, among other traumatic events, have been found to be related to the later emergence of borderline symptoms. However, it is becoming increasingly clear that, just as there is no single "borderline personality disorder," so there can be no single cause responsible for its development.

Biology as Destiny?

Descriptions of the borderline syndrome have moved away, over the past twenty years, from an emphasis upon its schizophrenic-like features and toward an affective symptomatology that stresses rage, depression, self-destructiveness (including suicidality), feelings of emptiness, and emotional lability, among other characteristics. According to this view, BPD is basically an atypical affective disorder whose core features—instability of mood and dysphoria—are responsible for a host of "borderline" symptoms (Kroll, 1993).

It may be no accident that such a transformation coincided with an increase in clinical interest in and appropriation of financial resources for research on the affective disorders (Kroll, 1988), or that the latter has resulted in the replacement of a tendency to overdiagnose schizophrenia with a tendency to overdiagnose the affective disorders (Aronson, 1985). The addition, in *DSM-IV* (1994), of "transient, stress-related paranoid ideation or severe dissociative symptoms" (p. 654) as the ninth and last criterion for diagnosis of BPD by no means signals a return of the diagnosis to its former meaning as the "borderline" between neurosis and psychosis. One can arrive at a BPD diagnosis many times over without reference to this new descriptive criterion.

The casting of the borderline diagnosis in affective terms and the increasing number of research studies linking affective illness with borderline psychopathology may be logical outgrowths of a long-standing battle between the psychodynamicists and the "affectophiles" (Kroll, 1988). Having subsumed many of the schizophrenic, anxiety, and minor depressive syndromes under

> a biologically-defined concept of affective disorder, and with the psychodynamic concept of neurosis greatly weakened, what is left for the neo-Kraepelinians to conquer? The personality disorders are the logical choice, and the prize among them is the most popular and largest grouping, the borderline personality disorder. The campaign to do this was initiated . . . by defining borderline personality disorder within Axis-II of DSM-III mainly in terms of depressive symptomatology. (p. 25)

Even when researchers dismiss the borderline label, as "an adjective in search of a noun" (Akiskal et al., 1985, p. 41) and declare that it does not specify a particular syndrome, they may go on to suggest that "the characterologic disturbances of borderline patients sometimes represent primary character pathology but more often are secondary to or concurrent with an affective disorder" (p. 47).

The battle between the psychodynamicists and the "affectophiles" is, in large part, an economic one, and the question to be asked is the following: Is BPD a condition that is actually on the increase, or are a variety of existing disorders being relabeled "borderline" (Kroll, 1988)? The "prize" of BPD is a substantial one because those individuals diagnosed borderline seem to represent a substantial portion of persons seeking outpatient mental health treatment. If BPD patients are grouped diagnostically with depressives rather than identified as individuals having trouble getting along in life, they naturally will require antidepressant medications and treatment by psychiatrists rather than by other, nonmedical, therapists. And what of the fact that a "depressive" group of patients/clients will tend to be female?

Gender is not mentioned as a relevant factor in these internecine wars. The stripping away in *DSM-III* (1980) of the transient psychotic and cognitive symptoms that had formerly often been associated with borderline psychopathology[1] in favor of an affective loading may have opened the door not only for the overdiagnosis of BPD in both sexes but for the *overrepresentation of women in this category* as well. Cauwels (1992, p. 222) cites an interesting comment in a paper by Michael R. Liebowitz who took the affirmative side in the debate "Resolved: The Etiology of Borderline Personality Disorder Is Predominantly Biological," delivered at the May 1990 meeting of the American Psychiatric Association (APA): "Without affectivity, the pure form of borderline would be more toward the antisocial, impulsive, aggressive aspects of the illness." This remark points up how "masculine" the borderline disorder would appear if stripped of its affective features. The same APA convention featured a lengthy debate about the issue of biological etiology of BPD that pointed up the vehemence with which many researchers and clinicians hold to their biological theories of etiology.

The debate has by no means been resolved, and there is recent evidence that the manner in which research has been conducted has been biased in favor of the "affectophiles." Since researchers have rarely controlled for the baseline incidence of affective disorder in the "borderline" population under investigation, they have, unwittingly perhaps, introduced a selection bias into their research, much of which has been conducted in clinics for depression. One of the few studies that *did* control for depression found the incidence of affective disorder in BPD patients no greater than might have been expected in any inpatient population.[2]

Additional observations call into question another key assumption fundamental to earlier research, namely, that the depression experienced by borderlines is the same depression, qualitatively speaking, as that experienced by those suffering from an affective disorder. It does not seem at all clear that the dysphoria commonly described by borderline patients is depression as we currently define it. A special research program was set up in Larry J. Siever's hospital to compare depression in depressed patients and depression in personality disorder patients (Cauwels, 1992, p. 224). In order to enter the study, patients had to demonstrate, via structured interviews, that they had experienced classic depressive episodes. They likewise had to agree to be medication-free in their first two weeks of hospitalization. During these first weeks, the depressed patients remained the same or worsened. The majority of depressed patients *with personality disorders,* however, began to feel better within a few days in response—it was thought—to the care and attention of the hospital staff. By the end of the two weeks, less than 10 percent of the personality-disordered group still scored depressed on the Hamilton rating scale—an instrument commonly used to measure depression. This result was interpreted as signifying that mood reactivity is basically different in personality-disordered patients and depressed patients, and it calls into question the validity of diagnosing major depression in cases of personality disorder generally.

Borderline dysphoria is a primitive, painfully uncomfortable experience that is an admixture of anxiety, depression, emptiness, and rage—a state far different from some other depressive states (cf. interview with Rex W. Cowdry, cited in Cauwels, 1992, p. 80). A study of borderline adolescents showed that their depression differed qualitatively from that of depressed comparison subjects (J. Wixom, "Depression in Borderline Adolescents," Ph.D. dissertation, cited in Block, Westen, Ludolph, Wixom, & Jackson, 1991, p. 90). These teenage "borderlines" showed a type of depression centered around dependency, abandonment, aggression, and a sense of inner badness for which they criticized themselves. In this depression, sadness did not predominate. Evidence of this sort is important in countering the notion of BPD as affective disease, particularly since it is likely that all BPD patients experience some "depressive-type" symptoms (O'Leary et al., 1991). We shall return to a discussion of emotional dysregulation in Chapter 5.

Abuse Traumata and Psychological Distress

Despite the strong association between histories of child sexual abuse and psychological difficulties in adult men and women (Briere, Evans, Runtz, & Wall, 1988), it has only been in the past two decades that clinicians have begun to examine the extent to which victims of abuse are represented in a variety of mental health settings (Carmen, Rieker, & Mills, 1984). Freud's early theory of hysteria rested upon his belief in the veracity of his female patients' stories of their unwilling seductions. It was only later, when it no longer appeared feasible to believe that so many women could have been so cruelly victimized by so many men—particularly by men within the family circle—that Freud embraced the notion that the women's reports were merely fantasies of seduction. Freud's retraction of the seduction theory as significant in the etiology of hysteria in favor of the Oedipal complex explanation has had the unfortunate consequence, in the decades since, of effectively deemphasizing the role of catastrophic experience in the development of psychological disorders and, thus, diminishing the perceived importance of the social context in which individual psychology is embedded (Gelinas, 1983; Rieker & Carmen, 1986; Rosenfeld, 1979; van der Kolk, 1984).

General public awareness of child sexual abuse as a major form of child abuse did not emerge until the 1970s, when the combined efforts of the women's movement and the child protective movement brought it to the fore (Finkelhor, 1984). In a 1979 study by Finkelhor of a nonclinical sample of 796 college students, 19.2 percent of the women and 8.6 percent of the men reported histories of child abuse. Even at the time, Finkelhor believed that these statistics underestimated the prevalence of child abuse. The first national epidemiological survey of a random sample of adults, undertaken in July of 1985, found that 27 percent of the women and 16 percent of the men in a sample of 2,626 reported having been sexually abused as children (Finkelhor, Hotaling, Lewis, & Smith, 1990).

In the Minnesota Adolescent Health Survey of more than 36,000 adolescents, 25 percent of female senior high school students and 6 percent of male students reported having been physically or sexually abused (Harris, Blum, & Resnick, 1991). More girls reported both physical and sexual abuse; most boys reported physical abuse only. A third or more of the girls said that they had never discussed their abuse experiences with anyone.[3] Other studies have estimated the prevalence of child sexual abuse among women at anywhere from 15 to 38 percent. Incest, or intrafamilial child sexual abuse, has reportedly been experienced by 4 percent to 12 percent of adult women (Herman, 1981). Results of epidemiological studies have varied widely probably because of differences in methodologies employed—principally, variations in sample types, methods of data gathering, survey response rates, and definitions of sexual abuse (Haugaard & Emory, 1989).

Although not all victims of sexual abuse are permanently damaged by it (Herman, 1981), there is evidence, even among nonclinical populations, that a history of childhood sexual abuse may be predictive of high levels of psychological distress (Greenwald, Leitenberg, Cado, & Tarran, 1990). Girls in the Minnesota study (Harris et al., 1991) who had reported histories of physical and sexual abuse showed poorer school performance, were at higher risk for suicide,[4] and were more disconnected from familial support systems than those girls who had not reported abuse. Studies of inpatient populations show that anywhere from 14 percent to 51 percent of patients in psychiatric settings report having experienced childhood sexual abuse (cf. Brown & Anderson, 1991; Bryer, Nelson, Miller, & Krol, 1987; Carmen et al., 1984; Craine, Henson, Colliver, & MacLean, 1988; Emslie & Rosenfeld, 1983; Husain & Chapel, 1983; Rosenfeld, 1979), and studies of those seen in outpatient, inpatient, and emergency psychiatric settings show that a high percentage of patients have histories that include sexual and/or physical abuse (Briere & Zaidi, 1989; Chu & Dill, 1990; Surrey, Swett, Michaels, & Levin, 1990). Research has begun to focus upon the long-term psychological effects of such abuse, which include: difficulty coping with anger and aggression, impairments in self-esteem, an inability to trust (Browne & Finkelhor, 1986; Carmen et al., 1984; Craine et al., 1988), depression (Gelinas, 1983), self-destructive (impulsive) behaviors (Browne & Finkelhor, 1986; Gelinas, 1983; Westen, Ludolph, Misle, Ruffins, & Block, 1990); suicidality (Briere & Zaidi, 1989; Brown & Anderson, 1991); dissociative symptoms (Chu & Dill, 1990; Gelinas, 1983; Ogata et al., 1990), sexual problems (Briere & Zaidi, 1989), and drug and alcohol abuse (Briere & Zaidi, 1989; Brown & Anderson, 1991; Herman, 1981).

It is not yet clear whether the different kinds of childhood abuse have different consequences in adulthood:

> For example, incest was reported to have a worse impact than other forms of childhood sexual abuse in a nonclinical population but an equivalent effect in a clinical population. Herman and her colleagues have reported that abuse by a parental figure, forceful violation, and prolonged victimization were associated with more severe sequelae. Childhood physical abuse has received less attention in this literature and has often been grouped with sexual abuse; however, at least one study has suggested that the additive consequences of physical and sexual abuse are more adverse than either alone. (Shearer, Peters, Quaytman, & Ogden, 1990, p. 214)[5]

One study found an association between *physical abuse* and subsequent adult psychiatric symptoms, but no evidence for the association between sexual abuse and such symptomatology (Chu & Dill, 1990). Another study examined a large sample—947—of consecutively admitted largely middle-class adult inpatients for presence of childhood sexual and physical abuse histories. On the basis of their findings, the researchers were able to sketch out a patient profile common to those who reported physical abuse: "drug and/or alcohol abuse, suicidality on admission (often chronic), and character pathology (especially symptoms of borderline and self-defeating personality disorders) against a backdrop of family dysfunction and psychiatric illness (often alcoholism in the father or stepfather) and unsuccessful outpatient treatment before admission" (Brown & Anderson, 1991, p. 60).

Gender Differences and Sexual Abuse

There is little that can be definitively stated with respect to gender differences and abuse. That males are the most frequent perpetrators of child sexual abuse, regardless of the sex of the victim (Finkelhor, 1984) has been widely documented. A review of summaries of 190 consecutive psychiatric outpatients for evidence of physical and sexual victimization revealed that although about a third of the female clients had been abused, 29 percent of the males had been abusive to others (Herman, 1986). Most of the abuse was perpetrated within the family. This research provides some support for the pattern of boys and men as perpetrators and girls and women as victims in families. When boys are the victims of *sexual* abuse in particular, the abuse is more often perpetrated by strangers, whereas for girls, family members are most frequently the sexual abusers, a pattern that has been corroborated in the most recent and largest epidemiological study of the general population (Finkelhor et al., 1990). Although there is no doubt that females are the most frequent victims of child sexual abuse, male sexual abuse may be more widespread than imagined. A study of 125 consecutive adult male outpatients revealed a rate of sexual abuse about as high for male as for female patients (Swett, Surrey, & Cohen, 1990). Sexual victimization may be even more underreported for males than for females for several reasons, among them: "a) investigator assumptions regarding the 'typical' abuse case (i.e., an older male victimizing a young girl, and b) social phenomena that discourage male abuse disclosure, such as the expectations of self-reliance and avoidance of implied homosexuality" (Browne & Finkelhor, 1986, p. 458).

The impact of victimization upon boys is not well known, and there is little data on differences in the way in which girls and boys are affected by sexual abuse. A comparison study of abused male and female clients from a crisis counseling center showed the psychological impact of victimization to be equivalent for both sexes, despite reported differences between the male and female groups with respect to the severity and duration of the abuse (Briere et al., 1988). The authors hypothesized that given their finding that men with lower abuse levels experienced symptoms similar to those of women who had been more severely abused, sexual abuse might be even more traumatic for men than women.

Men may show the effects of the trauma differently than women (Briere et al., 1988). In a study by Carmen and her colleagues (1984), female inpatients with histories of abuse were found to be suicidal, self-destructive, and/or depressed, whereas the abused male patients were more likely to show aggressive behavior and/or disordered conduct, to have psychosomatic symptoms, and/or to have had prior involvement with the criminal justice system. The researchers concluded that whereas the female patients' self-injurious behavior was "related to feelings of worthlessness, hopelessness, shame and guilt," the males' outward displays of aggression "were defenses against intolerable feelings of helplessness and vulnerability" (p. 382). They added:

> It may be that, if the behavioral response pattern of the abused adolescent males seen in our population continues into adulthood, they become inmates in other structured environments, such as state mental hospitals and prisons. It is possible that these men are coerced into treatment only after they have become dangerous and assaultive, hence the treatment focus is on their abusive behaviors while their histories of victimization go unrecognized. (p. 383)

However, although boys and men may be at risk for remaining untreated, women are in danger of receiving treatment in the mental health system that may be unhelpful, inappropriate, or damaging.

BPD and Sexual Abuse

A high percentage of patients who have been abused seem to qualify for a borderline personality disorder diagnosis (Barnard & Hirsch, 1985; Brown & Anderson, 1991; Coons, Bowman, Pellow, & Schneider, 1989; Courtois, 1988; Earl, 1991; Herman, 1986; Herman, Perry, & van der Kolk, 1989; Ogata et al., 1990; Rieker & Carmen, 1986; Stone, 1985; Stone, Unwin, Beacham, & Swenson, 1988; Surrey et al., 1990; Westen et al., 1990; Wheeler & Walton, 1987; Zanarini, Gunderson, Marino, Schwartz, & Frankenburg, 1989). Westen et al. (1990) concluded that a history of sexual abuse is a distinguishing feature of borderline patients, since rates of physical abuse are high in patients carrying the diagnosis in most psychiatric research samples previously studied.[6]

Despite the apparent relationship between borderline psychopathology and a history of sexual abuse, however, it has yet to be shown whether sexual abuse produces a syndrome that is frequently misidentified as borderline personality disorder or whether sexual abuse has a causal connection to the disorder (Briere & Zaidi, 1989). Briere and Zaidi's study showed that women who had been sexually abused generally received a greater variety of diagnoses than other patients. They interpreted this to indicate that clinicians were uncertain as to what diagnosis to apply to these patients, and that the first of the two hypotheses—that a particular syndrome that results from sexual abuse is being wrongly identified as BPD—is the more accurate.

Abuse and Neglect

Emotional neglect as well as abuse may play a part in the development of borderline personality disorder. BPD patients in one study reported that they were unable as children to rely on their parents for emotional support (Perry, Herman, van der Kolk, & Hoke, 1990). Neglect alone, the researchers suggest, "may not be sufficient to account for the intensity of borderline rage; a history of active abuse may add a crucial, heretofore missing part of the explanation" (p. 42). It is the abuse, they maintain, that amplifies the effects of the emotional neglect, and many of the problems borderlines have in close relationships are related to reenactments of situations in which they have felt attacked, threatened, or abused and then became enraged: "The characteristic self-destructive and stormy interpersonal behaviors that follow are an attempt to cope with unbearable feelings of rage, shame, guilt, and terror associated with the symbolic reexperiencing of the trauma" (p. 40).

Zanarini and her colleagues (1989) in their study of outpatients found that exposure to chronically disturbed caretakers and histories of abuse were more discriminating features of BPD than were prolonged separations from caretakers or histories of neglect.[7] In addition to sexual and/or physical abuse, verbal abuse (defined as chronically devaluative and/or blaming statements) was quite common in the histories of the psychotherapy clients diagnosed with BPD. The researchers concluded that although abuse, neglect, and loss were prevalent in the BPD group, no one type of childhood experience could account for all the clinical features of BPD. Certain specific types of experience may be more closely associated with certain specific symptomatic manifestations, they maintain—early separation experiences with later abandonment concerns, for example.

Psychological Maltreatment

In the discussions of abuse that are so prevalent in our time, it is easy to forget that it is the psychological meaning of an act that renders it abusive, not the act itself. Psychological maltreatment is rarely discussed apart from its connection to other forms of abuse. Although few of us, if any, escape being an occasional perpetrator or victim of psychological maltreatment, maltreatment that is abusive is distinguished by its frequency, intensity, duration, and the degree to which it impairs the functioning of an individual who is exposed to it (Hart, Germain, & Brassard, 1987). Psychological abuse or maltreatment can consist in rejecting; degrading/devaluing; terrorizing; isolating; corrupting; exploiting; denying needed stimulation, emotional responsiveness, or availability; and unreliable and inconsistent parenting (Briere, 1992). It has been associated with diverse symptoms, including poor self-esteem,[8] dependency, incompetence or underachievement, emotional instability or maladjustment, depression, prostitution, and suicide.[9] Because of the way in which it can "distort perceptions and assumptions regarding self, others, the environment, and the future" and its presence in other forms of abuse, psychological maltreatment has a tremendous impact upon psychological and social adaptation and is, therefore, an extremely insidious and pernicious form of child abuse (Briere, 1992, p. 10). Although psychological maltreatment may occur along with physical or sexual abuse, it differs from these other forms of abuse in that it may operate indirectly. A child or adolescent may be maltreated and yet never be singled out for victimization.

How do we separate particular varieties of abuse and ascribe to any one of these causative significance in the formation of so-called borderline symptoms? The idea that abuse potentiates neglect suggests that psychological abuse alone is not capable of wreaking the sort of psychological havoc that is observed in the borderline patient. However, it would seem that it is psychological abuse that potentiates other manifestations of abuse, such as physical and sexual abuse, not the other way around. It is entirely possible that, for a given individual, the abandonment or neglect—"nonevent traumas" (Earl, 1991, p. 98)—that may accompany more observable forms of abuse may be the most distressing component of the abuse. Much depends on what we define as abusive and/or traumatic. Because of the dependency of children upon the protective function performed by their caretakers,

> even accidental and impersonally inflicted traumas often arouse painful feelings of disappointment and disillusionment that disrupt relationships. Any failure of empathy on the part of caretakers may compound the trauma itself, leading to a vicious circle of pain, blame, and social isolation. This secondary hurt, the failure of caretakers to protect, sometimes has more lasting consequences than the original injury. (Waites, 1993, p. 9)

It is more likely that there is no cause and effect relationship between sexual and/or physical abuse and borderline personality disorder. Rather, it would appear that abuse usually occurs in the context of other family problems, including parental alcoholism or affective disorder, physical impairment or death of a parent, and fragmentation of the family. Hence, abuse victims are also burdened with the legacy of genetic predisposition or multiple developmental traumas, which compound the specific effects of victimization. Abuse experiences may nonetheless prove to be characteristic of a significant subgroup of borderline patients. (Shearer et al., 1990, p. 216)

Development occurs within a context that is multiply determined. In further discussions about female socialization, we shall see how given contexts can create vulnerability to so-called borderline symptomatology.

The BPD/PTSD Controversy: Who's on First?

Posttraumatic Stress Disorder: A Brief History

Psychic trauma is said to occur "when an individual is exposed to an overwhelming event resulting in helplessness in the face of intolerable danger, anxiety, and instinctual arousal" (Eth & Pynoos, 1985, p. 38). Catastrophic experience has the effect of shattering several important implicit assumptions that we hold about ourselves and our world: "1) the belief in personal invulnerability; 2) the perception of the world as meaningful and comprehensible; and 3) the view of ourselves in a positive light" (Janoff-Bulman, 1985, p. 18). The stress that follows upon traumatic events is primarily accounted for by the tearing asunder of this "assumptive" world.

Freud, in "Moses and Monotheism" (1939), made the distinction between *positive effects* of trauma, which consist in attempts by the victim to remember, repeat, and reexperience the trauma and bring it into awareness, and the *negative effects*, or defensive reactions, such as avoidance, phobia, and inhibition, which serve to keep the trauma out of awareness. Building upon these ideas decades later, Horowitz (1976) suggested that if a traumatic event cannot be optimally processed, thoughts, feelings, and memories that attach to the event may be experienced as intrusive and repetitious and may result in a sense of emotional numbing. These effects are among the symptomatic criteria for the diagnosis of adult posttraumatic stress disorder (*DSM-IV*, 1994, pp. 427–428):

A. The person has been exposed to a traumatic event in which both of the following were present:

1. the person experienced, witnessed, or was confronted with an event or events that involved actual or threatened death or serious injury, or a threat to the physical integrity of self or others
2. the person's response involved intense fear, helplessness, or horror

B. The traumatic event is persistently reexperienced in one (or more) of the following ways:

1. recurrent and intrusive distressing recollections of the event, including images, thoughts, or perceptions
2. recurrent distressing dreams of the event
3. acting or feeling as if the traumatic event were recurring (includes a sense of reliving the experience, illusions, hallucinations, and dissociative flashback episodes, including those that occur on awakening or when intoxicated)
4. intense psychological distress at exposure to internal or external cues that symbolize or resemble an aspect of the traumatic event

C. Persistent avoidance of stimuli associated with the trauma or numbing of general responsiveness (not present before the trauma), as indicated by at least three of the following:

1. efforts to avoid thoughts, feelings, or conversations associated with the trauma
2. efforts to avoid activities, places, or people that arouse recollections of the trauma
3. inability to recall an important aspect of the trauma
4. markedly diminished interest or participation in significant activities
5. feeling of detachment or estrangement from others
6. restricted range of affect (e.g., unable to have loving feelings)
7. sense of a foreshortened future (e.g., does not expect to have a career, marriage, children, or a normal life span

D. Persistent symptoms of increased arousal (not present before the trauma), as indicated by two (or more) of the following:

1. difficulty falling or staying asleep
2. irritability or outbursts of anger
3. difficulty concentrating
4. hypervigilance

5. exaggerated startle response

E. Duration of the disturbance (symptoms in Criteria B, C, and D) is more than one month.

F. The disturbance causes clinically significant distress or impairment in social, occupational, or other important areas of functioning.

The individual exposed to chronic traumatic abuse is able to survive extremes of terror only by means of adaptation that render the unendurable endurable. As a result of the psychological and/or physical assaults, these trauma victims develop "deformations in consciousness, individuation, and identity" (Herman, 1992, p. 108). Under conditions of chronic child abuse,

> fragmentation becomes the central principle of personality organization. Fragmentation in consciousness prevents ordinary integration of knowledge, memory, emotional states, and bodily experience. Fragmentation in the inner representations of the self prevents the integration of identity. Fragmentation in the inner representations of others prevents the development of a reliable sense of independence within connection. (p. 107)

Finkelhor & Browne (1985) explain the traumatic impact of child sexual abuse in terms of the unique conjunction of four factors: what they call "traumatic sexualization," betrayal, powerlessness, and stigmatization. Nearly all children who have been sexually victimized, in addition to having been forced to accept "revised ideas about people, life, and the future," also experience "repeated visualizations or other returning perceptions, repeated behaviors and body responses, [and] trauma-specific fears" (Terr, 1991 p. 19).

Although posttraumatic stress disorder (PTSD) as a classification of mental disorder first appeared in the 1980 *DSM-III*, the idea that a traumatic event could beget symptoms not attributable to somatic pathology is far from new (Trimble, 1985). Two wars—the Civil War and World War I—were responsible for exciting interest in the concept of posttraumatic disorders. Neurologists treating casualties in these wars accepted a psychological approach both to the etiology and to the treatment of these disorders and frequently used techniques such as suggestion or hypnosis (Trimble, 1985). However, it was not until the Korean and Vietnam conflicts that PTSD received more widespread public attention. Perhaps because of its highly publicized association with the unpopular Vietnam War, it has, at times, been "unfairly called a fad or misdiagnosis" (Lindberg & Distad, 1985).

As it was originally defined and described in *DSM-III* (1980), PTSD was not limited to the short-term battlefront syndromes formerly termed "traumatic neuroses," and yet "the etiology and pathogenesis of posttraumatic stress disorder, in spite of its new suit of clothes, remains invisible," most likely because the history of the disorder has changed over time in response to shifting concepts of disease (Trimble, 1985, p. 13). PTSD research is still in its relative infancy.[10] In its present incarnation, PTSD owes a good deal to our current understanding of the impact of a broad spectrum of traumatic events—including child sexual abuse—upon the individual psyche. A traumatic event can affect psychosocial development differentially, depending upon the stage of an individual's development, the level of integration of personality and identity formation, and the severity of the traumatic event or events (Wilson, Smith, & Johnson, 1985). Despite recent challenges to the view that posttraumatic stress symptoms develop solely as the result of premorbid psychopathology, there remains widespread skepticism about the possibility that allegedly "healthy" individuals can have serious psychological problems in response to traumatic experience as well as a generalized disbelief in the possibility that responses to trauma can be delayed (Scurfield, 1985).

A review of the literature found that most studies showed no relationship between premorbid personality variables and posttraumatic disorders. Typical assessments of an individual's functioning prior to the trauma, however, "tend to focus on individual pathology. . . . Usually, there is inadequate assessment of the psychosocial contexts in which the behaviors occurred, and whether the behaviors may be as explainable by environmental as by individual factors" (Scurfield, 1985, p. 228). In the wake of sexual trauma, a female victim may find herself in a highly sexist environment in which "issues of self-worth, rage, feeling betrayed or abused, and other lingering reactions to the trauma" may be exacerbated (p. 231).

Although the rate of prevalence of PTSD in the general population is about 1 percent (Helzer, Robins, & McEvoy, 1987), the diagnosis has generally been associated with military combat and has only more recently been applied to victims of sexual abuse. There are only a few investigations that document the incidence of PTSD symptoms in victims of incest (Gil, 1988). Data in these small-scale studies, however, do confirm the high prevalence of PTSD symptoms in survivors of abuse (Armsworth, 1984; Donaldson & Gardner, 1985; Edwards & Donaldson, 1989; Lindberg & Distad, 1985). In a study of ninety-eight female psychiatric inpatients, Chu and Dill (1991) found dissociative symptoms in those patients who had abuse histories. The researchers point out that depression, anxiety, and paranoia, among other symptoms, are not restricted to those who have suffered abuse, but that dissociative symptoms are important markers of an abuse history.

It has been argued that dissociative phenomena cut across diagnostic categories and that the dissociative disorders were inappropriately isolated from other disorders when the *DSM-III-R* was devised (Waites, 1993). Dissociation manifests itself in symptoms ranging from "simple disconnections of motor functions that are usually integrated (so-called 'conversion' disorders), to the dissociation of emotionally toned and uninhibited behavior from intentional behavior (disorders of impulse control), to the dissociation of sexual behavior from cognitive control, affective pleasure, or personal awareness (sexual dysfunctions), to name only a few" (Waites, 1993, p. 115). Considering dissociation in this way opens up greater possibilities for thinking about variations in the degree to which different stressful events affect different individuals adversely.

Posttraumatic Stress Disorder or Borderline Personality Disorder? The Name Game

There appears to be considerable overlap between symptoms of BPD and those of PTSD (Courtois, 1988; Herman & van der Kolk, 1987; Scurfield, 1985), and about one-third of those with BPD also meet criteria for PTSD (Swartz et al., 1990). Since both disorders are marked by disturbances in the areas of "affect regulation, impulse control, reality testing, interpersonal relationships, and self-integration" (Herman & van der Kolk, 1987, p. 115), some have believed that PTSD may be a more useful diagnosis for many individuals with a sexual abuse history (Craine et al., 1988; Courtois, 1988; Surrey et al., 1990; Swett et al., 1990), because it serves to recontextualize the sexual abuse and its effects. The individual is not labeled "crazy" and the focus in treatment remains upon the integration of the trauma (Carmen et al., 1984; Courtois, 1988).

Some proponents of the PTSD diagnosis for those with abuse histories believe that the very application of the BPD diagnosis to these clients may stand in the way of effective treatment planning (Briere, 1984 paper, cited by Courtois, 1988; Craine et al., 1988; Gelinas, 1983). PTSD is a diagnosis that is often overlooked in such cases, however. In a study of state hospital patients, "although many of the patients who had been abused showed symptoms of posttraumatic stress disorder, none of these patients had received that diagnosis, either as a primary or secondary diagnosis" (Craine et al., 1988, p. 303). Even in cases where there is evidence of preexisting symptoms of a personality disorder, clinicians should not necessarily assume the existence of a personality disorder *rather than* a PTSD diagnosis (Scurfield, 1985).

There are those who believe that the current definition of PTSD is too restrictive and should be enlarged to take in neglect and "perceived abuse," or a group of events that in combination "generate a stable perception of trauma" (Earl, 1991, p. 98). Exposure to a "toxic" environment in which the individual is devalued over the course of development can produce symptoms very like those defined in the criteria for PTSD. Earl (1991) treated two groups of adolescent girls on his inpatient unit—one group of girls who had described having experienced an identifiable traumatic event or events and another group whose experience had been perceived by them as traumatic, although they had not specified a traumatic event. The two groups received treatment of the type generally given to trauma victims, and both responded well.

Gunderson (Gunderson & Sabo, 1993) points out that the overlap in the presentation of BPD and PTSD can blur very real distinctions that emerge when clinicians perform detailed histories of patients. Enduring PTSD symptoms, Gunderson claims, could be interpreted as personality disorder, and the *DSM-IV* presents the category "Personality Change After Catastrophic Experience" for those clients who have PTSD symptoms that persist after they are evoked by a severe stressor (Gunderson & Sabo, 1993). Gunderson, who would reserve a personality disorder diagnosis for those patients with persistent and enduring symptoms of early onset, claims that the PTSD diagnosis was never intended "to describe a childhood-initiated developmental process," and that BPD "exemplifies a type of personality whose formation is often partly shaped by childhood traumas—a type of personality that is keenly vulnerable to developing PTSD in response to what might for others be subthreshold stressors" (p. 23). In this view, vulnerability to PTSD symptoms arises from preexisting personality problems created under traumatic conditions experienced in childhood or latency.

Herman and her colleagues do not assume this dialectical interplay between earlier vulnerability and development of PTSD but conceive of BPD as "posttraumatic stress disorder which has become chronic and integrated into the victim's personality structure" (Herman, Russell, & Trocki, 1986, p. 1293). Herman (1992) has proposed a diagnosis called "complex posttraumatic stress disorder," which she claims includes criteria applicable to a large group of patients who come to the attention of clinicians.

But do childhood traumas cause BPD? Do the "brute facts of the abuse" overshadow all other possible determining influences (Kroll, 1993, p. 59)? Herman (1992) contradicts herself when she first holds that the nature of the traumatic event determines the degree of psychological harm and then later acknowledges the importance of individual differences in the determination of the form that this harm or disorder will take (Kroll, 1993). It appears that the stress inherent in a given traumatic event does not correlate strongly with the degree of subsequent psychological difficulty (M. Gibbs, "Factors in the Victim That Mediate Between Disaster and Psychopathology," cited in Kroll, 1993, p. 73). Therefore, other factors—gender, social support, and personality characteristics, among others—seem to affect the type and intensity of the response to a given stressor (Kroll, 1993).

The question arises in this, as in other discussions, as to whether "PTSD symptoms are being erroneously attributed to personality variables, with the implication of a persistent structural maladaptation that a personality disorder implies" (Famularo, Kinscherff, & Fenton, 1991). In my view, however, the more important question is whether clinicians and researchers can develop ways of looking at how temperament, family dynamics, and cultural forces combine to produce a variety of symptomatic pictures in women currently labeled "borderline." I concur with the view that the most important change that must be wrought in the treatment of these women—with or without the changing of diagnostic labels—is the development of a way of understanding what these women undergo in terms that underscore the normality of their responses to abnormal events (Linehan, 1993). Such an understanding in itself, I believe, helps to explain why so-called borderlines are not all alike. When Linehan talks about women diagnosed with BPD, she is clear about the fact that she is representing a parasuicidal subgroup. When Herman speaks of individuals given the BPD diagnosis, she is talking of a group that has experienced identifiable abusive stressors. Herman (1992) links BPD, multiple personality disorder (MPD), and somatization disorder because of their common origins in traumatic childhood events. However, the BPD patient who looks similar to a patient with MPD or somatization disorder does not resemble other BPD patients who come under clinical scrutiny. Some BPD patients much more closely resemble their "histrionic" and "dependent" sisters.

Westen et al.'s (1990) insistence on differentiating Herman's "complex" PTSD from "true" BPD seems moot if there is no "true" BPD but, rather, a constellation of diverse symptoms perhaps more usefully separated and possibly reclassified. The debates that currently rage over PTSD as chicken or egg should not obscure the central importance of the association between traumatic events and borderline psychopathology and should not hinder efforts to discover what manner of interaction between abuse and/or other contextual factors influences the child's development in what particular ways.

A particularly helpful way to explain the relationship between traumatic events and the subsequent development of chronic PTSD is to conceive of the nature and intensity of the stressful external event as primary in determining an individual's reaction and that, as the degree of stress intensifies, it will "break down" a larger number of individuals (Green, Lindy, & Grace, 1985).[11] Although the stressor may be conceived of as a *prima causa,* characteristics of both the individual and the environment in which that individual continues to exist—the "recovery environment"—interact with the processing of that stressor. According to this model, the person's previous coping style and the meaning the event has for him/her affect the processing of the currently experienced stressful event. There are multiple determinants, then, for the response that individuals have to a highly stressful event. The connection between personality disorder and PTSD admits of four distinct possibilities: (1) that there is *virtually no relationship* between the two; (2) that certain personality problems may *render individuals vulnerable* to develop chronic PTSD symptoms; (3) that personality problems *may act as a selector* of those who are exposed to high-risk situations that may become traumatic; or (4) that personality disorder *may emerge as a consequence of the trauma.* In this fourth case, a personality disorder may either emerge suddenly or develop from the coalescing of already-existing personality traits.

The Name Game

BPD, because of its relatively nonspecific criteria, has been in danger of overuse as a "wastebasket" category in situations of diagnostic uncertainty (Fernbach et al., 1989; Frances & Widiger, 1987; Reiser & Levenson, 1984), whereas, at the present time, PTSD "has been underutilized as a diagnostic category in general and with regard to incest in particular" (Courtois, 1988, p. 150). It has been thought that increased use of the PTSD rather than the BPD diagnosis might hold out the possibility of decreasing the diagnostic overuse of BPD, and also of eliminating the frequent, denigrating misuses and abuses of the term *borderline* (which we will discuss further in Chapter 7), which serve to blame the patient "who makes life difficult for the therapist or does not get better" (Aronson, 1985, p. 217). It may well be time for the term *borderline* to be consigned, like the term *hysteria,* to a musty archive. The value of PTSD as a diagnosis for those BPD patients who share its symptoms lies mainly in its connection between symptoms and situational causes (Kroll, 1993). Few diagnoses in the *DSM-III-R* or the *DSM-IV* can claim such associations. However, the heterogeneity and vagueness of both the BPD and PTSD diagnoses make it difficult to know what each is separately, let alone to ascertain whether they are one and the same thing (Kroll, 1993), and as we have previously discussed, new labels can take on old unfortunate associations.

Breslau, Davis, Andreski, and Petersen (1991) have identified the following as risk factors for the development of PTSD: separations in childhood, a history of antisocial behavior in the family, and *being female*. The vulnerability of women to both PTSD and BPD, as they are currently defined, cannot be explained simply by the fact that the preponderance of sexual abuse is perpetrated against women. Family studies (Gunderson, Kerr, & Englund, 1980; Walsh, 1977) have indicated that in as many as 20 to 40 percent of instances, BPD is not associated with abuse or abandonment. This evidence sharply contradicts the notion of the potentiating effects of abuse on psychological neglect. To go further in the exploration of so-called borderline phenomena requires the acquisition of additional tools.

Development of the Self, Developmental Psychopathology, and the Borderline Disorder

I contend that the spectrum of borderline disorders can result from events occurring and learning absorbed *over time*. Current ideas in recent developmental theory and developmental psychopathology form the background for this contention. We can no longer accept the idea that early problems in the relationship of infants or toddlers with their mothers forever alters their intrapsychic worlds. Newer developmental perspectives lend explanations that are more contextually based. The contextualization of personality disorder is particularly important for women, who have been truly disadvantaged in their relationship to the mental health system by the notion that the problems they have in living are purely intrapsychic in origin—"in their own heads." Women are all too ready to believe that in relationships the fault, blame, and responsibility belong to them. This is as true in their relationship to psychiatry, for example, as it is in other interpersonal relationships.

Developmental Psychopathology

Whereas developmental psychology has always focused on the essential continuity of human functioning throughout the life cycle, psychiatry has traditionally assumed there to be a more discontinuous pattern of functioning, with mental illness residing on one side of a psychiatric Mason-Dixon line and alleged normality on the other. *Developmental psychopathology*, in contrast, assumes neither continuity nor discontinuity; it focuses, instead, on "parallels and discontinuities between normal processes of adaptation and change on the one hand and abnormal responses to stress, trauma, and adversity on the other" (Rutter & Garmezy, 1983, p. 777). As a framework, it challenges the deterministic view that the phenomena of earliest childhood (Kegan, 1982) are capable of predicting an individual's later functioning. From the perspective of developmental psychopathology, patterns of adaptation or maladaptation at different developmental stages interact with changes in physiology to affect subsequent psychological development.

Development is an ongoing process—a "dynamic equilibrium"—and psychopathology, when viewed through a developmental lens, "is perhaps best seen on a continuum of pattern accumulation" (Stern, 1985, p. 261).[12] The fact that patterns have their origins at an "earliest" point does not make this earliest contribution necessarily any more significant in the development of subsequent psychopathology than any later contributions. Since each sense of self has a formative, or sensitive, period, it is true that insults in the environment that occur during the formative periods for each sense of self may produce relatively more serious or more entrenched pathology than do later traumata. Nonetheless, "because all senses of the self, once formed, remain active, growing, subjective processes throughout life, any one of them is vulnerable to deformations occurring at any life point" (p. 260). The developmental dialogue has moved from an emphasis on clinical developmental tasks as set out in a developmental stage theory such as Erikson's (1950) to an exploration of how the different senses of the self explain major changes in the infant's burgeoning social world. Clinical-developmental issues such as dependence, autonomy, and trust—among others—are developmental lines that are continuous throughout life and therefore do not occupy a position of ascendancy at any particular period of development when so-called fixations or developmental arrest could occur. Compensatory influences can, therefore, prevail at any period of the life span to inhibit the development of psychopathology or to affect the degree of its severity.

In object relations theory, "the phenomena of infancy become the context to which all further considerations of object relations throughout the life span are referred" (Kegan, 1982, p. 75), and of all the "phenomena of infancy," it has been primarily the poor quality of the mother-child relationship that has been presumed to influence the later development of psychopathology. Object relations theorists like Kernberg, who have attempted to describe how borderline psychopathology develops, have been accused of mother-blaming in a fashion "reminiscent of the infantile autism and schizophrenogenic literature of the 1940's" (Aronson, 1985, p. 216). They have ignored far more than the child's contribution to the mother-infant relationship, however. They have also largely ignored the pattern of experiences across several relationships that may have a greater impact upon personality development than any single experience, or even than a prolonged experience with one individual (Rutter & Garmezy, 1983).

The perspective of developmental psychopathology is essential to much of what I am going to posit about how what we now call borderline symptoms develop in women. The important empirical work of developmental psychologists such as Daniel Stern (1985), who has spent years researching the moment-by-moment nuances of infant-caretaker relationships, is a cornerstone of the discussion to come. Developmental psychopathology suggests ways of looking at development that give greater acknowledgment both to the significant effects of the press of later environmental events on people's lives and to the accumulation of patterns in the lives of individuals than the developmental arrest theories of the 1960s and 1970s. Moreover, the newer developmental perspective goes far toward dispelling the notion that psychological separateness is at the acme of "healthy" adult development.

Regardless of the service that developmental research in general and Stern's research in particular have performed in helping us to understand women's psychological functioning, it is important to note that nowhere in his book *The Interpersonal World of the Infant* (1985) does Stern tackle the subject of gender. This is both a surprising and egregious omission in such a careful and complete work. In Chapters 5 and 6 of this book, I will place female socialization within a developmental psychopathology framework so that its contributions to development of the psychological distress we now term "borderline" can be better understood.

The Self and the Other

Stern squarely distinguishes his developmental theory from that of Margaret Mahler (Mahler, 1971; Mahler & Kaplan, 1977; Mahler, Pine, & Bergman, 1985), whose stage theory has gained wide currency in the child development literature generally: That theory has served as the basis for more specific discussions concerning the development of borderline psychopathology, such as Masterson's. Mahler's infant moves from an earliest stage of fusion or symbiosis to one of increasing separation and individuation. However, whereas for Mahler, connectedness results from a failure in differentiation, for Stern, connectedness represents successful psychological functioning.

Empirical research shows that the infant's early experiences include the formation of a sense of a core self and a sense of a core other. To be with another, then, is an "active act of integration" rather than a "passive failure of differentiation." From the constructivist perspective, action, representation, and experience are all co-creations of the individual in interaction with the environment. The infant from the outset shapes and is shaped by her/his contact with the world.

Stern's (1985) infant research has led him to conclude that between birth and about thirty months an infant develops, sequentially, four senses of self—a sense of emergent self, a core self, an intersubjective self, and a verbal sense of self. Even prior to two months, "infants are not lost at sea in a wash of abstractable qualities of experience" (p. 67) but are already engaged in organizing information vital to the establishment of a core self and a core other. The infant is, from early on, truly a social being.

The Senses of Self

The Core Self. The core self can act (has a sense of agency), can feel (has a sense of affectivity), has coherence, and has a kind of nonverbal memory (has a sense of self-history). These are the "self-invariants"—experiences of self that are integrated and remain continuous throughout life, simultaneously "being built up, maintained, eroded, rebuilt, and dissolved" (Stern, 1985, p. 199). The core self can be in jeopardy at any particular time in life because it is in this state of "dynamic equilibrium." Individuals commonly have either the experience of or the fear of major disturbances in the core sense of self. Ruptures of agency can result in a paralysis of action or will; ruptures in ownership of feeling or affectivity can result in dissociation; ruptures of continuity can result in a sense of annihilation; and ruptures of coherence can result in a sense of fragmentation. We will return later to a discussion of some of these disturbances in the core sense of self in relation to the psychological adaptation of women.

The Intersubjective Self. Along with the formation of a sense of self and a sense of other, the infant actively constructs representations of interactions that have been generalized (RIGs). These representations are not representations of the caretaker or mothering person—the "self-regulating other"—alone, but of the *interaction* between the infant and that individual.[13] In Stern's (1985) thinking, this capacity for active construction of RIGs paves the way for the development of "intersubjective relatedness," or "the sharing of subjective experience between self and other and the influencing of one

another's subjective experience" (p. 203). It is with the development of intersubjectivity that the capacity for intimacy is born. Infant and caretaker
develop a shareable world.

This capacity for intersubjectivity emerges "just at the developmental
moment when traditional theory had the tide beginning to flow the other
way. In the present view, both separation/individuation and new forms of
experiencing union (or being-with) emerge equally out of the same experience of intersubjectivity" (Stern, 1985, p. 127).[14] Psychoanalytic theory, I
believe, has been paradoxically too intent on *separating* separation from the
matrix of being-in-relation. Separateness is always and only a question of
degree, and the relativity of the term has been consistently underempha-
sized by psychoanalytic theorists. Rather than separation/individuation,
then, perhaps we should talk about separation/connectedness.

The Verbal Self. The development of language capacities by the infant opens
up the possibility of new and varied opportunities for both self-definition
and shared meaning:

> Language is not primarily another means for individuation, nor is it primarily
> another means for creating togetherness. It is rather the means for achieving
> the next developmental level of relatedness, in which all existential life issues
> will again be played out.
>
> The advent of language ultimately brings about the ability to narrate one's
> own life story with all the potential that holds for changing how one views
> oneself. (Stern, 1985, pp. 173–174)

The capacities for language and symbolic thinking open up possibilities
both for distorting and transcending reality: "Prior to language, all of one's
behaviors have equal status as far as 'ownership' is concerned. With the advent of language, some behaviors now have a privileged status with regard to
one having to own them. The many messages in many channels are being
fragmented into a hierarchy of accountability/deniability" (p. 181).

In Stern's (1985) view, some psychologists have yielded to the temptation
to give too much weight to the "level of intersubjective relatedness as the
'critical' or 'sensitive' period for the origin of empathy-related failures in
self-development"(p. 220), which are characteristic of the borderline disorders. The "self" as we conceive of it clinically is structured at all three levels—that of core relatedness, of intersubjectivity, and of verbal relatedness.
If we eschew the notion that one period—in this case, the period of intersubjective relatedness—is responsible for failures in self-development, and if
we understand how each sense of self both influences and is influenced by

the environment as well as how each sense of self both affects and is affected by other senses of self, then we are better able to appreciate the complexity inherent in the development of what we currently call disorder.

What Now?

Current theorists such as Herman point out that what Kernberg attributes to intrapsychic processes—inner representations and fantasy—may well reflect the realities of the interactional life of individuals (Herman, 1992; Perry et al., 1990; Waites, 1993). Even so, the notion of representation to which Herman adheres is based upon the idea of evocative memory,[15] an earlier notion that the infant calls up memories of the caretaker alone, whereas current research suggests that the evoked memory is the "experience of being with, or in the presence of, a self-regulating other" (Stern, 1985, p. 112). For the infant, this experience of being with the caretaking "other" becomes the template against which memories of other such episodes are compared, and this comparison serves to determine what contribution the current episode will make toward the revision of the template itself.

Such an idea of representation sets the stage for thinking about how experience is integrated across the life span. When Mitchell (1988) speaks of "developmental tilt," he refers to how object relations theorists have tried unsuccessfully to slide essentially relational concepts under the Freudian drive model in an effort to reconcile two essentially unreconcilable models. I referred (Chapter 3) to his description of the debate as one in which the notion of "earlier" is equated with "deeper" or "more fundamental." Theories of the present decade, however, are not immune from these basic confusions. For example, Gunderson trusts in the "earliness" of onset of borderline traits (Gunderson & Sabo, 1993) to help differentiate borderline from posttraumatic conditions: "If certain traits (namely, borderline criteria 5, 6, and 8 and the newly proposed criterion 9) . . . are not documented parts of enduring patterns, they could be considered symptoms rather than personality traits. Their use as criteria for a personality disorder rests on their having an early onset and their being persistent qualities that endure across many situations" (p. 21).

Gunderson recommends that clinicians perform extensive and thorough histories in order to ascertain the "earliness" of the onset of difficulties. Like many studying borderline psychopathology today, he discusses the influence of traumata, separations, and neglect in the creation of borderline symptoms. At the same time, however, he subscribes to the idea that the earlier

the trauma, the more severe it is and the more productive of characterological effects, not to mention the fact that "beyond . . . observable reactions, . . . traumas evoke immature or primitive defenses that can persist
well after the stress is over" (p. 22). Discussions of the relationship of situational factors in the development of BPD are not infrequently accompanied
by this sort of unquestioning acceptance of a notion of "primitive defenses"
that tips its hat to—or, more accurately perhaps, borrows the hat from—
Kernberg. Gunderson's insistence upon distinguishing PTSD *symptoms*
from borderline *traits* is based upon a strong allegiance to earlier intrapsychic explanations for the etiology of BPD. It may be that the attempt to reconcile the notion of early injury and primitive defenses with an essentially
developmental psychopathology perspective constitutes a sort of second-
generation "tilt." There are, I believe, more theoretically accurate and consistent ways to understand the contributions of the interplay between the
intrapsychic and the interpersonal to the development of what we currently
call borderline symptoms, and we shall explore these shortly.

What, Then?

Given the human tendency to engage with the same issues (e.g., love and
hate; dependency and autonomy) throughout the life span, there is no
dearth of early experiences that bear a structural similarity to adult experiences; however, it is a mistake to attribute causation to these structural parallels, claiming that an earlier phenomenon underlies or has caused the later
one (Mitchell, 1988), as tempting as it might be—and has been—for many
theorists to do so. The questions we must ask about BPD are clearly different from those embedded in the developmental priority debate, for beyond
the drive and the developmental arrest models,

> a third, more fully interactional option is to regard developmental continuity
> as a reflection of similarities in the kinds of problems human beings struggle
> with at all points in the life cycle. Being a self with others entails a constant di-
> alectic between attachment and self-definition, between connection and dif-
> ferentiation, a continual negotiation between one's own subjective reality and
> a consensual reality of others with whom one lives. In this view the interper-
> sonal environment plays a continuous, crucial role in the creation of experi-
> ence. The earliest experiences are meaningful not because they lay down struc-
> tural residues which remain fixed, but because they are the earliest
> representation of patterns of family structure and interactions which will be
> repeated over and over in different forms at different developmental stages.

Understanding the past is crucial, not because the past lies concealed within or beneath the present, but because understanding the past provides clues deciphering how and why the present is being approached and shaped the way it is. (p. 149)

According to this model, "difficulties in living would be regarded with respect to the degree of 'adhesion' to one's early relational matrix and, conversely, the relative degree of freedom for new experience which that fixity allows" (Mitchell, 1988, p. 277). The questions to be asked would be:

How rigid is the self-organization forged in early interactions? How much range of experience of oneself does it allow? How adhesive are the attachments to archaic objects? How exclusive are the loyalties demanded by them? How compulsive are the transitional patterns learned in these relationships? How tightly do they delimit actions within a narrow border fringed with anxiety? (p. 277)

Since human beings are at the same time self-regulating and field-regulating, the dialectic between the definition of self and the connection with others is complex, a dialectic in which these self-regulating and field-regulating processes are sometimes compatible and sometimes in conflict with each other: "The intrapsychic and interpersonal are continually interpenetrating realms, each with its own set of processes, mechanisms, and concerns" (Mitchell, 1988, p. 35). "What dimensions of the infinite variety of human connection become dynamically central and conflictual for any particular person depends strongly on the particularities of the cultural and familial context and the specific constellation of talents, sensitivities, and rhythms the individual discovers in himself [sic] within that context" (p. 62).

Gunderson's statement that "beyond the more easily identifiable traumas of physical or sexual abuse, desertion, and abandonment are the less obvious 'microtraumas' such as emotional neglect, humiliation, or misattribution of blame" (Gunderson & Sabo, 1993, p. 23) is on the wrong side of a figure/ground dilemma. Neglect, humiliation, and their kin are, as we have discussed, the soil in which abuses flourish. Such are the confusions that emerge from theoretical constructs that are not adequately contextual. Many newer theories about the development of borderline psychopathology either ignore the particular socialization experiences of girls or explore them in a cursory way. In this sense, few go far enough in meeting the need for a truly context-based explanation.

Since not all those who develop so-called borderline symptoms have suffered physical or sexual abuse and not all of those who have been abused go
on to develop BPD, we must keep the "big picture" of overall contextual factors in mind in the attempt to understand which aspects of socialization put
some women at increased risk for development of "borderline" symptoms
and which may offer protection against them (Kroll, 1993). In the following
chapters we will do both.

5

Through the Looking Glass: Female Socialization and Personality Disorder

"Beauty is in the eye of the beholder." What a pat speech. Why do my beheld beauties vanish and deform themselves as soon as I look twice?

—Sylvia Plath, *Journals*

In the Looking Glass

The art historian John Berger maintains that a woman's psyche is divided in two by virtue of her need to be simultaneously both actor and observer. He says of the woman:

> She is almost continually accompanied by her own image of herself. Whilst she is walking across a room or whilst she is weeping at the death of her father, she can scarcely avoid watching herself walking or weeping. From earliest childhood she has been taught and persuaded to survey herself continually.

And so she comes to consider the *surveyor* and the *surveyed* within her as the two constituent yet always distinct elements of her identity as a woman." (J. Berger, *Ways of Seeing,* quoted in Showalter, 1985, p. 212)

The "looking glass self" (Cooley, 1902), defined as a self constructed from the mirrored appraisals of others, has literal as well as metaphorical meaning for girls and women.

There is . . . , for women, an ambivalence between fascination and damage in looking at themselves and images of other women. The adult woman near to-tally abandons the love which the little girl had for her own image, in the pe-riod of narcissistic glory. But this culture damages the glory and turns it into a guilty secret. The girl-child discovers herself to be scrutinized, discovers herself to be the defined sex, the sex on which society seeks to write its sexual and moral ideals. (Coward, 1984, p. 81)

In their provocative book about women writers and writing in the nine-teenth century, *The Madwoman in the Attic,* Gilbert and Gubar (1979) ex-amine closely the Brothers Grimm fairy tale "Little Snow White." This story has a good deal to say about how girls and women face their own and society's representations of themselves in ways that lead to greater and greater constriction as they become the objects of sexual desire.

At the beginning of the story, a queen sits at her window, looking out at the falling snow while she works on her embroidery. She pricks her finger and, upon watching three drops of blood fall on her needlework, she ex-presses a wish for a child "as white as snow, as red as blood, and as black as the wood of the embroidery frame." The queen does, indeed, bear a child, but dies when the child is born. One year later, the king takes another wife, Snow White's new stepmother, a "proud and overbearing" woman. To Gilbert and Gubar, the queens are the two aspects of woman—woman prior to sexualization and woman after she is sexualized. The stepmother is viewed, then, not as a separate individual, but as a representation of the original queen, now sexualized and, therefore, evil:

When we first encounter this "new" wife, she is framed in a magic looking glass, just as her predecessor—that is, her earlier self—had been transformed in a win-dow. To be caught and trapped in a mirror rather than a window, however, is to be driven inward, obsessively studying self images as if seeking a viable self. The first Queen seems to have had prospects; not yet fallen into sexuality, she looked outward, if only upon the snow. The second Queen is doomed to the inward search that psychoanalysts like Bruno Bettelheim censoriously define as "narcissism," but which . . . is necessitated by a state from which all outward prospects have been removed. (Gilbert & Gubar, 1979, p. 37)

The sense of inward-turning is further emphasized by the complete absence of the king from the story, so that the tale is dominated by the "conflict in the mirror between mother and daughter, woman and woman, self and self" (Gilbert & Gubar, 1979, p. 37). But there is one important means through which we and the stepmother/queen come to hear the king, for his is the voice in the mirror,

> the patriarchal voice of judgment that rules the Queen's—and every woman's—self-evaluation. He it is who decides, first, that his consort is the "fairest of all," and then, as she becomes maddened, rebellious, witchlike, that she must be replaced by his angelically innocent and dutiful daughter. . . . To the extent, then, that the King, and only the King, constituted the first Queen's prospects, he need no longer appear in the story because, having assimilated the meaning of her own sexuality (and having, thus, become the second Queen) the woman has internalized the King's rules: his voice resides now in her own mirror, her own mind. (p. 38)

Stretching this analysis to cover the territory of female adolescence, we could say that the first queen represents the time during a girl's life when initiative is strong and prospects seem open to her. With the advent of adolescence and adulthood, the woman, now a thoroughly sexualized being who is defined by others, particularly men, may view herself principally through the eyes of others. If so, opportunities to experience her true self are foreclosed. She is, as the story is written, represented to herself and others as a less acceptable version of her former "self"—as the evil queen—and as a version of herself once removed—a "stepmother." She is trapped in the mirror—in an inauthentic, unnurturant relationship with herself. The stepmother/queen's attempts to kill her daughter represent the killing off of that authentic self that is the true offspring of the first queen.

In the last of three attempts to kill Snow White, the evil queen believes she has finally succeeded. Snow White has partaken of the poisoned apple and has ceased to breathe. The seven dwarfs, who arrive home only to find they cannot resuscitate her, cannot bear to bury her under the ground. For this reason "they . . . made a coffin of clear glass, so as to be looked into from all sides" (Grimm, 1886/1989, p. 220) and placed it above ground. Although the glass of the coffin is clear, like the glass of the window through which the first, young queen had gazed, Snow White has no prospects, for, even though the dwarfs remark upon her lifelike appearance, she is still and mute. She cannot look out, although she is an object of the gazes of all comers. One such is a prince who, on seeing Snow White, insists he must have her, coffin and all. The following conversation then takes place between him and the dwarfs:

"Let me have the coffin, and I will give you whatever you like to ask for it."

But the dwarfs told him that they could not part with it for all the gold in the world. But he said,

"I beseech you to give it me, for I cannot live without looking upon Snow-white; if you consent I will bring you to great honour, and care for you as if you were my brethren."

When he so spoke the good little dwarfs had pity upon him and gave him the coffin, and the king's son called his servants and bid them carry it away on their shoulders. Now it happened that as they were going along they stumbled over a bush, and with the shaking the bit of poisoned apple flew out of her throat. It was not long before she opened her eyes, threw up the cover of the coffin, and sat up, alive and well.

"Oh, dear! where am I?" cried she. The king's son answered, full of joy, "You are near me," and, relating all that had happened, he said,

"I would rather have you than anything in the world; come with me to my father's castle and you shall be my bride."

And Snow-white was kind, and went with him. (pp. 220–221)

Snow White owes her very life to the prince who viewed her, through the glass of the coffin, as something to be possessed, and although *he* expresses strong feelings about needing to "have" her, *she* expresses no such desire or longing. As the story goes, she agrees to go with him because she is "kind." Throughout the tale she is never able to seize the initiative: First she is driven from her home by the queen; then she seeks asylum in the home of the dwarfs in exchange for taking care of them; later, she agrees to be "possessed" by the prince out of a sense of compassion or duty. She remains, as it were, under glass, just as she was in death: The coffin and the mirror are essentially the same imprisoning entities. The girl/woman gives herself over to the man in reality ("And Snow-white was kind, and went with him") or responds instinctively to his voice, now internalized (the voice of the king's judgment in the mirror). To return to our discussion of the mirror, it is fair to say that women do not merely appraise themselves with reference to the "voice" in the mirror; they also "have served all these centuries as looking glasses" themselves, "possessing the magic and delicious power of reflecting the figure of man at twice its natural size" (Virginia Woolf, *A Room of One's Own,* p. 36; quoted in Ussher, 1992, p. 254).

The poet Sylvia Plath, in her early journals, accuses herself of being "in love only with myself" (Plath, 1982, p. 34). In large block letters she writes to herself in her journal: "CAN A SELFISH EGOCENTRIC JEALOUS AND UNIMAGINATIVE FEMALE WRITE A DAMN THING WORTHWHILE?" (p. 35). "I can only love (if that means self-denial—or does it mean self-fulfillment? Or both?) by giving up my love, of self and ambitions" (p. 39). And yet Plath subjects herself over and over again to "the terrifying hellish weight of self-responsibility and ultimate self-judgment" (p. 61). She repeatedly excoriates herself for her needs and ambitions. The apparent self-absorption of which she continually accuses herself is not something innate, but a struggle with the demons of self-blame rooted in social conceptions of who she must be. As she feels herself to be "drowning in negativism, self-hate, doubt," she desperately lists alternatives to what she fears is an impending episode of madness: "devoting the rest of my life to a cause—going naked to send clothes to the needy, escaping to a convent, into hypochondria, into religious mysticism" (p. 61). Plath's list is a compendium of some of the time-honored alternatives to madness for women.

How does the girl become the woman who learns to listen obediently to the voice in the mirror? How is it that some women are able to manage their coming of age in such a way to enable them to achieve satisfaction in the twin spheres of love and work while others struggle with self-blame and self-retaliation so dreadful as to render them powerless in pursuit of these goals? Why is it that so-called borderline women travel such a terrible path in pursuit of intimacy and in pursuit of a future? For these women, the struggle to balance care for others against care of themselves has become a mortal combat of the self, and it is in the ground of female socialization that the seeds of the conflict have been sown.

From Childhood to Adolescence

In our society, girls and boys grow up in significantly different contexts for psychological learning, and the differences in these learning environments may importantly influence the later psychological functioning of both sexes (Block, 1983). The socialization process can affect various dimensions of the self-concept differently, resulting in the internalization of quite dissimilar values by boys and girls (Rosenberg & Simmons, 1975). Girls are raised in a more structured, directed, and predictable environment than are boys (Block, 1983). They receive more supervision and ask for, as well as receive, more help in problem-solving situations, even when it may not be needed (Block, 1983; Fagot, 1978; Rothbart & Rothbart, 1976). From infancy throughout the preschool years, girls seek physical closeness to others more than do boys and are rewarded for this behavior by mothers and teachers (Goldberg & Lewis, 1969; Serbin, O'Leary, Kent, & Tonick, 1973; Wasserman & Lewis, 1985).

Parents give more reinforcement to actions initiated by boys, provide more physical stimulation for boys than for girls throughout the years of childhood (Block, 1983), and give more attention to the assertive acts of toddler boys (Fagot & Hagan, 1985). With their sons, they emphasize achievement and competition as well as control of feelings, whereas with their daughters they encourage physical expressions of affection as well as trustworthiness, truthfulness, and polite behavior (Block, 1976, 1983). Boys are encouraged to be curious and to explore the environment independently (Block, 1983). In contrast, practices employed in the rearing of girls are responsible for a style of "personality and cognition that in its observable outcome is not dissimilar to the effect of repression [in a psychoanalytic sense]" (Lerner, 1974, p. 112).

Given the paucity of genuine biologically based differences that exist between the sexes (Maccoby & Jacklin, 1974), and accounting for the impact of stereotyped notions of masculinity and femininity, the process of socialization can be understood as one in which actual or, more often, *perceived* sex differences in children's behavior elicit differential treatment, thereby resulting in further differences in behavior, which, in turn, produce perceptions of more pronounced sex differences, and so on.

Whereas in childhood, it is boys who are more often seen in mental health settings and who are generally perceived as having more psychological problems, by adolescence, girls seem to be more distressed (Eme, 1980). Sex differences in depression, for instance, begin to appear at about age fourteen, when there is an increase of reported depression among girls, and when female adolescents seek out psychiatric services and hospitalization more often than their male counterparts (Nolen-Hoeksema, 1990). Nolen-Hoeksema suggests that the increase in fear of abuse and actual rates of abuse of girls may contribute to the increase in rates of depression. When families are under stress it may be boys who are more at risk in childhood and girls who are most at risk in adolescence (Elder & Caspi, "Studying Lives in a Changing Society," cited in Gilligan, 1991). Andrulonis (in interview in Cauwels, 1992) says of female adolescent borderlines:

If deprived or abused, these girls react more resiliently than boys until adolescence breaks them down. Through grades seven to nine, a borderline girl will start to show depression, eating disorders, acting out, or other symptoms of her personality disorder. She then enters the mental health system, where she will be hospitalized more often than a male borderline and may receive antidepressants or lithium. (p. 144)

But why does adolescence break girls down? Why do girls seem to suffer in resiliency around puberty? Andrulonis does not say. Why does gender appear to be a "risk factor" (Waites, 1993)? Why do "some girls, who in pre-adolescence demonstrate a solid sense of self, begin in adolescence to renounce and devalue their perceptions, beliefs, thoughts and feelings" (Stern, 1991, p. 105) and go on to develop psychological symptoms? The discussion that follows attempts to answer some of these questions as it takes issue with the premises of others. The evidence *does* support the adolescent "breakdown" notion while at the same time the theory from which the evidence derives suggests that the breaking down is a result of processes at work throughout girlhood.

Self-Concept in Adolescence

Harter (1990) describes the intriguing and complicated transitional period of adolescence as one that is

marked by the emergence of newfound cognitive capacities and changing societal expectations that . . . profoundly shape and alter the very nature of the self-concept. . . . Failure to chart these waters successfully may result in a number of potential psychological risks, among them a distorted or unrealistic self-concept, failure to integrate the self across multiple roles, conflict over seeming contradictions within the self, maladaptive or distressing displays of false selves, and definitions of the self that rely primarily on the standards and desires of others. Any one of these may preclude the development of an integrated, internalized sense of self that will foster the search for a meaningful identity. (p. 354)

The advance in cognitive abilities during adolescence[1] that enables the teenager to describe herself in more abstract terms may bring with it certain liabilities, since such descriptions are more remote from observable actions and behavior and are, therefore, "more susceptible to distortion" (Harter, 1990, p. 355). The reader will recall here our discussion of how the "verbal self" develops—how the capacities for articulation and abstraction bring with them the capacity to distort and to transcend reality. It is possible for adolescents to develop inaccurate self-perceptions that may, in turn, lead to various forms of maladaptive behavior. Both in those individuals whose need is "to protect a fragile and unrealistic sense of competence" and in those who devalue their abilities, this behavior may manifest itself in a general avoidance of challenges (p. 356). This latter group may also experience emotional distress in the form of anxiety or depression, which can further impede functioning.

For many girls, ruptures in the core sense of self—ruptures of coherence and agency—have their origins in adolescence. The developmental task of differentiating and then integrating a number of self-concepts can be a risky one, for if such integration is not accomplished, the self may remain in a state of pathological fragmentation that can result from an assault on the sense of coherence of the core self. It is possible that "the conflict caused by one's awareness of multiple self-concepts may not abate," resulting in persistent distress (Harter, 1990, p. 359). This conflict over the different attributes necessary for the fulfillment of different roles seems to ease up in the latter stages of adolescence for boys, but not for girls (Harter, 1990). Boys seem to see their roles as more distinct from one another and, therefore, less needful of fitting into a harmonious whole (Gilligan, 1982). There is complexity inherent in the consolidation of identity for girls, "to the extent that [they] . . . may attempt to establish identities in a greater number of domains" than do their male counterparts (Harter, 1990, pp. 380–381). As the options for women multiply, so does the potential for greater confusion and conflict (Harter, 1990). However, there are many women who are not equipped to straddle, like Colossus, the many continents of choice—for whom *restriction* of choice, a gender-related phenomenon—is itself a stressor. Poverty, lack of training, resources, and/or affordable child care, as well as the prevalence of abuse in the lives of many women all serve to narrow the field (Waites, 1993). Pressures to conform to gender roles and concern over penalties for violating gender norms may lead many girls to carve out less than favorable life paths for themselves in the world (Nolen-Hoeksema, 1990).

Instrumentality appears related to feelings of self-efficacy. The self-concept of boys, more often than that of girls, reflects a sense of personal mastery over the environment (Block, 1983). These differences in the perceived sense of competence appear to have their origins in adolescence and to extend into adulthood (Eme, 1980; Nawas, 1971), affecting how members of each sex meet the challenges of adult life. A recent study by Stake (1992) that examined differences and similarities in men and women's self-concepts in their work and family life experiences found a pattern of gender differences "consistent with traditional gender-role expectations and stereotypes":

> Girls and women are expected to place an emphasis on developing positive, harmonious relations with others, whereas men are expected to focus their energies on developing their instrumental abilities. The individual's history of socialization and current social pressures influence the type of accomplishments the individual strives for and, thus, indirectly affect the individual's experience of successes and failures; these, in turn, affect the individual's perceptions of personal strengths and weaknesses. (p. 361)

This sort of research evidence suggests that many girls are not being raised much differently from their mothers and grandmothers, despite increased options in the workplace.

Gender and Self-Esteem

As we discussed earlier, differences in goals and methods of parenting each sex not only influence the very different notions at which both sexes arrive about how responsive the world will be to their actions but also have implications for the development of self-esteem. Although there has been only mixed support for the "androgyny equals adjustment" hypothesis (Kelly, 1983),[2] the positive correlation of masculinity and self-esteem has been quite widely demonstrated (Adams & Sherer, 1985; Antill & Cunningham, 1979; Jones, Chernovetz, & Hansson, 1978; Whitely, 1983).

Of all the characteristics that contribute to our liking of ourselves—men or women—physical appearance appears to top the list not only in adolescence but throughout the life span (Harter, 1990). Girls' feelings about their attractiveness seems to have a great deal to do with their self-esteem. The mirror becomes, in adolescence, the teller of ugly "truths." It is not surprising that since looks are more critical for girls during adolescence than they are for boys, and since teenage girls "experience greater discrepancy between their perceived physical attractiveness and the importance that they attach to appearance," girls generally have lower self-esteem than do boys (p. 367). Girls appear to hold a group of related ideas about their physical appearance that include "a less favorable body image, greater self-consciousness, feelings of unattractiveness, and more negative attitudes toward their own gender, which, in consort with the value placed on appearance, take their toll" (p. 367). Because girls also report more physical changes with the advent of puberty and have more trouble adjusting to those changes than boys do, they are apt to have more disturbances and fluctuations in self-concept (Harter, 1990).

Overall, it would appear, coming of age in our culture poses more risks for adolescent girls than for adolescent boys. Since low self-esteem paves the way for emotional and behavioral problems, it is not surprising that in adolescence girls are prey to a variety of problems—eating disorders, poor body image, suicide attempts and suicidal thinking (Harter, 1990; Peterson, 1988), chronic dieting, and higher levels of emotional stress than boys experience (Harris et al., 1991). The results of the Minnesota Adolescent Health Survey, administered in 1986–1987 to 36,284 young people in the seventh to twelfth grades, gives us a picture of girls who are far more unhappy with themselves than are boys (Harris et al., 1991). Concern over and dissatisfaction with their physical appearance increased with age for girls in this large sample. The girls showed significant distortion in body image, and one-third of them had experienced episodes of binging and purging. The authors concluded that over half the junior high and 65 percent of senior high girls in the study were at risk for developing an eating disorder, as against 29 percent of the boys. More of the girls had attempted suicide, although the suicide attempts made by the boys were more lethal. The expressions of the girls' significant distress, when taken together, formed a pattern that the researchers called "self-directed, quietly disturbed behavior," which contrasts starkly with the kinds of externalized expressions—delinquent behavior, aggressive behavior, substance abuse, and extremes of risk-taking—to which boys have been found to be more prone (p. 129). For both boys and girls, the strongest buffer against the "quietly disturbed" internalized expressions of distress was a feeling of being cared about by and connected with their families.

The developing orientation of girls toward others in adolescence, a social tropism ingrained through the experiences of early socialization, brings with it a magnified self-consciousness and consequent increase in fear of displeasing others. This results in a greater sensitivity to criticism or disapproval, generally, than exists in boys (Rosenberg & Simmons, 1975). Low self-esteem produces a vulnerability in many adolescent girls that leads to a reliance upon others for validation of self-worth, which in turn produces vulnerability, "a pattern which is consistent with the female stereotype" (Franks, 1986, p. 225). Another label for this vulnerability is "dependency"; yet another name for extreme dependency, as we shall discuss later, is psychiatric disorder. There is evidence that women experience greater fearfulness and anxiety than do men (Block, 1983).[3] Uncertainty in women may have its origins in the dependence on others for validation of self-worth. Belenky, Clinchy, Goldberger, and Tarule's (1986) study of female cognitive development emphasizes the difficulty many women have in shaking off the yoke of authority of others' knowledge and opinions. Even the sex-related differences in help-seeking behavior, which may propel more adolescent girls than boys into mental health treatment,

> may both lead to and derive from circular processes involving differential attributions and expectations about the need for help, and the "real" differences in willingness to ask for help and in the response to requests for assistance. These, then, both lead to and produce sex-related differences in self-appraisal, which lead to further differences in help-seeking behavior, thereby fulfilling initial social expectations. (Piliavin & Unger, 1985, p. 178)

Selfless behavior and low self-esteem are frequently paired. A strong emphasis upon the capacity to nurture—even, in some cases, upon self-abnegation—in the socialization of many daughters drastically reduces the chance that women will choose to act on behalf of self over acting on behalf of others. To label such behavior "masochistic," and then to define masochism as an innately female tendency, is to ignore the contribution social learning makes toward the development of that behavior (Caplan, 1985). The model of maternal powerlessness to which many women have been exposed—a model that defines woman as "mother" and "loser" (Chesler, 1972)—is a fixture in the inauthentic environment built up around the societal values of obedience and good behavior (Ruddick, 1980). The requirement for good behavior, defined as an excessive concern for the needs of others, can alienate women from their genuine desires and feelings and stand in the way of achievement and self-fulfillment (Rosenberg & Simmons, 1985).

Although there is much in female relatedness that is nurturing to both self and others, it is often the destructive properties of connection that are emphasized. Such an emphasis is seen not only in the construction of the myth of women's masochism (Caplan, 1985) but equally, as we shall see later, in the male mythology of women's neediness, manipulativeness, and, ultimately, destructiveness, which has had expression recently in films like *Fatal Attraction*.

A Case of Privileged Meaning: The Reification of Autonomy

There is a Victorian precept that in sexual relations "a lady doesn't move." The modern psychoanalyst has to recognize this role, not as passivity, but as a desperate form of activity—a drastic inhibition required to play this inactivated part. The inhibiting may be carried out unconsciously and supplemented by conscious aversion, and the groundwork for this behavior would have to have been laid in early childhood, but it is activity nonetheless, at least as much as anything else is. It is from Freud particularly that we have learned about this unconscious activity. Yet, although Freud the clinician was ever alert to the many forms unconscious activity takes in the lives of women, Freud the theoretician, when dealing with the development of sexual identity, named this inhibition passivity and made it the crux of femininity. (Schafer, 1974, p. 482)

Without empirical foundation, some special theoretical meanings become elevated to positions of prominence, while others are minimized and/or discouraged (Hare-Mustin & Marecek, 1988; Lerner, 1988b). This has certainly been the case in reference to the meanings of separateness, differentiation, and autonomy. Although in our culture these have been deemed prerequisites for healthy growth (Kegan, 1982), the glorification of autonomous functioning has been achieved by excluding a sense of relatedness from the pantheon of cultural values. By extension, since a woman is more influenced in her sense of self by her relational experience, she is consistently "defined out" of the world of effective beings when an equation is made between dependency and pathology. Such an equation defines effectiveness and competence as achievable only through individual action and/or competitive action; these attributes are not to be derived through emotional connection. Even the ways in which relationships are generally described contain spatial elements (e.g., closeness and distance) that emphasize the importance of assessing degree of separateness at the expense of examining the quality of those relationships (Miller, 1991a). There is, then, a poor fit between the outcome of female socialization and the values of the larger culture (Linehan, 1993).

We now know that the world of the infant is an interpersonal one from its earliest days (Stern, 1985). This idea of a "core" self as a self-in-interaction flies in the face of the Mahlerian notion that the very young infant exists in a state of fusion or merger with her caretaker (Miller, 1991a). When applied to adult relationships, such terms as *merged* and *symbiotic* can be devaluing, since they imply a connection between intense interpersonal involvement and a primitive, regressed state (Jordan, 1991). However, developmental theorists, from Erikson (1950) onward, have tended to see

all of development as a process of separating oneself out from the matrix of others. . . . Development of the self presumably is attained via a series of painful crises by which the individual accomplishes a sequence of allegedly essential

separations from others, thereby achieving an inner sense of separated individuation. Few men ever attain such self-sufficiency. . . . They are usually supported
by wives, mistresses, mothers, daughters, secretaries, nurses, and other women
(as well as other men who are lower than they in the socioeconomic hierarchy).
Thus, there is reason to question whether this model accurately reflects men's
lives. Its goals, however, are held out for all, and are seen as the preconditions
for mental health. (Miller, 1991a, p. 11)

The prevalent models are powerful because they have become prescriptions
about what *should* happen. They affect men; they determine the actions of
mental health professionals. They have affected women adversely in one way in
the past. They are affecting women in another way now, if women seek "equal
access" to them. (p. 12)

Moreover, the psychological notion of the separate self, which is an artifact
of modern culture (Kleinman, 1988), fits well with the prevailing American
ideologies of individualism and capitalism, making it "feel right," whether or
not there is evidence to support it (Jack, 1991). Kleinman (1988) makes the
point that Western society has intensified a critically observing *metaself*
that is

alienated from unreflected, unmediated experience. By internalizing a critical
observer, the self is rendered inaccessible to possession by gods or ghosts; it cannot faint from fright or become paralyzed by humiliation; it loses the literalness
of bodily metaphors of the most intimate personal distress, accepting in their
place a psychological metalanguage that has the appearance of immediacy but
in fact distances felt experience; and the self becomes vulnerable to forms of
pathology (like borderline and narcissistic personality disorders) that appear
culture-bound to the West. (p. 50)

There are implicit dangers in the way that psychological theories consistently
commingle the construct of the "self," culturally defined in the way we are
describing, and the construct of "mental health" (Linehan, 1993).

It is commonly accepted that women are the largest consumers of the so-
called self-help literature. This literature puts up another mirror in which
women must view themselves. Beginning with the "me-generation" hype of
the 1970s and proceeding to the codependency literature of the 1980s, many
of the self-help books have exhorted women to be "self-aware" and have used
the dominant idea of an independent, proactive self, fully capable of choice
to emphasize to women their responsibility for their own well-being while simultaneously holding them accountable both for staying in "wrong" relationships and for seeking viable ones. All of this occurs without helping

women to understand better the grip that female socialization has on their alleged "choices"; and it occurs in a context in which they are blamed for their tolerance of unhealthy relationships and for the behavior that enables such relationships to flourish.[4] Such "help" can only contribute to the strengthening of women's critical internal observer.

Continuities and Discontinuities in Women's Coming of Age

Freud and others have contended that for girls adolescence is a time of contraction rather than expansion. The message that a girl's perceptions and desires as well as her ability to be aware of and to use her powers fully may bring her into conflict with others is a constant throughout her growing up, but it is at no time more strongly experienced than during adolescence. The sense of self-as-agent that she had experienced very early in life is gradually eroded and supplanted with a sense of herself as one who must defer to the needs and desires of others (Miller, 1991a). This lesson of "others first" not only implies the lesser importance of her own needs but also raises the possibility that her needs will never be met, or that they will be met only in exchange for meeting the needs of others (Jack, 1991).

In 1938 the anthropologist Ruth Benedict wrote an article, "Continuities and Discontinuities in Cultural Conditioning," in which she stressed the extreme discontinuities in our society, as contrasted with other cultures, between childhood conditioning and expectations for adult behavior. In the article, Benedict speaks of how, whereas "the child is sexless, the adult estimates his virility by his sexual activities"; how, whereas "the child must be protected from the ugly facts of life, the adult must meet them without psychic catastrophe," and how, whereas "the child must obey, the adult must command this obedience" (Benedict, 1938/1955, pp. 21–22). The three contrasts that she emphasizes are those of a responsible versus a nonresponsible role, dominance versus submission, and asexuality versus sexuality.

Other than the apparent physiological differences between child and adult, Benedict argues, these differential expectations for child and adult are "cultural accretions" or "dogmas" that are not shared by all other cultures. As a society, she avers, we expect that an essentially sexless, irresponsible, submissive child will by some means develop into a sexual, responsible, and authoritative adult. No wonder, she continues, adolescents in this culture experience a period of intense Sturm und Drang, if we consider that "adult activity demands traits that are interdicted in children and that, far from redoubling efforts to help children bridge this gap, adults in our culture put all the blame on the child when he fails to manifest spontaneously the new behavior or, overstepping the mark, manifests it with untoward belligerence" (Benedict, 1938/1955, pp. 29–30).

Clearly Benedict was referring to boys rather than to girls in her discussion.[5] However, although the discontinuities that she delineates are based on male rather than female development, I would like to extend her discussion in order to illuminate the nature of the perilous passage women make from adolescence and adulthood. Had Benedict written with girls and women in mind, her conclusions in 1938 might have been quite different. At the time she wrote this article and throughout the century preceding it, there existed substantial *continuities* rather than discontinuities between girlhood and womanhood. Like girls, women were not expected to display their sexuality overtly, nor were they expected to dominate or to take on responsibilities other than the domestic and maternal duties in which they had been well rehearsed earlier in life.[6] Coexisting, however, with these apparent continuities were contradictory messages about the *advisability* of following these cultural prescriptions.

The Victorian cult of domesticity came into existence as the economic life of the country moved from farm to city. For the middle classes, home became the "haven in a heartless world" to which weary husbands returned after a pressured day at the office. As wives lost the economic role in the family that the agricultural life had demanded of them, their place in that home was redefined to include a considerably expanded emotional role in the family (Lasch, 1977). Not only was the Victorian wife expected to nurture her children physically and emotionally, but she was to nurture her husband emotionally as well. This sort of imperative to nurture, then, has been in existence for at least a century (Westkott, 1986).

In the nineteenth century, the feathery domestic shawl that appeared to offer women protection from the chill and menacing world of male activity did not shield them from the tension of contradictions inherent in their adult duties. Women were to submit to the authority of men and, at the same time, to nurture them and their children: They were expected to be "both strong and weak, self-reliant and dependent, maternal and ladylike, responsible for men and deferential to them" (Westkott, 1986, p. 26), sexually available to their husbands and yet uncontaminated by their own sexuality. Whereas expectations for men, in Benedict's terms, were discontinuous from boyhood to manhood, women's duties, while *apparently* continuous, required adult women to maintain contradictory behaviors and attitudes. In the twentieth century, although the distinction, long-maintained, between the "bad" sexual woman and the maternal, asexual "good" woman became less pronounced and the attainment of the goal of sexual attractiveness became increasingly important for all women, in marriage the "expectation for mutual sexual fulfillment did not replace other ideals of married life; instead, it was added onto them in ways that produced conflict" (pp. 44–45), as the contradiction between the need to let go of sexual inhibitions clashed with the continuing expectation that women would mother men.

Over the decades, women have found a variety of ways to reconcile these clashing expectations. Depending on the extremity of the contradictions, women may resort to more or less "pathological" means for their resolution. Westkott's *The Feminist Legacy of Karen Horney* (1986) adds substantively, I believe, to our understanding both of the historical and the social contexts in which women's psychological conflicts are embedded and of the transformative effects of these sociocultural forces upon personality. Although Horney intended her work to apply equally to men and women, Westkott interprets it as a theory of women's psychology and uses Horney's "feminist voice" to articulate a new social psychology of women (p. 5). Westkott's exposition of and expansion on Horney's psychological theory provides several key elements that will further our discussion of the development of borderline personality disorder in women. Before we can make proper use of these elements, however, let me put forward some of the major premises upon which Horney's theory rests.

Safety and Satisfaction

In Horney's view,[7] safety and satisfaction are key principles governing human behavior:

> The concept of safety introduces social and ethical elements to Horney's theory of human development. Whereas satisfaction refers to the need for an object world—a world of people, and food and other things that are the objects of one's needs and desires—safety refers to conditions that others must create. From the perspective of the developing infant, safety implies caretakers and a human community. The theoretical primacy of safety suggests that the human infant is not simply—or even primarily—a bundle of desires but a being at rest, dependent upon the ethical conduct—the care—of others. (Westkott, 1986, p. 69)

Parents who are vulnerable to the pressures of our society may create conditions within the family that come closely to mirror those they fear in the outside world. When parents' capacity to care is compromised by self-preoccupation, children may be exposed to dangers that take the form of physical or sexual abuse or, even more pervasive than these, dangers that take the form of a lack of genuine feeling for the child, Horney maintains. Children respond to these dangerous family environments with fear—an understandable reaction to dangers over which the child has no control. "Powerless and devalued, he or she feels weak, helpless, and worthless" (Westkott, 1986, p. 74). Along with the fear, the child experiences hostility toward the parents who devalue and/or abuse her or him. Horney perceives the anger as a healthy means of fighting back—of giving expression to the self in the face of a sense of worthlessness. Whereas hostility itself is not problematic, the repression of this legitimate protest does create difficulties, and in many cases children have no choice but to inhibit their rage in order to avoid further endangerment when a parent or parents respond to it "by employing the same abusive or devaluing means against which the child is protesting." Thus, "out of fear of reprisal or loss of love, the child represses hostility; the feared and resented parent becomes admired and the child becomes the object of his or her own hostility" (p. 75). In this way, conflict is eliminated and danger diffused. But "this shift from essentially true and warranted accusations of others to essentially untrue and unwarranted self-accusations [has] far-reaching effects" (Horney, 1942, p. 50).

The suppression of legitimate anger increases fear. The rejection of protest signals acceptance of a reliance on the good will of others. The child, in conceding her vulnerability to danger, enters into a pretense that all is well. At the same time, however, feelings of defenselessness arise. What Horney refers to as *basic anxiety* is generated out of the child's perception that the world is a dangerous place populated by menacingly powerful others. It is this anxiety that forms the basis for the development of character disorder (neurosis). "The neurotic feels threatened by a menacing environment, which in turn generates additional feelings of defensive hostility. A cycle is created: fear and anxiety lead to hostility, which is projected and experienced as an external threat. This heightens anxiety, provoking hostility in defense" (Westkott, 1986, p. 77).

The primary dangers to which children are exposed, Horney implied, are devaluation and sexualization. Westkott takes the convincing position that not only is Horney's description of the childhood experiences that may provoke development of neurotic character structure essentially descriptive of the female experience but that the "neurotic types" that she delineates appear to emerge more clearly out of that same female experience. The primary "solution to the anxiety created by childhood danger is compliant affection and repressed hostility," a character type that Horney calls "dependent." The remaining two character types, the hostile-domineering and the detached types, seem more intelligible when considered as secondary characteristics of the dependent type, Horney's concept of modern woman. Domination and detachment emerge in this type, as a protest against powerlessness, only after the core dependent character is formed. They are essentially attempts to claim power or establish restitution for past mistreatment. They remain repressed in the face of the dangerous parental power but appear later under social conditions in which the individual becomes able to exercise some power over others or independence from them. (Westkott, 1986, p. 87)

The core dependent character, then, comes to be created in many women as a result of a process of acculturation both to general social expectations and to specific family contexts. The conditions are set whereby the "protest against powerlessness" will not be successful, because of distortions in the capacity to express anger that develop. These distortions account, at least in part, both for the symptomatology of a variety of "female" psychological disorders, including borderline personality disorder, and for the increase in adolescent girls' psychological distress.

As we have seen, the rise in the rate of psychiatric problems among adolescent girls appears related to a decline in self-esteem over the course of girlhood, which results from a gradually eroding sense of competence. For girls, this sense of unworthiness is strongly experienced just at a time in their lives when societal expectations for autonomous functioning is increasing. Demands for autonomy—that is, our Western notion of independence defined as placing care of the self over care for others—may not be at all welcome to or manageable by girls who have been raised in contexts that do not offer them either adequate or appropriate tools for making this transition. And yet is the transition one that we really expect them to make? As we have discussed, the demand that they take responsibility for others is more or less constant for many women from girlhood to womanhood.

Mothers, Daughters, and the "Nurturing Imperative"

In focusing on sexualization and devaluation as the most dangerous of the external stimuli to which girls are exposed, Horney is able to keep herself from making one of the most egregious errors committed by some feminist theoreticians: assuming the utter centrality of the mother/daughter relationship and, thereby, failing to give adequate explanatory weight to other social/familial forces. Westkott (1986) points out that the ego psychologists and object relations theorists have abstracted the mother/child relationship "from the contexts of family and culture in which [it is] embedded" (p. 68). As Horney herself wrote, "In fact cultural conditions not only lend weight and color to individual experiences but in the last analysis determine their particular form. It is the individual fate, for example, to have a domineering or a self-sacrificing mother, but it is also only because of these existing conditions that such experiences will have an influence on later life" (1937, p. viii).

Chodorow and Contratto (1992), in their argument for the incorporation of interactive theories of development, make the point that recent feminist writing on motherhood is based on certain psychological themes, one of which is "a sense that mothers are totally responsible for the outcomes of their mothering, even if their behavior is in turn shaped by male-dominant society. Belief in the all-powerful mother spawns a recurrent tendency to blame the mother on the one hand, and a fantasy of maternal perfectibility on the other" (p. 192). Another feminist assumption is that mother and child are set apart from others, both physically and psychologically. This isolation is then used to explain and even justify the effects of mothering, as well as to substantiate and reinforce the inordinate significance commonly ascribed to the mother/child relationship—the idealization and blaming that are "two sides of the same belief in the all-powerful mother" (p. 203). We are still left with the "fantasy of the perfect mother," who, if the effects of "male dominance, lack of equality in marriage, and inadequate resources and support . . . were eliminated, . . . would know naturally how to be good" (p. 203).

Chodorow (1978) maintains that mothers form closer identifications with their daughters than with their sons because of the gender likeness. Since in the course of growing up, a girl must learn not only to identify with her mother but, eventually, to differentiate herself from that same mother, as Chodorow sees it, girls have more difficulty achieving separation from their mothers than do boys, for whom identification and differentiation need not be accomplished within the same relationship. Chodorow argues that, for these reasons, the need for affiliation becomes a part of girls' experience of themselves in a way that it does not for boys, and according to Westkott, the "nurturing imperative becomes embedded in the female psyche" (1986, p. 124). However, because this "nurturing imperative" is an outgrowth of historical developments that created a male entitlement to nurturing by women, "the development of a need to care for others is not a structural issue of mothers identifying with their daughters who then develop 'permeable' ego boundaries . . . but the result of parent-child relations premised on the cultural belief that all females should be nurturant" (p. 131).

Although the influence of the feminist relational theorists has had the positive effect of valuing caring and connectedness as important aspects of women's experience, to go as far as to call caring and connectedness female *traits* or *attributes* is to underemphasize how the subordination of women contributes to the distorted expression some women give to these relational needs. As Westkott points out, the personality characteristics that are currently identified as female—those emphasizing the need for affiliation (Miller, 1976), the tendency to be nurturing (Chodorow, 1978), and the sense of responsibility for others (Gilligan, 1982) emerged from a historical devaluation of women. I share her concern "that, in the absence of contextual understanding, the traits [are] mystified and unreflectively idealized as an inherent female essence, thereby undermining a tradition of feminist scholarship that takes gender patterns to be historically created, contingent, and thus subject to change" (Westkott, 1986, p. 2).

Caring for others is inextricably bound up with a sense of powerlessness. The female voice of moral responsibility of which Gilligan (1982) speaks "is an expression of a contradiction of powerless responsibility, a duty to care for others out of subordination to them" (Westkott, 1986, p. 141):

> Female altruism is hardly the ideal that Gilligan implies this different morality to be. . . . [It] is rooted in premature renunciation of needs, deprivation, reversal of nurturing roles, conversion of anger into compliance and of self-assertion into caring for others. Female altruism is loaded with unresolved issues of basic anxiety and hostility: fear of the power of others, of abandonment, or ones' own hostility and that of others. In this respect, caring for others as an expression of selflessness is a peace offering to devaluing authority. It is self-protection through self-denial. (pp. 142–143)

Devaluation and Sexualization

The twin phenomena of female sexualization and female devaluation have everything to do with why many girls need to achieve this self-protection of which we are speaking. Girls in our society are seen first and foremost as sexually attractive entities. Within the family, girls may be sexualized in more or less obvious ways:

> Furtive, fragmentary, yet part of everyday family life, the sexualization of girls seems commonplace yet so elusive, routine yet undefined. To speak of it invites disbelief. To call it sexual aggression sounds hysterical, delusional. To identify it as the "real danger" appears an overreaction. How does one speak of something that fades from scrutiny, denies its own existence, or pretends that it is something else at the same time that it merges with the routines of daily living? (Westkott, 1986, p. 112)

Incest is an extreme form of this general and universal treatment. . . . The sexualization usually hinges upon a power difference between the adult older male and the young girl. It is therefore an expression of what Horney . . . called the confounding of "terror and tenderness" in adult sexual exploitation of children (Horney, 1937, p. 84). The girl's sexuality comes to derive its meaning from her powerlessness, and her powerlessness is confirmed in the sexualizing treatment. . . . The power difference between adult and child is compounded by the prerogative of gender, the socially sanctioned right of all males to sexualize all females, regardless of age or status. (pp. 94–95)

Sexualization, then, is always present in the experience of girls, but the forms it will take and the intensity of it may vary. Depending upon the severity and intensity of their sexualization, girls may, as they move toward womanhood, need to find ways of protecting themselves. Seductiveness and sexual submissiveness are both essentially self-protective strategies employed by women: Whereas submissiveness is a passive attempt to gain safety, seductiveness presents the appearance of desire with the underlying goal of safety (Westkott, 1986). Thus it is not desire that informs seductiveness but the need to make oneself desirable and to find safety in being chosen. As we have seen, Snow White gains a protector in the prince by submitting to his desire, just as her stepmother—or sexualized self—must maintain her attractiveness/desirability in order not to be cast off by the king.

Devaluation is, of course, inseparable from sexualization. Earlier in this chapter we spoke of the ways in which many girls are handicapped as they face adulthood by constriction of choice and intention and the lack of freedom to act according to their own self-interest. These limitations result from a social process that consists in the devaluation of whatever qualities or abilities deemphasize a girl's sexuality and/or femininity. This "devaluation of aspirations and capabilities is not simply a destruction of will; it is a reinforcement that she is nothing more than a sex object" (Westkott, 1986, p. 122). The imperative to nurture, then, is the quintessential devaluation. In some families, a role reversal can occur when mothers, themselves undernurtured, call on their daughters for "reinforcement, care, and validation" (p. 139). Some of the help that mothers call upon daughters to provide is assistance in taking care of their husbands. Fathers in some families, too, have expectations of care from their daughters when they look to them for emotional validation and use them as objects for their own sexualized aggression (Westkott, 1986). This latter exploitation finds its most extreme expression in incest. Even in families where the girl's experience of devaluation and sexualization is mild, the requirement that she "be good" chokes off opportunities she might have to arrive at a critical judgment of what is occurring in the family or possibilities for "the self-defending expression of hostility for injuries received. It is this feminine behavior, demanded overtly and subtly, that forms the foundation of the idealized self and sustains the conviction of utter worthlessness. All this goodness serves only to sustain the rage at being undernurtured, a rage that is also feared" (p. 139).

Many girls grow up, then, suppressing their need for care. In this way they not only avoid their mothers' resentment and gain something resembling love, but they protect their mothers' fragility as well (Westkott, 1986). But why, Westkott asks, would a daughter nurture her parents if doing so means foregoing her own needs? The answer lies in Horney's explanation of the need for safety: Devaluation of a girl's needs leads to fear that she will lose safety and love; that fear, in turn, leads to anger toward those who do not value her true self. Since fear supervenes over anger in the face of parental strength, the girl turns the anger against herself, admiring those who devalue her and complying with their wishes in order to conceal her own sense of inferiority. Being needed and being loved become intertwined. Snow White goes with the prince because he must have her. The result of parental demands that the girl's anger be suppressed is what Westkott calls "self-contemptuous altruism."

> Female altruism, from this perspective, is a contradiction in which the undernurtured nurturer gives what she does not have in order to be "loved" by those who have disregard or even contempt for her true self and needs. It is a precocious and in some ways *spurious strength* that denies the self and attributes greatest importance to the needs of others. Consequently, the woman or girl needs to "affiliate" with others in order to validate that she is who she should be, *her idealized nurturant self.* (Westkott, 1986, pp. 139–140; italics mine)

Any discussion of the development of what is called female psychopathology, I believe, must refer to the two elements of which Westkott speaks—illusory strength and the idealized self. The "apparent competence" that Linehan (1987, 1993) believes to be a core presentation of "borderline" women is, in part, an outgrowth of the burden of nurturance that some women have had to bear as girls and teenagers. Families in which sexualization and devaluation are dominant forces create what Linehan (1993) calls "invalidating environments." Invalidating environments can engender the development of a false self because, in these environments, an individual is encouraged to bring into play only those aspects of her inner experience that fit the inner experience of another. In that case, the "shareable interpersonal world" that emerges from the development of intersubjectivity may demand the suppression of other legitimate parts of an individual's inner experience, and confusions of identity may ensue.

In invalidating family environments girls' communications of private experiences are responded to erratically, inappropriately, and in an extreme fashion (Linehan, 1993). There is no validation for inner experience; painful emotions and what are perceived by the individual as causes of her emotional distress are not legitimated, and the expression of negative feelings is often punished or minimized. There is a premium placed upon putting a good face on things. The individual is not prized, and her needs remain unacknowledged. She is told, in effect, that she is wrong in her assessment of what underlies her experience—emotionally, cognitively, and behaviorally. In addition, her experience is attributed to unattractive and unacceptable personal characteristics or traits. In this context, she may be told

> that [she] . . . feels what she says she does not . . . , likes or prefers what she does not, . . . or has done what she said she did not. Negative emotional expressions may be attributed to traits such as overreactivity, oversensitivity, paranoia, a distorted view of events, or failure to adopt a positive attitude. Behaviors that have unintended negative or painful consequences for others may be attributed to hostile or manipulative motives. Failure, or any deviation from socially defined success, is labeled as resulting from lack of motivation, lack of discipline, not trying hard enough, or the like. Positive emotional expressions, beliefs and action plans may be similarly invalidated by being attributed to lack of discrimination, naiveté, overidealization, or immaturity. (Linehan, 1993, p. 50)

The girl's growing capacity to use language and to think in symbolic terms brings with it the capacity to develop representations or symbolic constructs of experience that may distort reality (Stern, 1985). "Characterological blame" (Janoff-Bulman, 1979), is predominant in invalidating environments, just as it is in psychological theories of women's psychopathology. The self-blame to which women are, to differing degrees, so prone and that forms the basis for much of the self-injurious behavior to which women diagnosed borderline are prone results from the impossibility of reconciling their thoughts, feelings, and behavior with the attributes of the idealized nurturant individual many women believe they should be. The particular distortions in experience to which they have been exposed that have helped to create these thoughts, feelings, and behavior have a strong influence upon the story they tell themselves over time about themselves. The "narrated self" constructs a story from all aspects of the core sense of self—agency, affectivity, coherence, and self-history (Stern, 1985), and the story women tell themselves has much to do with the way they learn to experience dependency and the way they learn to express anger.

6

Anger, Dependency, and Fear: Women at the Border

Carson McCullers's *The Member of the Wedding* (1946) is more than just a girl's coming-of-age story: It is the story of a girl whose history catches up with her, much in the same way that suppressed grief, anger, fear, emptiness, and despair catch up with many of the adolescents who develop borderline symptoms. "The risk in adolescence, the risk of taking one's love and one's need to love into the world outside" (Lane, 1990, p. 50) summons all that the adolescent has come to know about trust in love.

Member of the Wedding

"It happened that green and crazy summer when Frankie was twelve years old. This was the summer when for a long time she had not been a member. She belonged to no club and was a member of nothing in the world. Frankie had become an unjoined person who hung around in doorways, and she was afraid" (McCullers, 1946, p. 1). Frankie Addams was to have a hard summer, that summer of the change from childhood to adolescence. This was the summer her father said she was too old to sleep in his bed; it was the summer when she was not invited to become a member of the club that included girls from the neighborhood—thirteen-, fourteen-, and fifteen-year-old girls. "It was the year when Frankie thought about the world. And she did not see it as a round school globe, with the countries neat and different-colored. She thought of the world as huge and cracked and loose and turning a thousand miles an hour" (p. 20). "She was afraid because . . . the world seemed some-how separate from herself" (p. 21). Prior to that summer, she had not been afraid or "dirty and greedy and mean and sad" (p. 20) and different from other people. But now, because she could not dispel the fear,

> she would hurry to do something. She would go home and put the coal scuttle on her head, like a crazy person's hat, and walk around the kitchen table. She would do anything that suddenly occurred to her—but whatever she did was always wrong, and not at all what she wanted. Then, having done these wrong and silly things, she would stand, sickened and empty, in the kitchen door and say:
> "I just wish I could tear down this whole town." (p. 23)

We are told that Frankie's mother died when she was born and that her fa-ther is tired and preoccupied. At the time we meet her, Frankie spends most of her time hanging around the kitchen where the family's black house-keeper, Berenice, is to be found, along with Frankie's young cousin, John Henry West. When Frankie finds out that her brother, who has been away in the service, is to be married, she is devastated. This event confirms for Frankie her abandonment in a frightening world. Upon hearing the news about her brother and his fiancé,

> Frankie closed her eyes, and, though she did not see them as a picture, she could feel them leaving her. She could feel the two of them together on the train, riding and riding away from her. They were them, and she could feel this part of her own self going away, and farther away; farther and farther, so that a drawn-out sickness came in her, going away and farther away, so that the kitchen Frankie [the Frankie who hung around the kitchen] was an old hull left here at the table. (McCullers, 1946, p. 27)

A sense of acute deprivation and inner emptiness assails her. As she stands outside at twilight, her attention is captured by the sound of someone play-ing a horn:

> The tune was low and dark and sad. Then all at once, as Frankie listened, the horn danced into a wild jazz spangle that zigzagged upward. . . . She stood there on the dark sidewalk and the drawn tightness of her heart made her knees lock and her throat feel stiffened. Then, without warning, the thing happened

that at first Frankie could not believe. Just at the time when the tune should be laid, the music finished, the horn broke off. All of a sudden the horn stopped playing. For a moment Frankie could not take it in, she felt so lost.

She whispered finally . . . : "He has stopped to bang the spit out of his horn. In a second he will finish."

But the music did not come again. The tune was left broken, unfinished. And the drawn tightness she could no longer stand. She felt she must do something wild and sudden that never had been done before. She hit herself on the head with her fist, but that did not help at all. (McCullers, 1946, pp. 41–42)

Frankie's "wild" and sometimes self-destructive actions consist of futile attempts to stave off the anxiety that arises when she comes too close to the essential sadness, aloneness, and fear inside her. She finds an anchor for her unmoored self in the fantasy of being absorbed into the marriage soon to take place between her older brother and his fiancée, telling herself: *"They are the we of me."* In truth, she has little connection to either of these two, and her lack of knowledge of them permits her to idealize them and their plans for the future. Her attachment to the idea of leaving with the bride and groom after the wedding helps her to feel more connected to herself and to other people.

Frankie, having renamed herself F. Jasmine Addams, walks around town, telling strangers of her plan to leave with the bride and groom directly after the wedding. Whereas in the old days she had taken delight in dressing up in a costume and pretending to these same strangers that she was someone other than she was, on this day before the wedding she "was not trying to trick people and pretend; far from it, she wanted only to be recognized for her true self. It was a need so strong, this want to be known and recognized, that F. Jasmine forgot the wild hard glare and choking dust and miles." The world itself had changed: It seemed close, rather than loose and cracked and spinning, "layered in three different parts, all the twelve years of the old Frankie, the present day itself, and the future ahead" (McCullers, 1946, p. 56). Part of the fear and emptiness experienced by Frankie is the lack of connection to herself—and, by extension, to others—that arises from her sense of not being known.

Frankie swears that if her brother and his new wife will not take her with them, she will kill herself. Berenice accuses her of "falling in love with a wedding" (McCullers, 1946, p. 77). In truth, she is falling in love with the idea of wedding *herself* to something that will make her feel solid, that will finish the melody, that will anchor her in space. Of course, this connection to the wedding cannot hold, and Frankie's salvation is temporary, much the way that the so-called borderline woman's way of holding onto the other is but a temporary solution to the dysphoria that frequently assails her when she experiences a lack of connection to herself. For Frankie, as for many young women, the transition into adolescence not only brings with it the inevitable biological and psychological changes of this period but also provokes a profound and inchoate longing for a connection that they often do not fully comprehend and do not always have the tools to acquire. Witness Frankie's retrospective of events as she returns home, desolate, after making a spectacle of herself at the wedding:

> She stood in the corner of the bride's room, wanting to say: I love the two of you so much and you are the we of me. Please take me with you from the wedding, for we belong to be together. Or even if she could have said: May I trouble you to step into the next room, as I have something to reveal to you and Jarvis? And get the three of them in a room alone together and somehow manage to explain. If only she had written it down on the typewriter in advance, so that she could hand it to them and they would read! But this she had not thought to do, and her tongue was heavy in her mouth and dumb. (p. 137)
>
> The rest was like some nightmare show in which a wild girl in the audience breaks onto the stage to take upon herself an unplanned part that was never written or meant to be. You are the we of me, her heart was saying, but she could only say aloud: "Take me!" And they pleaded and begged with her, but she was already in the car. At the last she clung to the steering wheel until her father and somebody else had hauled and dragged her from the car, and even then she could only cry in the dust of the empty road: "Take me! Take me!" (p. 138)

Frankie is not trying to make a scene; she is merely unable to speak her need to be taken care of. Her behavior is inexplicable to the onlookers, and it might have appeared to them that she deliberately set out to ruin her brother's wedding. The difficulty of allowing herself to be known to herself and to others that arises out of prior experiences of indifference and invalidation keeps her tongue heavy and dumb in her mouth and precipitates her seemingly wild and bizarre behavior. By the end of the novella, however, Frankie is clearly out of the woods, psychologically speaking, and looking toward a more tranquil and productive future. Her behavior, which looked so "borderline," seems to have been the artifact of a troubled early adolescence, but one within the normative range. The reader might ask whether Carson McCullers fooled herself into thinking—or wishing—that Frankie's impulsivity was just a phase or whether "borderline" and "adolescent" behaviors have a closer relationship than we might previously have imagined.

Block and her colleagues (1991) have tried to answer this question. They believe that adolescent behaviors most likely fall somewhere along a continuum of borderline features, at the "healthier" end of which the differences between "normal" and "borderline" adolescents are strikingly pronounced. The Block study compared female borderline adolescents with both normal and disturbed adolescents[1] and found similarities between typical adolescent and borderline phenomena on a number of characteristics—moodiness, problems dealing with impulses and strong wishes, and "unrealistic and transitory representations of self and others" (p. 91). The "borderline" group "appeared ill-prepared for the normative conflicts and affective ups and downs of adolescence, and [they] responded with severe difficulties in terms of emotional upheaval, impulsivity, and massive disruptions in functioning" (p. 102). Certain features clearly distinguished the "borderline" teenagers from the adolescents in the control groups. Although the other groups showed some self-destructive symptoms and constriction in their behavior, the "borderlines," who seemed to use acting out as a way to manage overwhelming affect—particularly rage—used repeated, self-destructive acting out, manipulation, and self-mutilation much in excess of their counterparts. These teenagers, too, often seemed unaware of the rage underlying their behaviors. Although the "normal" adolescent sample showed considerable impulsivity and poor planning, they were more able than the "borderlines" to use social supports and self-talk to control their impulses and avoid being overwhelmed. The "borderlines," albeit struggling with typical adolescent impulsivity, moodiness, depression, and irritability, seemed compelled to act and frequently felt that they were being taken over by feelings. These girls suffered from a pervasive depression that often seemed to reflect "a sense of primitive badness, emptiness, or abandonment" (p. 96) with little sense of how they felt and why, whereas the "normal" group's moodiness and boredom seemed more linked to specific situations they encountered and was more explicable to them.

The "borderline" teenagers had particularly severe conflicts and concerns over autonomy and separation. They likewise had difficulties with boundaries in relationships. Many admitted, on the one hand, to being terrified of being alone and denied, on the other hand, any desire to be cared for. The researchers' findings strongly support the hypothesis that the requirement to nurture their own caretakers and/or the need to act as their own primary caretakers were centrally important in the engendering of relationship difficulties:

Many borderlines found being alone intolerable. A borderline girl, when asked if it bothered her to be alone, replied, "I always avoid getting home before my mother; if I'm in the house alone I feel really panicky."

. . . Concomitantly, borderline adolescents typically bristle at the thought of being cared for. Many had been parentified children who had to care for their mothers, women whose own dependency needs and boundary disturbances were pervasive. Others had documented histories of neglect and spoke wistfully of wishing for a real childhood or, conversely, strongly denied any desires to nurture or be nurtured. Not uncommon was a pseudomaturity expressed in the girl's sense of her own role as caretaker. Asked if it bothered her to be cared for, one subject replied, "I don't like it at all. I'm the caretaker at home and I like it that way. My mom wants me to be strong." (Block et al., 1991, p. 98)

Studies of so-called borderline families have shown that children in such families often have assumed pseudomature managing and caretaking functions in response to parental neglect and unavailability (Gunderson, Kerr, & Englund, 1980; Walsh, 1977):

This adaptation promoted a serene relatedness to the parents whose superficiality became evident in their progeny in adolescence. In adolescence the heightened demands for autonomous function glaringly revealed the failures of ego maturation and parental function. The critical problem was not, however, withdrawal of libidinal support by the parents in response to separation-individuation. It is more that the borderline adolescent's inability to negotiate relationships and regulate his [sic] drives is unmasked and then is exacerbated by the failure of his parents to respond constructively. These families are probably similar to those found by other investigators where the parents see the children as too dependent. (Gunderson et al., 1980, p. 32)

Lerner (1983) has questioned whether women are, in fact, dependent *enough.* In doing so, she defines the term as positively related to the meeting of legitimate needs for support and nurturance. The parents Gunderson et al. describe, however, appear to find the requirement for meeting such needs an inappropriate demand and, therefore, label their children "too dependent" rather than labeling themselves, for example, "undernurturant." When a child who has long been expected to nurture others and to deny her own feelings, needs, and desires enters adolescence with little in the way of social support, it is not so surprising that she may choose to kick over the traces, as it were, and make her statement of need in the only way she knows—that is, behaviorally. This is not to say that she is aware of the feelings she is trying to communicate or that her means of communication are effective; it is simply to say that they are the only means she has available.

Autonomy Revisited: Personality Disorder and Ideas About Autonomy

Shapiro (1981) views all psychopathology as related to compromises and distortions of autonomous functioning, but nowhere does he see such compromises and distortions more evident than in the personality disorders. He claims that the capacity to objectify the world is necessary for the achievement of self-directed action, and that the "development of self-direction and individual autonomy is at the same time the development of the capacity for abstract thought" (p. 36). When men are believed to have cornered the market on higher-order thinking—when Ophelia is truly mad but Hamlet is merely in acute metaphysical distress (Showalter, 1985)—this pairing of a capacity for abstract thinking with initiative and initiative with autonomous function appears to render the capacity for intelligent action a primarily male preserve.

Schafer (1984) employs the language of male initiative versus that of female passivity when he describes chronic psychological distress as characterized by the "pursuit of failure" in males as opposed to the "idealization of unhappiness" experienced by chronically distressed females. Men would seem, in this parlance, to be actively engaged with the world—albeit on a self-destructive mission—while women sit and weave tapestries of their despair like saddened Penelopes reveling in the sacrifices they make for an absent Odysseus. It is possible, however, that, far from idealizing her unhappiness, the chronically distressed woman finds despair in her certainty that the act of pursuing or questing is in itself fruitless. The unconscious bias that attaches to women who follow cultural prescriptions (Hare-Mustin, 1983; Kaplan, 1983) related both to dependency and to the expression of anger has contributed to the process of labeling some forms of dependency and anger as "personality disorder."

Anger, Dependency, and Personality Disorder

The essential feature of the dependent personality disorder, as explicated in *DSM-IV* (1994), "is a pervasive and excessive need to be taken care of that leads to submissive and clinging behavior and fears of separation" (p. 665) beginning in early adulthood. The *DSM-III-R* (1987) included such features as: the need for excessive advice, difficulty in taking initiative, and a need for reassurance when decision-making is required. Individuals with the disorder were said to feel helpless when alone, to go along with things in order to be liked, and to be so fearful of abandonment that they are devastated when relationships end. The *DSM-IV* made just a few notable adjustments to the *DSM-III-R*'s criteria. "Fear of loss of approval" (p. 668) is substituted for the *DSM-III-R*'s "fear of being rejected" (p. 354). The *DSM-III-R* criterion "is easily hurt by criticism or disapproval" has been deleted from *DSM-IV.* The *DSM-IV* candidate for a dependent personality disorder diagnosis is no longer "preoccupied with fears of being abandoned" (p. 354); she "is unrealistically preoccupied with fears of being left to take care of . . . herself" (p. 669). She no longer "feels devastated" when close relationships end, but "urgently seeks another relationship." It would appear that several of the changes in diagnostic criteria represent efforts to make the diagnosis more distinct from the BPD diagnosis (e.g., eliminating the idea of fear of abandonment and toning down language in such a way that urgency or intensity is lessened).

The "histrionic" individual tends toward "pervasive and excessive emotionality and attention-seeking" (*DSM-IV*, p. 655) beginning in early adulthood. Hers is a more active dependency than that of the woman diagnosed with dependent personality disorder. She "may seek to control [her] partner through emotional manipulation or seductiveness on one level, whereas displaying a marked dependency on them at another level" (p. 656). She is "at increased risk for suicidal gestures and threats to get attention and coerce better caregiving" (p. 656); she is "easily influenced by others" (p. 658), inappropriately sexually seductive, and overconcerned with physical attractiveness.

As one might expect in the case of the more "feminine" disorders, both the histrionic and dependent classifications rely heavily upon interpersonal criteria for their diagnosis. In terms of our cultural stereotypes, BPD resembles its sisters—the dependent and histrionic personality disorders—in a number of aspects. Despite the widely acknowledged overlap among criteria for the three disorders (cf. Chapter 2), however, the relationship between the disorders is not made much of in the literature. Because of the recent emphasis on the relationship between BPD and the trauma of sexual abuse, much of the recent discussion of BPD has focused on the relationship between BPD and posttraumatic stress disorder as well as other disorders such as multiple personality disorder, whose traumatic etiologies are well known.

Many of the symptoms listed in the current BPD diagnosis are indices of the difficulties some individuals have in meeting their dependency needs and expressing their anger. What else do difficulty tolerating aloneness, engaging in self-destructive behavior, and proneness to outbursts of rage indicate if not that? The problems women have with dependency and anger lie along a continuum, at the less extreme end of which are these "symptoms": the sense that taking care of oneself is "selfish," a readiness to accept blame and/or emotional responsibility for what goes wrong in relationships, and difficulties with assertiveness, among other dilemmas. Many BPD symptoms are severe manifestations of the problems commonly reported by "normal" women.

Discussions of the traumatic antecedents of BPD tend to focus on flagrant physical and sexual abuse. The shocking realities of the sexual exploitation of girls and women in our society are undeniable; nonetheless, traumatic events in the lives of some borderline and nonborderline women should not blind us to the continuities of female experience that bind us all—the perhaps less overtly shocking but no less entrenched conditions that affect many more than "borderline" women and that can produce "borderline"-type behaviors in "normal" women as well. I cannot count the number of women I have talked to, both inside and outside of my office, who have become convinced that there was something horribly wrong with them because they had become enraged over something "minor" in a discussion with their partners and had done something they later experienced as shameful. "Am I going crazy?" they ask. "Why did I do that?" It is not surprising to me (although it initially is rather surprising to them), when the incident is explored, to find as the basis of their reactivity a statement or behavior that seemed abandoning, even though it may not have been intended to be. (I am not implying here that there are not other bases for this type of reactivity, but that fear of abandonment is often a precipitant.)

Trauma has a societal as well as a familial context. We must consider that the abuse of women takes place against a cultural backdrop of female devaluation and sexualization to which all women are exposed—to varying degrees—and of dependency needs and emotions imperfectly realized during girlhood and adolescent socialization. We should not allow the intensity of the distress and concomitant severity of symptoms that are characteristic of so-called borderline women to distract us from the more pervasive difficulties many women have in giving voice to strong feelings or desires of many kinds. Let us not think, then, of BPD or the borderline client as a "special case," unique and strange, as something or someone that needs to be put at a remove. The women who suffer from a spectrum of symptoms we currently call "borderline" can offer us a unique opportunity to understand our own emotional struggles and the context from which they emerge.

What is important to stress, then, is that such important associations as *have* been made by researchers among BPD, abuse, and the dissociative disorders should not obscure the connection between BPD and the histrionic and dependent personality disorders. The present classification of disorders is a *categorical* model; a *dimensional* model that defines dimensions of personality that underlie both normal adaptive and maladaptive traits (Cloninger, 1987; Widiger, Trull, Hurt, Clarkin, & Frances, 1987) might well place the dependent, histrionic, and borderline disorders on a continuum of severity (Gunderson, Links, & Reich, 1991). As Millon (1987) points out, groups of BPD patients have very different histories, and there are multiple pathways through which the "disorder" may develop. The BPD that has more in common with the histrionic and dependent personality disorders is, in my view, at the beginning of a continuum of severity; at the end of that continuum is the BPD that has commonalities with the dissociative disorders. The BPD that is cousin to the first two personality disorders is more easily observable as kin to all female experience; by understanding this kinship, we can come to accept how the socialization of women brings us all somewhat closer to the "border" that is now called borderline than we might imagine. To reach that understanding, we must know that BPD is not one disorder but an aggregate of symptoms; to understand how that collection of symptoms is a "female" one, we must further explore how female experience is shaped by training in dependency and the inhibition of anger and we must look at the reciprocal relationship of these two.

Female Dependency in Context

Over the years, the term *dependent* has been used in a variety of ways: "to describe a need state (longing, oral needs), an affective state (feelings of helplessness, neediness), and even a personality trait (passive-dependent, oral)" (Stiver, 1991a, p. 141). As psychoanalytic theory would have it, dependency needs originate in the earliest, oral, stage of development. A fixation at the oral, or dependent, stage signifies a failure on the adult's part to have attained maturity (Stiver, 1991a), and since, without empirical foundation, women are assumed to be more dependent on men than men are upon women, they are also often presumed to be less mature and less psychologically "healthy" than men. Although the dependent behaviors of little girls are not held to be pathological (Franks, 1986) and the dependency of men and boys upon wives or mothers is not considered deviant (Hare-Mustin & Marecek, 1988), the dependent behaviors of some adult women have merited designation as personality disorder. Kaplan's (1983) discussion of the *DSM-III's* (1980) views on dependency are just as relevant to *DSM-III-R* or *DSM-IV*:

DSM-III makes three major assumptions about dependency. One is that there is something unhealthy about it. Another is that dependency's extreme expression in women is reflective not simply of women's relationship to (e.g., subordinate position in) society but also of women's behavioral, psychological, or biological dysfunction. A third assumption is that whereas women's expression of dependency merits clinicians' labeling and concern, men's expression of dependency does not. (p. 790)

"Ironically," Westkott (1986) points out, "female dependency is the developmental consequence of the historically created adult male dependence on women's physical and emotional caretaking" (p. 140). The requirement that a daughter be a caretaker, denying her own needs and her true self, does not generally arise out of intentional cruelty on the part of parents, but reflects a tendency toward devaluation of girls and women that is general in the society (Westkott, 1986). If dependent behaviors were differently defined as the means for getting others to meet one's needs, then the question would not be whether or how women in this society become overdependent, but whether women are dependent *enough* (Lerner, 1983).

In a society in which many women are encouraged "to suppress anger and placate those on whom they depend" (Hare-Mustin & Marecek, 1988, p. 459), it is not difficult to mistake social learning for intrapsychic phenomena and thereby to end up equating "overdependency" with mental illness. Of course, judgments concerning which behaviors are too dependent rest in the eye of the beholder. Talking about dependency as an intrapsychic phenomenon diverts attention from the means by which cultural conditions such as poverty, physical illness, and/or domestic violence promote the dependency of women (Jack, 1991, p. 19).

It is important, therefore, to make a clear distinction between the popular notion that attachment *is* dependency or, more accurately, that an interest in being or remaining connected with others through relationship is dependency, and the extremes to which some individuals may go to meet dependency needs—extremes of behavior that are presently called psychiatric illness. Stiver (1991a) differentiates dependency from the boundary confusions and fear of loss of self experienced by those whose wish to merge with another that results from a lack of cohesive self. The press toward merger occurs, not because of a failure to separate, but because of an inability to remain connected with others while forming or asserting a distinct sense of self (Gilligan, 1982). This, then, constitutes a failure of connectedness, *not* a failure of autonomy. Even if people define themselves in relation to others, they must have some sense of the "part" they are in the relation to the "whole" in order to achieve interdependence in relationship.

There are some excellent reasons why some individuals find it so easy to label others "too dependent":

> What are currently considered pathologically dependent behaviors may be more a function of the underlying rage about unmet needs than of the "dependency" itself. Those who are called "too dependent" are often those who ask for help in a way that makes it very difficult to respond because of the communication of underlying rage at both self and others. . . . When one feels . . . that no matter what one does, the other's discomfort is not allayed one is apt to become angry and quickly label that person "too dependent." (Stiver, 1991a, p. 147)

It is not the request for help, then, "that is so problematic, but the ease and comfort with which one is able to identify what one wants and then ask for help" (p. 147). The ability to make themselves known through the assertion of their legitimate needs is especially difficult for those individuals who feel themselves to be the most unworthy, and the boundary between assertiveness and aggression may be particularly ill defined for women who do not feel they have the right to make legitimate demands of others, creating a predicament potentially fraught with anxiety and guilt (Barbara Kirsch, "Status and Verbal Power Assertion: Does Gender or Popularity Better Predict Directive Use?" [Ph.D. dissertation cited in Franks and Rothblum, 1983]).

Women's Anger

Adolescent girls soon discover that expressing anger may expose them to criticism and isolation. For women, the experience of anger itself can bring with it a sense of separateness, difference, and aloneness (Lerner, 1988a). Depending upon the strength of the inhibition against its direct expression, anger can take forms that range along a continuum, one pole of which is self-destructive behavior (Westkott, 1986). The suppression of anger results in both frustration and inaction, producing a sense of weakness and a lack of self-esteem, further contributing to a sense of unworthiness and inferiority that, in turn, generates yet more anger (Miller, 1991b). Women often report feeling filled with unwarranted, irrational anger, and although this description does not relay an accurate picture of their psychological situation, it is one "that the external world—so-called 'reality'—is only too ready to confirm, because any anger is too much anger in women. Indeed, the risk of expressing anger can appear grave and disorganizing. All this can end in a kind of self-fulfilling prophecy" (Miller, 1991b, p. 185).

I recently noticed, mounted high above a local throughway, a billboard advertising a city florist. At the bottom, in bold lettering, was written the question, "Exactly how mad *is* she?" and above it were three bouquets—one very small, one medium-sized, and one quite lush and large. It would be difficult, I thought, to conceive of a male version of that advertisement, even without the flowers. The question, "Exactly how mad is *he?*" is a far more dangerous one to ask. In our society, it is angry men who are most to be feared, angry men who are most often mollified—usually by women. However, the alleged logic of the advertisement speaks to the fear of women's anger. Angry women are pathologized, rejected, or ignored far more often than they are propitiated, with or without bouquets.

Even during the period of infancy, the identical perceived negative emotion in females is more often labeled "fear," whereas in males it is more commonly described as "anger" (Condry & Condry, 1976). Expressions of anger and aggression, even in the post–women's liberation era, continue to be thought unfeminine in women and masculine in men (Lerner, 1988a; Macaulay, 1985). Women's anger may be labeled pathological when it is not deployed in the service of others (i.e., when it runs counter to gender norms), despite the fact that the conditions of many women's lives are such as to stimulate a good deal of it (Carmen et al., 1981). The psychoanalytic and psychodynamic schools have long endorsed a view of angry women as women who have "identity problems, are rejecting their proper sex role, are being poisoned by bottled-up anger, or are being destroyed by aggression turned inward—or all of these at once" (Macaulay, 1985, p. 199) and have fostered a perception of women as more innately passive and dependent than men (Hare-Mustin & Marecek, 1988; Macaulay, 1985). The psychopathologizing of women's anger came to a full, pernicious flowering in the naming of the "angry woman syndrome," a condition said to be characterized by a woman's extreme, angry displays of temper unrealistically misdirected against others—most frequently, her benighted husband (Rickles, 1971). Not only some allegedly unsuspecting husbands, but some psychotherapists as well, may share the common fear of women's anger that exists in our culture (Carmen et al., 1981). An aggressive female patient may be said to be "acting out" or be called a "bitch," "delinquent," or "castrating," and acting-out female patients are frequently diagnosed as having personality disorders (Waites, 1993, p. 107).

Whereas the direct expression of anger by women is thought to be socially unacceptable, its sanctioned inhibition (Lipshitz, 1978) may contribute to a stereotyped view of women as whining, petulant, seductive, manipulative, and covertly controlling (Carmen et al., 1981; Lerner, 1988b; Macaulay, 1985)—in point of fact, *histrionic*. In describing the "inappropriate" expression of exaggerated emotion said to characterize the histrionic personality disorder, the *DSM-III-R* and *DSM-IV*, as is customary, bypass any explanations for such behavior that may lie, not in the intrapsychic realm, but in the social context in which women may find themselves. Women may find their "efforts to be heard and truly listened to . . . intensely frustrating when the other person seems emotionally impervious. The result . . . is often an escalation of intense feelings with increased loss of focus and defusion [sic] of intense affective expression" (Stiver, 1991b, p. 263).

BPD and the Core Dependent Personality

Understanding dependency is critical to understanding the borderline woman because the core dependent personality is integral to the "borderline" personality (just as it is to the "dependent" personality and the "histrionic" personality).[2] One might say that the socialization that most women receive is necessary but not sufficient for the development of the core dependent personality, just as the existence of the core dependent personality is necessary but not sufficient for the development of BPD. As we discussed in the previous chapter, the "feminine type" is essentially dependent. As Westkott (1986) sees it, for the "feminine type,"

> dependency is, on the one hand, a characterological solution to childhood sexualization. It involves submission as confirmation of a degraded sense of self, the need to merge with a powerful other, and attraction to intimate relationships as salvation. Dependency is also . . . the consequence of childhood experiences of devaluation. It is the response of the female altruist who needs the appreciation of others to assure herself that she is not the contemptible and selfish person she fears she is. Together the experiences of sexualization and devaluation foster the development of a dependent character structure that is dominated by the idealized self. (p. 145)

The dependent individual believes she is worthless, and she experiences this sense of worthlessness as hatred of her body, as the tamping down of real feeling, and as dislike of those characteristics that form her sense of her true self. Despising what she sees as her real self, she composes another, idealized, self, made up of stereotypical and abstract feminine characteristics. In this way she has unwittingly achieved the internalization of culturally prescribed notions of femininity.

A dependent woman literally lives "in the eyes of others," concerned with how others respond to her and judge her, watching others watch her. "The question 'Am I attractive?' is inseparable from another one, 'Am I lovable?'" for many women (Horney, 1950, p. 138). If she exists only in the eyes of others, then it stands to reason that she finds it difficult to be alone. She only has a self if she is interacting with others. For her, "being alone means both the loss of identity and the proof of being despicable. . . . To ward off the indignity and escape the terrifying loss of self that being alone can invoke, the dependent one may seek out the company of others with a compulsiveness that disregards their needs for privacy. . . . The need for others, felt to be so overwhelming, becomes a claim upon them" (p. 160). Such is the developmental trajectory of the woman who may be called "needy" by friends, family, or the therapeutic community. Her vulnerability to criticism, to expressions of disinterest, or to disagreement makes any of these feel like an extreme attack and leaves her prone to feeling victimized in ways that often transcend, in their intensity, the provocation of the moment. What others call a "hypersensitive" or "unreasonable" response may appear only proportionate to the affront she perceives. Because she is dependent on those who might mean her harm, her ability to discern harmful or abusive conditions is compromised, and she deals with such conditions by alternating between accusing the other and accusing herself (Horney, 1937).

In some women, because the internal pressure to be self-effacing and the pressure to be expansive are in competition for supremacy, intrapsychic conflict is particularly severe:

The adaptive defenses of dependency stifle the release of hostility, undermine self-esteem by adopting the appearance of softness, and permit others to triumph over the self through criticism, exploitation, or success. Indeed, the compliance necessary for dependency creates conditions that heighten the feelings of being abused; hostility is increased, but the inhibitions of dependency forbid its release. On the other hand, release of hostility in the vindictive abuse of others arouses anxiety over abandonment and loss of love. . . . Behavior and feelings may then seesaw between insecurity and hostility, alluring compliance and explosive rage, helplessness and fury over feeling humiliated or disrespected by another. . . .

. . . Behavior is simultaneously incited and inhibited, validated and punished. Inhibitions that foster dependency are upheld and bitterly denounced at the same time. If the denunciation is strong enough, the inhibitions will be temporarily rejected. Indignant rage may be the response; but the rage is not only a release of hostile strivings but also a severe violation of dependent inhibitions. (References to Horney, 1937, p. 225; 1950, pp. 233–234, in Westkott, 1986, p. 179–180)

What would render one woman more likely than another to fight with herself in the particular way we now call "borderline"? When conditions during the course of socialization are such as to create extreme mistrust of those on whom she must depend, an individual is more likely to remain emotionally off-balance in an ongoing argument with herself about her own "badness." The harder she is on herself, the more ashamed and/or blameworthy she feels, the less likely it is that she will be able to tolerate the self-laceration, and when the point of satiation is reached, she may lash out at others. Self-accusation and other-accusation are flip sides of the same emotional coin.[3] Emotions may come to be known as other than they are. Borderlines eventually internalize the invalidation of emotional responses and respond to a welling up of affect with the secondary negative emotions of "shame, criticism, and punishment" (Linehan, 1993).

The "feminine type" of whom Horney speaks—that is, the woman who has developed a dependent character structure—wages an ongoing inner conflict with her anger. Her idealized self continuously demands nothing short of self-abnegation, altruistic accommodation, and physical beauty. Not only does she berate herself constantly for failures to reach perfection, but because of her perfectionism, she also finds her efforts to reach this ideal ridiculous. Yet, although the ideal self cannot be mollified, neither can the authentic self be permitted to emerge:

> It is not just that the real self falls short of the abstract ideal, but that it preserves a rage that the ideal of sweet femininity cannot permit. The real self as a repressed possibility represents more than anger, but because anger is the feeling that required the real self to go into hiding in the first place, it predominates as the terrifying secret of one's being. This is why the release of anger is experienced by the feminine type as a momentous and self-threatening expression of her fundamental being, and conversely why shaking off the shoulds of perfectionism touches deep anger in the real self's striving for assertion. (Discussion of Horney, 1942; 1950a in Westkott, 1986, p. 167)

Attempts to allow the real self to find expression generate hostility and a sense of worthlessness. The individual feels abused, and no wonder: "She *is* abused. While this condition may have originated in response to others, it becomes internalized as a continuing aspect of her character" (Discussion of Horney, 1951, in Westkott, 1986, p. 168).

All is not inner struggle, however; the individual's dependency on others can breed hostility toward those powerful others as well as a wish for them to take control of her life and protect her (Horney, 1937). This anger toward others feels to her as something that is coming from outside her:

> The externalization of inner abuse mirrors the process of externalized living. Dependent individuals embrace and internalize the expectations and judgments of others and experience themselves as living "out there" exposed to and under the power of others. The abuse one actually directs toward oneself is therefore experienced as a consequence of perpetually trying to meet others' expectations, a consequence of their power. (Westkott, 1986, p. 169)

The sense of victimization, in tandem with an extreme sensitivity to anything that deviates from unconditional validation, creates an experience of being a victim that can color her entire experience of life and may contribute to an inability to judge accurately what situations are actually dangerous so that she may take steps to protect herself.

Borderline women, not unlike many women who do not suffer from the disorder, have not developed a capacity to trust in themselves. Cotroneo (1986) defines *trust* as "a stance toward reality, shaped by a balance of giving and receiving that enables a person to discern, in every concrete situation, what is authentically and normatively human and helps him/her to respond in that situation with care, competence, and an attitude of fairness" (p. 414). The capacity to trust others underlies the ability of any individual to display what Cotroneo calls *functional trust*—trust that can be activated in a given situation "to enhance one's capacity to handle inevitable failure and disappointments, to rework unrealistic expectations, to integrate complexity, to make new claims on relationships, and to sustain ongoing commitments" (p. 415).

The environments in which borderline individuals are raised fail to help them adopt a balanced "stance toward reality." As a result of being unable to name private experiences and to modulate emotional arousal, these women have great difficulty tolerating internal distress and setting realistic goals for themselves. They are constantly responding to cues in the environment about how to act and think and feel, rather than learning how to trust their own experience (Linehan, 1993). And it is this lack of trust in what is inside them that leads to a failure of *functional*, or situational, trust. Turning constantly outward for information on how they should feel or act engenders identity confusion that may stem, not from the failure to experience their own autonomy, but from *a failure to experience their own relatedness* (Linehan, 1993).

Recall Mitchell's (1988) comment (cf. Chapter 4) that "being a self with others entails a constant dialectic between attachment and self-definition, between connection and differentiation, a continual negotiation between one's own subjective reality and a consensual reality of others with whom one lives." If one's subjective reality *is* the consensual reality of those around one, and no such dialectic exists, then there can exist little sense of separateness or of relationship. There is a disturbance in the core sense of self when interactions with others, repeated over and over again throughout a childhood and an adolescence, become internalized in a faulty way. Since infants not only represent a separate "other" but also internalize a representation of the interaction of "self" *with* "other" (Stern, 1985), it is clear how, as children grow, the shape of the distortions in invalidating relationships becomes the template for future relationships. The core self—which is a self-in-relation—has little sense of agency, little ownership of feeling (sense of affectivity), and, because of these deficits, may not experience itself as a unified, coherent entity.

Recall also Mitchell's suggestion that the range and flexibility of self-organization is created out of patterns of interactions occurring over time and depends on the extent to which old attachments are "adhesive"—how much loyalty is extracted by them and to what extent they constrain action. Clearly, for women on the border, there is little flexibility within the self to draw upon; there is barely a self to call up. If one believes, as I do, that the greatest inducements to loyalty are either fear or love, the borderline's "old attachments"—her family—extract the ultimate in loyalty through the instillation of fear of the loss of love.

BPD and the Regulation of Emotion

Many of those diagnosed borderline would have no difficulty relating to Jane's statement (in *Jane Eyre,* chapter 4): "It seemed as if my tongue pronounced words without my will consenting to their utterance: something spoke out of me over which I had no control."

In Linehan's (1993) view, BPD is, in the main, a disorder of emotional dysregulation, and most borderline behaviors stem either from attempts to regulate intense emotion or are the results of affect dysregulation. Paradoxically, then, "emotional dysregulation is both the problem the individual is trying to solve and the source of additional problems" (p. 59). Linehan's theory of the etiology of BPD symptoms rests upon biological as well as social learning foundations. The case for the borderline individual's emotional vulnerability does not have to be made biologically, however. Whereas Linehan argues that a predisposing emotional vulnerability is exacerbated by environmental experience, one can as easily argue that the environmental presses to which borderline women are subject when they are growing up are sufficient to produce the kind of vulnerability that results in the borderline's extreme reactivity, emotional intensity, and difficulty in returning to what Linehan calls an "emotional baseline" following arousal.

Social learning, then, in itself can help to create emotional vulnerability. The patterns of adaptation adopted by individuals in order to enable them to fit their environments can leave them "differentially vulnerable to adult disorders" (Sroufe & Rutter, 1984). We have previously explored how gender itself can render individuals vulnerable, and how specific family contexts activate that vulnerability to an extreme degree. In some cases, the contextual factors of devaluation and sexualization may create the vulnerability that is ascribed to the "emotional regulation system" (Linehan, 1993, p. 43).[4] There is no question that "poorness of fit" (Chess & Thomas, 1986) between child and family can be based upon temperamental factors in interaction with environmental factors, but this in itself does not imply that there is always a major biological component to the borderline personality disorder (cf. Gunderson's negative position in the debate, "Resolved: The Etiology of Borderline Personality Disorder Is Predominantly Biological," at the 1990 APA annual meeting, cited in Cauwels, 1992, pp. 226–227). The evidence, as we shall see, that the timing and seriousness of psychological, sexual, and/or physical injuries to the developing child relate to the severity of psychopathology is more persuasive than a purely biological hypothesis. However, the relationship between exposure to risk and symptom development is quite complex.

Adolescence, Risk, and Protection: The "Borderline Break"

Too little has been made of the developmental connection between the period of adolescence and the emergence of borderline symptoms. This failure is especially surprising given the dearth of evidence that there is truly such a thing as a "borderline child." A recent literature review (Lofgren, Bemporad, King, Lindem, & O'Driscoll, 1991) finds no conclusive evidence for the predictive value of a childhood borderline diagnosis. The prospective follow-up study of "borderline" children performed by Lofgren et al. supports this conclusion. Children who were diagnosed borderline did not appear, later in life, to have symptoms that fit the *DSM-III-R* (1987) description of BPD. Many of the "borderline" children followed into late adolescence and adulthood who *did* adapt poorly in adulthood suffered from a range of personality disorders, but did not have comorbid Axis I affective or schizophrenic disorders. It is striking that all the subjects whose adult functioning was adaptive were found to be living in currently stable family situations, despite the fact that several of them as children had lived in extremely chaotic family environments. The authors hypothesized that interventions in the children's family situations even as late as latency may have influenced their development positively.

There are no absolute answers to the question of what promotes resilience in individuals exposed to serious risks. Although often persons who later develop disorders have experienced "accumulations of greater risks . . . over longer periods of time" than others, there are also factors that can modify an individual's vulnerability to risk situations (Rutter, 1990, p. 209). Some protective processes that seem to operate are as follows:

> (a) those that reduce the risk impact by virtue of effects on the riskiness itself or through alteration of exposure to or involvement in the risk, (b) those that reduce the likelihood of negative chain reactions stemming from the risk encounter, (c) those that promote self-esteem and self-efficacy through the availability of secure and supportive personal relationships or success in task accomplishment, and (d) those that open up opportunities. (pp. 209–210)

The individual's reasonable disposition (e.g., activity level, sociability), minimum average intelligence, competence in communicating, and internal locus of control also appear to offer protection against risk. A longitudinal study of 698 infants born in 1955 showed that risk and protective factors had different impacts at different developmental stages (Werner, 1989). At each stage, the balance shifted "between stressful life events that heightened an individual's vulnerability, and protective factors that enhanced resilience" (p. 80). Gender also shifted the balance, so that boys were more vulnerable than girls in the first decade of life and girls were more vulnerable during the second, with the balance shifting back again at the beginning of the third decade.

The environment in which the so-called borderline woman has been reared does not include the protective processes named by Rutter. Risk, psychological and/or physical, is persistently experienced, and the supportive relationships and opportunities for competence, if they are available at all, are available only to girls who fill the narrow role of caretaker. Competence in caretaking, however, when it is achieved early in such environments, is fragile and may not furnish the sense of agency and self-efficacy that some other skills may provide. What girls often take with them out of these contexts is an illusory strength whose protective function cannot persist in the face of the pressures of adolescence and leads only to what Linehan (1993) calls "apparent competence" in adulthood.

When we examine the relationship between developmental changes and psychopathology, it becomes clear why there is so little evidence for the premise that a so-called borderline child becomes a borderline adult (Lofgren et al., 1991; Palumbo, 1982). Children who show no apparent signs of behavioral or emotional problems may develop severe disorders in adulthood (Sroufe & Rutter, 1984). That does not mean that such disorders spring forth as if from the head of Zeus and have no points of origin in the past, however. The continuity exists, as Sroufe and Rutter put it, "in lawful relation to later behavior, however complex the links" (p. 21). The maladaptation that is disorder is related to the adaptational history of the individual: "Change, as well as continuity, is lawful and therefore reflective of coherent development" (p. 22). Thus, adaptation that serves an individual well at one developmental phase "may later compromise the child's ability to maximally [sic] draw upon the environment in the service of more flexible adaptation" (p. 23). Patterns of adaptation can be considered pathological only "if the adaptation compromises the normal developmental process whereby children are increasingly able to draw emotional support from age-mates (as well as give it), and to stay engaged in social commerce despite the frequent emotional challenge of doing so," in which case "the individual may be sacrificing an important buffer against stress" (p. 23). Adaptation is a continuously transforming experience; adaptational failures at one point affect how the individual adapts at the next phase. The "lawfulness" of an individual's adaptational history exists in the connections that he/she makes between earlier and later adaptations. As yet, the adaptational antecedents of most disorders are not known. However, it does seem that failure to resolve adequately certain developmental issues can predict later *behavior*, and the failure of children to move from a position of emotional dependency and be able make use of adults and peers as resources is highly predictive of their behavior later on in life (Sroufe & Rutter, 1984).

There may well exist a "common developmental pathway" for a number of adolescent problems, including mental illness, comprised of both individual and contextual factors that weaken the capacity of an individual to cope with the challenges of life as well as phases of life that pose inherent challenges to that individual (Ebata, Petersen, & Conger, 1990). The movement into and out of adolescence may itself pose inherent developmental challenges (1990, p. 318). A consistent finding in the long-term follow-up studies of borderline patients has been that most show substantial improvement in their symptoms as they approach the age of thirty.[5] Kroll (1993) believes that central nervous system maturation accounts for this finding, but we must also consider that those pressures and challenges posed most strongly in the transition from childhood into adolescence and from adolescence into young adulthood may recede somewhat in the late twenties and early thirties.[6]

Adaptive efforts made during adolescence "influence and perhaps constrain the likelihoods of particular future trajectories, not just in terms of adaptive capacity but also in terms of life 'choices' and patterns of adaptation in the roles and responsibilities expected of young adults: for work and self-sufficiency, involvement in an intimate relationship . . . , and parenting" (Ebata et al., 1990, p. 321). There are two transitional periods in adolescence: the one that takes us into the period and the one that takes us out of it. Demands upon children increase as they enter adolescence, and no child has yet completely developed the skills to meet them. Some children, however, are even less prepared than others for this new developmental venture. Whereas during infancy and childhood *contextual factors* are critical in determining how individuals adapt to their social environment, children approaching adolescence must depend on their own *individual abilities and interests* to select those situations and experiences that may influence their continued development (Ebata et al., 1990). The kind of context-dependent learning, then, that spells protection and even survival for females during childhood does not necessarily serve them well in the teenage years. Girls who have been exposed to extreme forms of sexualization and/or devaluation have not developed a sense of their own capacities and desires. For them, adolescence poses special risks, including the risk of taking their love and their need to love into the outside world (Lane, 1990).

7

"Borderline" Self-Destructiveness and Therapeutic Breakdown

Anne Sexton, the Pulitzer prize–winning poet who eventually committed suicide after struggling for her entire adult life with episodes of debilitating depression, ragefulness, dissociation, anxiety, and impulsivity,[1] found a way to speak of both her "mad" self and her more conventional, quotidian self in the poem "Her Kind":

> I have gone out, a possessed witch,
> haunting the black air, braver at night;
> dreaming evil, I have done my hitch
> over the plain houses, light by light:
> lonely thing, twelve-fingered, out of mind.
> A woman like that is not a woman, quite.
> I have been her kind.
>
> I have found the warm caves in the woods,
> filled them with skillets, carvings, shelves,
> closets, silks, innumerable goods;
> fixed the suppers for the worms and elves:

> whining, rearranging the disaligned,
> A woman like that is misunderstood.
> I have been her kind.
>
> I have ridden in your cart, driver,
> waved my nude arms at villages going by,
> learning the last bright routes, survivor
> where your flames still bite my thigh
> and my ribs crack where your wheels wind.
> A woman like that is not ashamed to die.
> I have been her kind.
> —Anne Sexton, *Her Kind,* 1960

In her poem, Sexton, using a double "I" identified with madness but set apart from it through insight, renders distinct the difference between pain itself and the representation of pain (Middlebrook, 1991, p. 115). In each stanza, there are two points of view—that of the one acting or acting out, and that of the observing "I" who, in the refrain, steps out to "witness, interpret, and affirm her alter ego" (p. 114). As the poem begins, Sexton is the witch/madwoman, alone, frightening to others ("haunting the black air") by virtue of her mad abnormality (she is "twelve-fingered" and "out of mind"), but also lonely and frightening to herself. She views herself as others view her at these times—as not quite human ("not a woman, quite"). In the second stanza, she is the nurturer—gathering provisions, cooking, arranging, creating warmth. She is, however, an unhappy caretaker ("whining"). Unlike Snow White, who finds both escape and vocation in caring for the dwarfs (here, "elves"), Sexton's "kind" is the housewife socialized to her role but discontented with it. She is "misunderstood," perhaps because no one sees in the wife/mother either the pain of her madness or her unhappiness with the conventional role of caretaker, nor does anyone acknowledge her capacity for creativity that is the other aspect of her mad witchery—the "magic craft" (p. 115) of poetry. In the third stanza, Sexton sees herself as one who has experienced both happiness ("bright routes,") and carnal passions (the "flames [that] still bite my thigh"). Passions and excitements, however, have the power destroy her. The tumbrel in which she rides will one day lead her to her death, as it has previously taken her close to it, through her attempts at suicide.

So-called borderline women have much in common with Sexton's "kind." If they are frightening, disturbing, or merely off-putting to others, they are equally so to themselves; if they are temporarily lost in impulsive urges and passions, they are more often made miserable and, in some cases, destroyed by them. Although socialized to be good girls and compliant women, they have been taught by those who do not themselves nurture well, and therefore they often bitterly disappoint themselves by buckling under the mandate to nurture, seeking nurturance in unhelpful ways that others then call selfish, manipulative, and attention-seeking. It is no wonder that such women may come to believe that "a woman like that is not a woman, quite."

In this chapter, we shall explore the difficulties many "borderline" women encounter in trying to live and be understood, the urges toward self-destruction they experience, and the ways in which these women represent this "madness" to others. The representations of their troubles and the ways in which others interpret that experience are not generally the stuff of poetry or poetic interpretation (as they were not always for Sexton), nor do they lead to the most salutary interventions.

Self-Injury and BPD

The propensity of many so-called borderlines to harm or to threaten to harm themselves is a source of agonizing mystery to those close to them. Professionals, although less mystified by the self-destructive acts of borderline patients, are often no less frustrated by them and frequently no less at a loss in their attempts to help their patients bring these urges under control. Although many women diagnosed as having BPD drink too much, shop too much, have eating problems, and/or engage in sexually promiscuous behavior, these behaviors are easier to conceal and are more likely to be viewed as variants of "normal" behaviors, whereas cutting, burning one's skin, or trying to kill oneself are not.

Self-injurious behavior (SIB) (cf. Kroll, 1993) may take the form of self-mutilation through cutting, burning, or other means; risk-taking behavior that could lead to self-harm; impulsivity in the form of substance or food abuse; or actual suicide attempts. If SIB is the "behavioral specialty" of the borderline (Gunderson, 1984), of all forms of self-injury, chronic self-mutilation is unarguably the behavior most readily recognized as "borderline," even though it is by no means restricted to the borderline patient (Favazza, 1987). In this discussion, I will focus particularly on self-cutting and suicide attempts, as these are thought to be prototypical of the disorder.

Self-injurious behavior is more common among individuals who have an external locus of control—those who believe that they cannot effectively influence their lives through their own actions (Jack, 1992, esp. pp. 61–67). Class and gender play a compelling role in determining whether a person will adopt an internal or an external locus of control (Jack, 1992), and an external locus of control is a more characteristic outgrowth of women's socialization than it is of men's. Women's greater tendency toward self-injury is not, therefore, surprising. They have generally been more prone to aggress against themselves than against others.

It may seem odd to consider some forms of self-injurious behavior as more deviant than others, but when behavior is matched against gender norms, deviance does become a question of degree. Just how deviant is it for women in our culture to torture themselves with dieting? How deviant is it for young adult men in college to drink until they black out and boast of it the next day? These behaviors share a cultural "normalcy" that some others do not. There is a point, however, beyond which the acceptability of certain self-injurious behaviors is challenged within the culture. Here we are faced with the paradox of a society's disapproval of behaviors whose *goals* are actually socially sanctioned. The labeling of anorexia nervosa as mental illness is an example of society's disapproval of self-starvation that occurs in response to that same society's more or less constant encouragement of young women to become thinner and thinner (Kroll, 1993). How far will the psychiatric profession go, Kroll asks, in "defining socially undesirable, including indirectly self-destructive, behaviors as medical disorders" (Kroll, 1993, p. 84)?

In order for a woman's self-destructive act to be true to feminine stereotype, it should ideally be private. To the extent possible it should not involve or implicate others. Dangerous activity in the service of being accepted or acceptable (e.g., rigorous dieting, promiscuous behavior, self-mutilation through breast enlargement surgery) is more easily tolerated in women than are acts that dramatize other inner states such as anger. Although socially sanctioned forms of SIB, both religious and secular, have existed throughout the ages—sacrifice and propitiation to the gods, hunger strikes, self-immolation, and the like—the resolution or dramatization of personal conflicts by self-mutilation has not been viewed as having any socially redeeming value. When certain behaviors have no institutionalized meaning, they and the persons who engage in them are viewed as deviant—most likely mentally ill (Kroll, 1993).

Functions and Origins of SIB

In order to understand the association between women, BPD, and self-destructive behavior, we must first make a distinction among the functions SIB

serves for the individual, the motives that are ascribed to it, and the response
that others make to it. Self-mutilation serves as "an attempt to correct or prevent a pathological, destabilizing condition that threatens the community,
the individual, or both. . . . At the deepest, irreducible level it is prophylactic
and salubrious for groups and for individuals threatened by death, disorganization, disease, and discomfort" (Favazza, 1987, p. 191). Seemingly unendurable psychological tension can be rapidly relieved by self-injurious behavior such as skin-cutting (Favazza, 1987). Cutting "works" in the short run,
and in the absence of more functional methods for reducing the tensions of
extreme discomfort, it may be employed over and over again, sometimes es-
calating in frequency and severity (Briere, 1992). Dissociative experiences often accompany such attempts at self-injury (Favazza, 1987; Kroll, 1993;
Waites, 1993).

   Childhood physical and sexual abuse figure prominently in the histories of
those who are prone to SIB (Bryer et al., 1987; Courtois, 1988; van der
Kolk, 1989; van der Kolk, Perry, & Herman, 1991), not all of whom are diagnosed as having borderline personality disorder. In individuals who have
histories of abuse, the ability to regulate emotional states is "disrupted by
traumatic experiences that repeatedly evoke terror, rage, and grief. These
emotions ultimately coalesce in a dreadful feeling that psychiatrists call 'dysphoria' and patients find almost intolerable to describe. It is a state of confusion, agitation, emptiness, and utter aloneness" (Herman, 1992, p. 108). Because of the consistent disruptions that Herman describes, individuals are
unable to call forth self-soothing behaviors to ease their extreme distress.
Self-injurious behaviors, or "pathological soothing mechanisms," as Herman
calls them, serve the function of regulating these emotional states (Briere,
1992; Favazza, 1987; Herman, 1992; Waites, 1993). The individual attempts to alter her feeling state by actively engineering an extreme change in
the autonomic system through a "jolt to the body" (Herman, 1992). Self-injury can produce a variety of changes in self-awareness such as trance states
or a numbness that anesthetizes feelings. Alternatively, it can produce pain of
sufficient intensity to stimulate awareness and affirm to the individual that
she can feel (Waites, 1993).

   In a recent study of the origins of SIB (van der Kolk et al., 1991), sev-
enty-four individuals (thirty-nine women and thirty-five men) with diagnoses of bipolar II disorder, BPD, and three other personality disorders—
antisocial, narcissistic, and schizotypal—were monitored for suicide
attempts, self-injury, and eating disorders. Of all the diagnoses under consideration, only BPD was significantly associated with suicide attempts,
cutting, and other self-injurious behaviors. People with histories of child-

hood sexual and/or physical abuse were found to be prone to cut their skin and/or to attempt suicide. Chronic self-destructive behavior was most frequent among those persons who had the most severe histories of separation and neglect and/or histories of sexual abuse. The researchers found that the character of the trauma and the age of the individual at the time of the trauma affected the nature and the severity of the self-destructive act. They discovered that disruptions in attachment (separation from parents, domestic chaos, physical and emotional neglect) were significantly associated with cutting but not with other self-injurious behavior or suicide attempts. From this evidence, they hypothesized that although trauma in childhood contributes substantially to an individual's beginning to act self-destructively, self-destructive behavior is actually maintained in instances where individuals lack ongoing secure attachments to others. The patients who had histories of prolonged separations from parental figures and those who had no memory of feeling cared about as children were least able, of all patients studied, to make use of inner resources to control self-destructive behavior.

SIB can become a central means by which borderline clients give expression to separation/abandonment conflicts (Perry & Cooper, 1986) and relieve the cumulative tensions arising from the struggle for expression of anger and other emotional needs (Favazza, 1987; Perry & Cooper, 1986; van der Kolk et al., 1991; Waites, 1993). Cutting the body may be conceived of literally as making an opening through which anger, tensions, anxiety, and a sense of badness can escape (Favazza, 1987). These emotions, "often accompanied by feelings of powerlessness," affect an individual's "sense of stability and well-being and may create the sensation of an impending bodily explosion" (Favazza, 1987, p. 195).

Self-Injury and Self-Blame

Cutting or burning of the skin inflicts harm on a body that has come to represent a self who deserves to suffer. Hurting is proof of survival in the face of threats to survival, but it also stands as proof of one's ability to control pain (Waites, 1993). Both the pain and the blood (or the serous fluid that oozes from a burn) are evidence of life and of the intactness of the body's boundary—the skin. Scar tissue marks the painful event and furnishes evidence of healing (Favazza, 1987). Some survivors of abuse dissociate feelings of being victimized and come to identify with the aggressor, attacking themselves as if they were both perpetrator and victim, in a reenactment of the traumatic situation(s) (Waites, 1993).

There is more than one pathway through which a woman can become her own victimizer. It is important to understand how the stage for this kind of disquieting relationship with the self can be set throughout girlhood through gender role socialization. The development of a double identity that includes an awareness of a self who is acting and a self who is acted upon is not unique to traumatized individuals who dissociate. In our discussion of female socialization, we have explored the particular forms that girls' self-awareness takes in adolescence. The mirror bears critical witness to the objectified self. Even women who have not been physically or sexually abused by others have had to cultivate, from early on, an acute self-awareness that frequently includes a strong sense of self-blame.

For many women the rigidities of perfectionism are as tyrannical as any human abuser could be, and it is sometimes in reaction to extreme self-imposed controls that women engage in impulsive, self-destructive behaviors such as bulimia, promiscuity, substance abuse, and the like. Women tend to blame themselves for their misfortunes, whereas men tend to blame circumstances (Franks, 1986). In addition, women are not only *blamed* more for their bad fortune by others than are men, but the blame is affixed to the woman's character, whereas in the case of men, the blame is attached to their behavior, *not* their character (Howard, 1984). Self-blame is the result of the representation of a critical self that is a by-product, over time, of generalizing the representation of self mirrored in interaction with important others who have been abusive, dismissive, and/or invalidating. One can only assume that women more easily fashion and maintain that critical observer, not because they necessarily have more to criticize in themselves than do men, but because their upbringing fosters such a construction.

There is a valuable distinction to be made between *behavioral* and *characterological* self-blame (Janoff-Bulman, 1979). In the case of the former, an individual considers that behaviors can be modified by her or his own efforts and thus that victimization can be avoided in the future; in the case of the latter, the individual maladaptively remains in the past, focusing on the issues of deservedness or worthiness. The woman who believes her character to be at issue may have difficulty protecting herself from maltreatment in the future, and she is likely to have difficulty taking care of herself in other important ways.

Private Agony and Public Response

Kroll (1993) makes a distinction between public and private aspects of self-mutilation. He sees the public component of self-mutilation as a demonstration "of one's wounds with the expectation of eliciting a response, usually supportive, from others. The self-injurious behavior in these cases is the individual's method of making a public statement" (p. 85). Some "borderline" women aggress against themselves in ways that are quite deviant. Their self-mutilation and suicide attempts evoke strong reactions from others. Families and institutions such as hospitals and halfway houses are more compelled by the *public* dimension of the act and, as a result of their attention to this dimension, ignore the "private anguish" (p. 86) and operate on the assumption that the behavior is merely an attention-getting ploy. Individual psychotherapists, in contrast, pay attention mainly to the *private* dimension—the internal distress that engenders the behavior—and ignore the public statement (cf. pp. 85–86). There are dangers in ignoring either aspect. Concentration on the public component can result in blame and compassionless control, whereas focus only on the private struggle may cause a therapist to overlook portions of the message the client is giving, since in therapy, self-injurious behavior may indicate panic, rebellion, or fury. The message from the client may be an ambivalent one, in which appeals for rescue are accompanied by the insistence that she is in control and not in need of the therapist's help. Self-injury can be an attack on the therapist, who is compelled to look on helplessly as the client proceeds to destroy herself. It may, however, be an invitation to explore secrets, such as a history of self-abuse or earlier abuse by others.

Kroll draws a fascinating parallel between medieval asceticism and the SIB of the group of women he refers to as PTSD/borderlines. In both cases, self-injurious behavior has been performed by young women while in a state of heightened emotional arousal in an effort to alter their mood or state of consciousness. He contends that in former times, as now, society has given to SIB symbolic meaning and legitimacy, and he seems to fear that with the growing acceptance of a connection between childhood trauma and later self-destructive behavior, as well as with the development of greater empathy for those who struggle with self-injurious impulses, clinicians may fail to help clients modify that behavior. He states:

> Ritualized SIB, performed in our society by PTSD/borderlines, is interpreted as a meaningful symbolic act and is simultaneously reinforced and discouraged. An examination of SIB by medieval ascetics suggests that, in medieval society, too, there was public ambivalence. The medieval populace was as suspicious yet intrigued by excessive SIB as we are. Yet, in each society, the prevailing value system gave the self-injurious persons the vocabulary and the conceptual tools to develop asceticism or symptoms as a meaningful behavior.
>
> In both societies, caring professionals . . . are caught in the paradox that their very understanding and sympathy for the suffering and aspirations of the

young persons who engage in SIB have the effect of supporting and reinforcing the SIB. At the same time that sympathy is offered, there is also recognition in both societies of an unhealthy narcissism to heroic SIB that feeds on the intense self-centeredness accompanying SIB and on the public fascination drawn to such persons. (p. 96)

Psychiatric patients' public display of SIB would appear to flout societal norms, but Kroll argues that, paradoxically, defining this public display as an understandable outgrowth of various childhood traumata has created new norms for how formerly abused persons are expected to behave. I cannot agree. In my view, Kroll, on the one hand, grossly overestimates the number of professionals who truly understand self-injuring clients and, on the other, wrongly makes the assumption that the expression of understanding or empathic concern on the part of those who treat such patients will inhibit the process of working toward change.

It hardly seems likely that the small steps therapists have taken in recent years toward understanding self-destructive behaviors will, of necessity, lead to a wholesale acceptance of these behaviors. If anything, endless discussion about "patient management" has scarcely created a cozy therapeutic world for the "borderline." Surely, nothing distances us so thoroughly from clients as the consideration of their "management," and nothing brings up the discussion of so-called management issues as swiftly as self-injurious behavior. Such discussions hark back to the domestication of insanity by the psychiatric profession during the Victorian era, when "'moral insanity' redefined madness, not as a loss of reason, but as deviance from socially accepted behavior . . . [and] 'moral management' substituted close supervision and paternal concern for physical restraint and harsh treatment" (Showalter, 1985, p. 29).

The Marked Woman

When self-injury is viewed primarily as a manipulative way to garner attention, it is no wonder that repeated episodes can arouse anger and increasing frustration on the part of those close to the borderline. It is but a small step from the perception that the behavior is manipulative to the experience of it as a personal affront. The question that may be tacitly or overtly asked of the self-destructive individual by professionals or intimates is: How could you do this to me after all I have done to help you?

There have always been "marked women" in our culture, but they have not marked *themselves;* they have been set apart and marked by the society that named their behavior deviant. Like Hester Prynne of the *Scarlet Letter*, women have been shunned and stigmatized for real or perceived social transgressions, generally sexual. As a society, we are accustomed to doing the marking of women *ourselves;* when "borderline" women mark themselves through self-mutilation, they draw attention to themselves in ways that only they have determined. On an institutional level, the self-marking of women by cutting or burning may be responded to as manipulative primarily because it is presumed to be a challenge to the control of others. By marking these women officially through label or diagnosis, others may reassert control over them. The perception of manipulation itself is the ascription of power to individuals who themselves feel least powerful.

Counterpoised to the assumption that "borderlines" are flagrantly out to get attention by the most shocking means possible is ample evidence of the difficulty they have in commanding the attention of other people. The connection between inflicting harm on the self and "getting attention" (a euphemism for harming others by worrying them, punishing them, and so on) is much more complicated than the equation of self-harm with purposefully controlling ("manipulating") behavior. Manipulation is not characteristic of borderline patients; in fact, their means of influencing others tend to be direct, forceful, and clumsy:

> Often the most influential behavior is parasuicide or the threat of impending suicide; at other times, the behaviors that have the most influence are communications of intense pain and agony, or current crises that the individuals cannot solve. . . . The central question is whether or not borderline individuals purposely use these behaviors or communications to influence others artfully, shrewdly, and fraudulently. Such an interpretation is rarely in accord with borderline individuals' own self-perceptions of their intent. (Linehan, 1993, pp. 16–17)

The interpretation of their behavior as manipulative may, in fact, be a "major source of their feelings of invalidation and of being misunderstood" (p. 17).

In *Girl, Interrupted* (1993), Susanna Kaysen, who years later discovered that she had been diagnosed "borderline" when she was hospitalized in her late teens, describes the "perverse" behavior that led to her commitment to a mental hospital:

> My ambition was to negate. The world, whether dense or hollow, provoked only my negations. When I was supposed to be awake, I was asleep; when I was supposed to speak, I was silent; when a pleasure offered itself to me, I avoided it. My hunger, my thirst, my loneliness and boredom and fear were all weapons aimed at my enemy, the world. They didn't matter a whit to the world, of

course, and they tormented me, but I got a gruesome satisfaction from my suf-
ferings. They proved my existence. All my integrity seemed to lie in saying No.

So the opportunity to be incarcerated was just too good to resist. It was a
very big No—the biggest No this side of suicide.

Perverse reasoning. But back of that perversity, I knew I wasn't mad.
(p. 42)

Others could well have interpreted Kaysen's behavior as "manipulative" and
"attention-getting"; she herself clearly did not perceive it that way.

The sense that many borderline patients have that their pain is worse than
anyone else's may well be justified: "It's colored by both the need to be special—in this case to be specially in pain, to achieve that distinction through
suffering—and a sense I have that there's some truth to it. These dysphoric
states that are triggered in borderlines are in fact exquisitely painful experiences. Just because we may not feel that the trigger justified the response, this
does not mean that the response is not excruciating" (cf. interview with Rex
W. Cowdry, cited in Cauwels, 1992, p. 80). The well-worn line from the
song, "Nobody Knows the Trouble I've Seen," is true on more than one level.
On the one hand, the individual believes that no one *cares* to know the trouble, as no one has cared in the past; on the other hand, she believes that no
one can ever *know* the trouble because others have never felt anything like
the kind of pain that she has experienced. For a woman at the border, the
sense that no one can comprehend the extent and intensity of her suffering is
an understandable consequence of the sense of never having *been known*. She
is saying to those around her, *not* "I want you to suffer as I have suffered,"
but "it is through my pain you shall know me."

Borderline Women and the Dialogue of Suicide

Historical Implications of Women's Suicide

If suicide is an interpretation whose "subject-object has always been identity
and *ethos*" (Higonnet, 1986, p. 71), how we currently interpret women's suicidality accurately reflects the temper of the times. In the classical world, the
suicides of women like Antigone and Cleopatra were viewed as heroic, masculine, voluntary, and, often, political acts. However, the last of these female
suicide heroes was the French revolutionary martyr Charlotte Corday. By the
beginning of the eighteenth century, suicide, as a "violation of social

norms[,] is treated as a malady; the victims of suicidal depression are subject to 'vapors'" (p. 70).

Higonnet reminds us that "to medicalize suicide is to feminize it. Since much of the scientific literature perceived woman as an abnormal man, the link between her genetic defect and suicidal illness was readily made. Furthermore, the traditional perception of women's weak character . . . helped assimilate them to the image of suicide as a phenomenon of mental breakdown" (p. 70). In the nineteenth century, the earlier vision of heroic self-sacrifice yielded to one of disintegration and social victimization, and women's self-destruction was often perceived to be a surrender to an illness resulting from love—*le mal d'amour:* "Gradually, in what we may call the Ophelia complex, the suicidal solution is linked to the dissolution of self, fragmentation to flow. The abandoned woman drowns, as it were, in her own emotions" (p. 71). Men die for their political ideals; women for love. "If Brutus commits suicide for the nation, Portia commits suicide in order not to live without Brutus" (p. 73). Women lose themselves in relationships quite literally.

Although it was known during the nineteenth century that men committed suicide at a rate about double that of women, women have borne the "literary burden" of suicide (Higonnet, 1986). In novels, women are more often depicted as committing suicide than men. Portrayal of the suicidal heroine is as an involuntary casualty of suicide, her "quest for autonomy . . . replaced by the breakdown of identity" (p. 81).

More women *attempt* suicide; more men actually kill themselves. A study of male and female college students found that both men and women who completed suicide were considered by others to be more masculine and powerful than those who made attempts (Linehan, 1973); little wonder, then, that suicide "attempters" are described in denigrating, "feminine" terms: "manipulative," "hysterical," "inadequate" (Jack, 1992).

Borderline Women and Suicide

> *But suicides have a special language.*
> *Like carpenters they want to know* which tools.
> *They never ask* why build.
> —**Anne Sexton, from** *Wanting to Die,* **1960**

The rate of completed suicide in borderline personality disorder is roughly 9.5 percent,[2] a rate as high as that found in the major psychotic disorders

(Stone, 1990). Suicide gestures and serious attempts are by no means ubiq-uitous in BPD patients, however; in fact, the combination of an affective disorder or substance use disorder with BPD may carry a substantially higher risk for suicidal behavior than BPD alone (Fryer, Frances, Sullivan, Hurt, & Clarkin, 1988b). Fryer and her colleagues raise the possibility, based on the results of their review of 180 charts of individuals diagnosed with BPD, that whereas suicidal *gestures* are related to borderline psy-chopathology alone, serious *attempts* may be related to the combination of BPD and affective and/or substance use disorders. Whereas van der Kolk et al. (1991) found an association between childhood trauma and suicide at-tempts and a corresponding association between cutting and childhood ne-glect, Shearer, Peters, Quaytman, and Wadman's (1988) tentative profile, generated from data on 40 women hospitalized for BPD symptoms, sug-gests the following predictors of suicide lethality: advancing age, number of previous suicide attempts, family history of substance abuse, and presence of an eating disorder. In this study, family history of suicidal behavior, early loss of a parent, physical abuse, and incest were among the variables *not* pre-dictive of suicidality.

Self-mutilation and suicide attempts arise from different needs (Favazza, 1987). Suicide attempts by "borderlines" may well be guided by interper-sonal communications,[3] whereas cutting primarily serves to regulate inter-nal emotional states (van der Kolk et al., 1991). Linehan and her colleagues work with chronically parasuicidal individuals who meet the criteria for di-agnosis of BPD (*parasuicide* refers to behaviors that are frequently termed "suicidal gestures," or "manipulative" suicide attempts). Linehan (1993) be-lieves that parasuicidal behaviors constitute an attempt, albeit a maladaptive one, to gain control over unbearably painful, overwhelming negative affect. Suicidal behavior can also be an effective means—in some cases, the only means—for getting others to help these individuals handle their intense pain. It is likewise an effective way for a nonpsychotic person to get admit-ted to a psychiatric hospital or to have increased contact with her therapist, and many of the clients in Linehan's program reported that one aspect of their drive to engage in parasuicidal behavior was an intent to alter their en-vironment. From the point of view of patients,

> suicidal behavior is a reflection of serious and at times frantic suicide ideation
> and ambivalence over whether to continue life or not. Although the patients'
> communication of extreme ideas or enactment of extreme behaviors may be
> accompanied by the desire to be rescued by the persons they are communi-
> cating with, this does not necessarily mean that they are acting in this man-

ner in order to get help. . . . Function does not prove intention. (Linehan, 1993, p. 17)

It has traditionally been assumed by sociologists that a clear distinction could be made between the "genuine" suicidal *act*, aimed exclusively at death, and suicide *attempts* of various kinds, aimed at survival (Taylor, 1982). Research into suicide and suicide attempts has shown, however, that often only the most minute of differences separates death from survival—that most suicidal acts are "characterized not by the certainty of death, but by the possibility of death, and the majority of these are 'risk-taking' acts" (p. 148).

Taylor (1982) concluded that "suicide is more likely to the extent that individuals are either psychologically immune from the opinions, feelings and wishes of others or are psychologically unprotected from the opinions, feelings and wishes of others" (p. 178). There are two basic types of suicide, in his view: one that is directed inward and one that is directed toward others. The first constitutes a monologue; the second, a dialogue, which represents a "communication *through* suicide" (p. 180). The borderline woman's suicidality would seem to be of the latter type. Taylor calls this type of act an *appeal* suicide.

In an appeal suicide, others tell the individual "everything about himself [sic]. That is, without others', or a particular other's, good opinions, love, respect, or even mere presence, the individual feels that [her] own existence is problematic. . . . [She] has no 'real' existence independent of others' favorable validation of [her]" (Taylor, 1982, p. 178). The individual is unprotected from the judgments and needs of others. For the female "borderline" who is suicidal, the act is a gamble with death. She cannot kill herself "for real" because then she will never find out the other's response to her death, but she cannot *not* kill herself, for there are no other means of validation, no other means of attaining certainty as to the other's (or others') persisting and complete attachment to her or attaining certainty as to the meaning of her existence to the other (or others). She gambles, holding out some hope that [she] might live and yet be responded to as if [she] had died" (p. 180). The nature of the other's (or others') response—and the individual's interpretation of it—are frequently critical in determining whether she will repeat the suicidal behavior. Although Taylor is not a clinician, his direction for sociological inquiry has interesting implications for the psychotherapist working with parasuicidal borderline patients: "Our analysis here would direct us to enquire whether or not the subject's uncertainty had been resolved" (p. 185).

Treatment at the Border

It is not my goal to discuss here how to conduct psychotherapy with border-line clients. There are a number of individuals who are refining treatment approaches, and I have cited several of them.[4] It is my aim, rather, to indicate important treatment considerations for both therapist and client.

In a study of the treatment of 790 BPD[5] patients by eleven experienced therapists, 44 percent terminated treatment precipitously, the vast number against the advice of their therapists, and half of these because of therapeutic impasse (Waldinger & Gunderson, 1984). Only 10 percent of the entire sample were thought, by termination, to have been treated successfully. A later study (Gunderson et al., 1989) supports the fact of consistent dropout of borderline clients from psychotherapy, generally within the first six months of treatment. In that research effort, 60 BPD patients were studied in the hospital. The majority of these (77 percent) were female, and their average age was twenty-five. Of these, 36 terminated prematurely. The largest group of them cited as reasons for ending treatment (1) that they were feeling worse as a result of the therapy (angrier, more depressed, more nervous); (2) that they were in basic disagreement with their therapists about what they needed; and (3) that their therapists were cold, uncaring, critical, judgmental, and/or distant.[6] The therapists, explaining their patients' decisions to terminate, maintained that their patients were denying problems that they needed to confront, and that it was confrontation that had led to conflict in the therapeutic relationship. Interestingly, the severity of the patient's psychopathology did not determine whether she dropped out, leaving the authors to conclude that the therapeutic relationship itself may well be the most important factor in determining the client's continuation in therapy. This conclusion is supported by evidence that most "borderline" clients, when they do terminate therapy, have the motivation to seek out treatment elsewhere (Kroll, 1993).

Clinicians and the Investigation of Trauma

It is all too common for researchers and clinicians to seek "an explanation for the perpetrator's crimes in the character of the victim" (Herman, 1992, p. 116). For clients diagnosed with BPD who have been sexually abused, the two characteristic elements of the response to trauma—reliving aspects of the trauma or avoiding all stimuli that might relate to the trauma—take the form of recapitulating traumatizing relationships and, alternatively, attempting to avoid close relationships entirely (Perry et al., 1990). Treatment of these women must be informed by an understanding of the role played by childhood trauma in the development of the disorder (Herman, 1992: Perry et al., 1990). Such understanding

> provides the basis for a cooperative therapeutic alliance that normalizes and validates the survivor's emotional reactions to past events, while recognizing that these reactions may be maladaptive in the present. Moreover, a shared understanding of the survivor's characteristic disturbances of relationship and the consequent risk of repeated victimization offers the best insurance against unwitting reenactments of the original trauma in the therapeutic relationship." (Herman, 1992, p. 127)

What was formerly described as a "destructive force" emanating from the innate aggression of the client, which intruded repeatedly into the therapist/client relationship, may now be conceptualized as the reemergence of the perpetrator's violence in the treatment situation.

Clients rarely enter treatment presenting the direct sequelae of sexual abuse as their primary complaint. Briere and Zaidi (1989) reviewed 100 charts of nonpsychotic patients to look for references to sexual abuse in the clinical histories. Fifty charts were randomly chosen; fifty contained histories written by clinicians who were requested to ask about an abuse history. Only 6 percent of the random charts showed references to sexual abuse, as opposed to 70 percent in the charts of those patients who were asked. The lack of attention given to questions about physical and sexual abuse in clinical history-taking has disturbing implications for women who seek mental health services:

> Clinicians are largely unaware of the psychosocial consequences of abuse because the victim-to-patient process is an area of clinical research that has been underconceptualized. Thus, even when abuse is identified, clinicians' confusion about the role of abuse in psychiatric illness leaves them unprepared to implement special treatment approaches for what appears to be a large proportion of psychiatric patients. (Carmen et al., 1984, p. 378)

In the case of individuals who have been hospitalized, "the traumatic etiology of affective and behavioral disturbances . . . is easily overlooked. . . . During the hyperreactive phase, the management of these patients may prove to be so challenging that they may receive a psychiatric label that denotes more the frustrations of their management team than an accurate diagnosis" (van der Kolk, 1984, p. xiii). In a study of inpatients, despite the fact that patients who had histories of abuse were not easily distinguishable from nonabused patients at the time of admission, abused patients spent more time in the hospital than nonabused patients and experienced more treatment problems—difficulty trusting their therapists, perceiving themselves as worthy of treatment, and managing aggressive impulses toward themselves or others (Craine et al., 1988).

In the frequent instances where child abuse has not been disclosed promptly and the psychological sequelae of the original trauma not treated immediately, "secondary elaborations" tend to develop that "typically . . . constitute part of the symptom picture for which patients seek treatment" (Gelinas, 1983, p. 317). As a result of the long-term entrenchment of maladaptive coping patterns (Scurfield, 1985), symptoms are often not clearly recognizable as the aftereffects of traumatic victimization. What the clinician is likely to see many years after the occurrence of the abuse,[7] then, is a "disguised presentation" of symptomatology (Gelinas, 1983). In incest victims, for example, symptoms may appear in the form of "a characterological depression with complications and with atypical impulsive and dissociative elements" (p. 327). If this type of disguised presentation becomes the focus of treatment, the abuse history may well remain hidden and its effects inaccessible to treatment (Gelinas, 1983). When therapists fail to "recognize the behavior and the subtle clues that signal disconfirmation and transformation of the abuse" (Rieker & Carmen, 1986, p. 368), they run the risk of exposing the patient/client to a revictimization, or destructive recapitulation, of the trauma, wherein the individual again bears his or her pain in silence.

Recent research indicates that victims of sexual abuse who consulted mental health professionals have often found them unhelpful or even abusive. Fifty incest victims studied by Frenken and Van Stolk (1990) had each been in treatment with more than three professionals, and half of them had dropped out of therapy along the way. Over half the therapists of these women failed to explore the clients' incest experience after they told the therapists of it. The authors conclude, "However reluctant the women may have been to disclose their incest experiences, one is struck by the inability of the professionals to (1) detect sexual abuse, (2) explicitly diagnose it, and (3) keep it a subject of discussion" (p. 260). By the clients' accounts, those clinicians who did address the incest belittled the client's story, made light of the perpetrator's acts, or blamed the victim, among other unhelpful interventions (Frenken & Van Stolk, 1990). Armsworth (1989) refers to a 1987 paper in which Goodwin estimates that more than 30 percent of women with histories of incest who seek therapy are sexually exploited by helping professionals and, thus, revictimized. In her own study of 30 incest survivors, 7 (23 percent) had been sexually intimate with, or had been pressured to become sexually involved with, the clinician they consulted.

In the same study (Armsworth, 1989), women who had female therapists found their therapists significantly more helpful than did women who had male therapists. Armsworth suggests that because most women have been abused by male perpetrators, female therapists may not trigger as many reliving or dissociative experiences as do male clinicians. The fact that the women who had the less helpful male therapists stayed in therapy longer than their counterparts may be explained by the fact that "the absence of empathic understanding in the survivor's past may actually be the initial 'hook' that keeps the client returning to therapy even when it is exploitative or regarded as not very helpful" (p. 556).

Women Minding Madwomen: Nurses and "Borderlines"

In Charlotte Bronte's *Jane Eyre,* Jane, the orphaned young woman who seeks a position as governess, arrives at Thornfield, home of Mr. Rochester. Jane first assumes that Mrs. Fairfax, the woman who greets her, is, in fact, her employer but soon learns that she is merely housekeeper for the master, Mr. Rochester, a gentleman who spends considerable periods of time away from his estate. Mrs. Fairfax keeps the house in his absence, and as Jane is to learn much later, it is Grace Poole who minds the madwoman in the attic,[8] Mr. Rochester's wife, Bertha. All the women at Thornfield, including Jane, are without companions: "Women in Jane's world, acting as agents for men, may be the keepers of other women. But both keepers and prisoners are bound by the same chains" (Gilbert & Gubar, 1979, p. 351).

In the psychiatric hospital, it is psychiatric nurses, predominantly women, who are the keepers of "borderline" women. The nurses, like Mrs. Fairfax and Grace Poole, generally stand beneath men (i.e., male administrators and psychiatrists) in the hierarchical order of things. Just as, at Thornfield, much activity and emotion are aroused in anticipation of Mr. Rochester's visits home, so patients often eagerly await the attentions of their (mostly) male physicians. In the hospital, whereas nurses have a good deal of responsibility for caretaking, and some have more authority than others, none has the ultimate authority over treatment decisions. Nurses must perform the difficult tasks of enforcing limits and dealing with crises on the psychiatric unit, and they may or may not be treated with respect by the women they look after.

Sandwiched in the middle of the hospital hierarchy, the nurse may, at times, be in disagreement with the physician or feel resentment toward him for a variety of reasons. *She*, however, is not permitted to rage at him as many of her borderline patients do at her; *she* does not have the luxury of being "needy." It is little wonder that, at times, tensions between nurses and "borderline" patients boil over. Nurses are not supposed to rail at doctors who are tardy, arrogant, and/or dismissive; they are sometimes not permitted to "have a say" in treatment (i.e., to express their needs in a direct manner). Furthermore, even if such permission were the order of the day, many nurses could not take advantage of it, having been well socialized as girls and women to express their feelings indirectly or not at all. It is little wonder that some of them may not be able to identify with their patients' difficulties in expressing their needs and their anger, particularly when these difficulties take the form of "acting-out" behaviors.

A study of 113 registered nurses in five separate short-term psychiatric settings (Gallop, Lancee, & Garfinkel, 1989) found that nurses had very different responses toward hypothetical patients diagnosed borderline than they had toward patients diagnosed schizophrenic. The levels of empathy expressed toward these two groups of hypothetical patients were strikingly different. The "borderline" patients generated significantly more belittling or contradictory responses than did the "schizophrenics." The researchers hypothesized that the nurses may have justified their responses to the "borderlines" on the basis that their behavior, unlike that of schizophrenic patients, was "manipulative" or "bad" rather than "mad." The nurses were, likewise, less involved with the BPD patients on an emotional level. Since BPD patients "are not perceived as sick, compliant, cooperative, or grateful," nurses may resist becoming more involved with them, fearing that by doing so they are capitulating to manipulation (p. 819).

Therapeutic Implications of Cultural Assumptions About Women's Dependency and Anger

When a client is a woman and a therapist is a man, as is often the case, the inequitable power distribution that exists in other male-female relations is replicated (Carmen et al., 1981; Gannon, 1982). The bias reflected in formal classifications of mental illness is even more dramatically evident in our informal language (Stiver, 1991b). Such terms as *manipulative, seductive, controlling, needy, devouring, frigid, castrating, masochistic,* and *hysterical* have been used pervasively, primarily to describe female patients, with the clear implication that such patients are hard to tolerate and almost impossible to treat and that if one does not manage them carefully, one will be taken over, fused with, devoured, and so forth. Even when the perception of the patient is more benign, such labels as "dependent" and "seductive" are, at best, patronizing, and the result is that the patient is not understood and not cared about (Stiver, 1991b).

Too much is made of "borderline" anger and hostility, even though other emotions—sadness, anxiety, panic, shame, guilt, humiliation, and fear—are present for "borderline" women in great measure (Linehan, 1993). Whether much of what is considered "borderline" behavior is seen to be associated with anger seems to depend on who is doing the observing. Inferring anger and aggression from "borderline" behavior rather than desperation and fear may well be related to the sex of the clinician (Linehan, 1993). I perceive anxiety in many female clients—"borderline" or otherwise—as a secondary elaboration of suppressed anger. Many women, when they are confronting situations that are genuinely angering, experience acute anxiety either because they are not able to permit themselves to express the anger directly or because the suppression of anger has become so automatic that they actually do not experience the anger at all.

When women, as they often do, "express their conflicts and concerns . . . in relational terms," men may "need to defend against the intensity of their own feelings and yearnings for connection" (Stiver, 1991b, p. 260). Many descriptions of female patients are laced with implicit anger toward them. This same anger underlies countertransference attitudes held by many male therapists and may be experienced by those clinicians as a felt need to achieve greater distance in the therapeutic relationship in order to maintain a position of power and control. Likewise, the therapist's projections may constitute powerful grounds for labeling, as, for example, when sexual feeling for the client results in a client's being called "seductive" (Stiver, 1991b).

Female resistance to sexual advances has long been conceptualized as something that must be overcome by men. It is a resistance that is thought to conceal the passions raging just under the surface—the "dangerous sexuality" that must be neutralized (Ussher, 1992, p. 271). It is said that woman really want to be conquered in this way. When women display aggressive behavior that cannot be neutralized, they are perceived as powerful and dangerous, although they are by no means so. The model for the villainess in *Fatal Attraction*, whose rageful response to perceived abandonment had such potentially lethal consequences, bears less resemblance to a female borderline client than to a fearsome mannequin constructed from the materials of therapeutic countertransference. Whereas the movie villainess eventually moved from self-mutilation to a vicious attempt to kill, the "borderline" woman would be much more likely, under similar circumstances, to continue to harm herself.

Countertransference and BPD

"Borderline" is truly one of the most misused and abused of all psychiatric labels. It can—and has been—employed to blame the patient who makes life hard for the therapist or who does not get better (and to some therapists, these are one and the same) (Aronson, 1985). Herman (1992) calls it "little more than a sophisticated insult." Reiser and Levenson (1984) have catalogued a number of these abuses. "Borderline" may be used:

1. As an expression of countertransference hate that can serve to explain the breakdown in empathy between therapist and patient
2. As a mask for imprecise diagnostic thinking
3. To rationalize treatment mistakes or treatment failure
4. To legitimate inappropriate countertransference behavior

There are a number of rationales for coercive treatment of "borderline" patients:

> The therapist who is grandiose and seductive argues that he is introducing necessary "parameters" to treat "borderline" patients. The therapist who is rigid and unable to give offers the identical argument—invoking concepts of "limit-setting" and "rigid frames" in the treatment of borderline patients to prevent "devaluation" of the therapist and "primitive aggression." (Reiser & Levenson, 1984, p. 258)

As a result of seeing clients merely as "borderlines" and failing to perceive their individual characteristics, we run the risk of seeing few of them get better, confirming our impression that such patients are untreatable. Thus do some mental health practitioners overlook treatable conditions or treatable parts of conditions and end up with "an unwarranted sense of therapeutic cynicism and prognostic despair" (p. 255).

An example of how clinicians can utilize treatment difficulties to define the borderline disorder and how devaluing descriptions can become part of an allegedly scientific investigation is a large study conducted by Zanarini, Gunderson, Frankenburg, and Chauncey (1990). Zanarini et al. compared 120 patients with BPD and 103 patients with other personality disorders.[9] The researchers found seven features that they believe to be useful markers, taken together or separately, for BPD: quasi-psychotic experiences; deliberate physically self-destructive behaviors; manipulative suicide efforts; worries about abandonment, engulfment, and annihilation; demandingness/entitlement; treatment regressions; and the capacity to arouse inappropriately close and/or hostile responses in professional caretakers. It is noteworthy that the last two markers—"treatment regressions" and "the capacity to arouse inappropriately close and/or hostile responses in professional caretakers" are taken as indicators of the disorder even though they relate principally to treatment considerations. Do we declare treatment impasses and countertransference to be markers for other psychiatric disorders? Such considerations underscore how countertransference can affect criterion selection. Even the way other features are described reeks of countertransferential spillage. "*Manipulative* suicide efforts," for one, adds a debatable editorial component to a behavioral description.

The overlap of countertransference and criterion selection has clear implications for women diagnosed "borderline." In the Zanarini et al. study cited above, a number of symptoms—the manifold affective symptoms that accompany BPD, forms of impulsive behavior other than physically self-injurious behavior, difficulty tolerating aloneness, counterdependency, and unstable relationships, among others—were not unique to borderline patients but characteristic also of patients with other personality disorders. However, in a study of gender differences in *DSM-III-R* diagnosis of BPD (R. Stine, "Gender Difference in DSM-III-R Diagnosis of Borderline Personality Disorder," cited in Gibson, 1990), psychiatrists who were surveyed were in fundamental agreement that "unstable and intense interpersonal relationships" was the most indicative criterion for BPD diagnosis for both men and women. In this study, the criterion "inappropriate, intense anger or lack of control of anger" was found significantly indicative of the disorder for women but not for men. The question certainly arises here as to what part the opprobrium that attaches to angry women affects the frequency with which the BPD diagnosis is applied to women.

To some clinicians—particularly those who practice psychoanalytic or psychodynamic psychotherapy—theory dictates interpretations of client behavior that are inherently accusatory (Wile, 1984).[10] Wile believes, and I agree, that concepts such as developmental defects, resistance, and infantile impulses are pejorative. The confidence with which the interpretations are made belie the speculative nature of their theoretical foundation. In the psychodynamic scheme of things, angry or negative responses by the client to the therapist's interpretations are explained as predictable manifestations of resistance or negative transference. Many of these reactions, however, might be attributable not to intrapsychic factors but to the accusatory nature of the interpretations themselves.

Accusatory interpretations are by no means limited to psychoanalytic treatment, since even therapists who have not adopted the psychoanalytic model often perceive clients as dependent, narcissistic, regressed, manipulative, resistant, refusing to grow up, controlling, and the like. Wile states:

> Interpretations made from this frame of reference are inherently pejorative. A woman may already feel self-critical about her tendency at times to whine. She is likely to feel even more discouraged and hopeless if her therapist were to interpret her whining as an attempt to manipulate or control, an expression of masochism, an indication that she is very angry, a reluctance to take responsibility for her own needs and feelings, as a result of her failure to achieve separation-individuation, or a consequence of unresolved feelings toward her parents. (Wile, 1984, p. 357)

The numerous references in the clinical literature to the disorganizing effect wrought by these sorts of interpretations on some types of clients—and borderline clients are frequently cited—have brought with them recommendations for a less "uncovering" and more supportive approach with these clients. Good, analyzable "neurotics" will sit and tolerate pejorative and accusatory interpretations; some "borderlines" and psychotic patients will not. Client defensiveness and anger are easily explicable in the psychoanalytic model as: "1) the inevitable resistance with which clients respond to treatment or to disquieting revelations about themselves and 2) clients' efforts to maintain infantile gratifications and establish omnipotent control" (Wile, 1984, p. 359), not as responses to pejorative interpretations.

It is one thing to attribute a tantrum to underlying oral or anal sadistic drives and quite another to view a client's rageful outburst as a likely outgrowth of her inability to assert herself or express her anger because she does not feel entitled to do so (Wile, 1984). It may also be the case that "the overinterpretation of anger and hostile intent . . . can itself generate hostility and anger" (Linehan, 1993, p. 71). Demanding behavior may have less to do with the efforts of the client to exert "omnipotent control" over the therapist than her inability to exercise a normal degree of control within a relationship, therapeutic or otherwise.

A Case of "Sadomasochistic Transference"?

Lest we trust that the practice of making accusatory interpretations is a thing of the past, we can look to a 1991 article published in the *Journal of the American Psychoanalytic Association* and coauthored by two female psychiatrists (one the therapist in the case, and the other her supervisor) for evidence to the contrary. The article is entitled, "A Sadomasochistic Transference: Its Relation to Distortions in the Rapprochement Subphase" (Seelig & Person, 1991). Early in the case study, the authors characterize the patient and her problems thus:

> The patient had originally been diagnosed as a hysterical personality and was believed to be an almost ideal analytic patient. Only later did we discover that our patient, Miss T., had throughout her life invariably clung to a primary relationship considered by her to be the only meaningful one in her life, and characterized by a reciprocal victim-victimizer dynamic. For her, such a sadomasochistic interaction constituted the paradigm for any intimate relationship. Early on in the analysis she felt misunderstood and abused by the analyst, and accordingly felt entitled to be rageful in return . . . ; she became intensely angry, accusatory, guilty and guilt provoking. (pp. 939–940)

It is not such a stretch from "sadomasochistic interactions" to the *DSM-IV* description of the BPD criterion for unstable self-image: "These individuals may suddenly change from the role of a needy supplicant for help to a righteous avenger of past mistreatment" (1994, p. 651). As Linehan (1993) reminds us, since many women who meet the criteria for BPD have, in fact, been victims of sexual and/or physical abuse and neglect, it hardly seems appropriate to pathologize the stance they may take with regard to their injuries; nor does it seem reasonable to call "needy" those persons who have so much difficulty finding, developing, and maintaining interpersonal relationships outside of therapy, relationships that might offer them a better chance of obtaining emotional sustenance (Linehan, 1993).

In the analytic case, the client, Miss T., a twenty-two-year-old college senior who was described as insightful and very intelligent, after beginning analysis

> quickly developed an intense sadomasochistic transference regression, demonstrating borderline structural features . . . that had not been apparent in the initial evaluations—so much so that at times we questioned the validity of the initial neurotic diagnosis. It was only after some of the intense pregenital material was worked through in the transference that Miss T. presented a more classically neurotic picture. (Seelig & Person, 1991, p. 941)

By session nineteen, Miss T. was quite angry at the analyst:

> *Miss T.* I don't see what's the good of talking right now. It's not going to change anything. You're not going to say anything. Why bother: I don't understand anything from other days. Why should I now?

Analyst: You sound reproachful that you haven't learned much about yourself yet.

Miss T.: It's just making me angry—lying here like a fool. I'm wasting time just lying here. You never answer a question. It's always "What does it mean to you?" [pause]. If I leave here angry, I'll go home and have a fight with E. [boyfriend]. I guarantee it. (p. 944)

Miss T. did, indeed, return home and provoke a fight with her boyfriend. The analyst later interpreted her acting out as an attempt to express her rage toward the analyst and prove that the analyst was harming rather than helping her. In the words of Miss T.'s analyst, "This anger was not only not resolved, but continued to escalate in the early months of this analysis" (Seelig & Person, 1991, p. 945). The analyst noted that occasionally she was not able to retain her analytic stance in the face of her client's hostility, and "failures of empathy" resulted that further exacerbated Miss T.'s anger. The analyst continued to find intrapsychic explanations for her client's rage.

At no time did the analyst attribute Miss T.'s "transference regression" and her resultant rage to the method of the treatment itself. When Miss T. said, "I don't think it'll be a good analysis, but there's no choice, so we'll stay in this battle for years and years," the analyst viewed her statement as "a transference statement that appears to have been related to a failure in the rapprochement subphase of the separation-individuation process" (Seelig & Person, 1991, p. 952). It never occurred to her that Miss T. might have had some genuine reasons for being unhappy with the analyst's remoteness and pejorative interpretations, for feeling that the analyst did not really understand her, and that she may have wanted to leave therapy for those reasons but, perhaps, felt unable to do so. Far from feeling "entitled to be rageful," this client had no sense of entitlement to her feelings. If she had, she clearly would have expressed them more directly and more appropriately.

The analyst also noted that her client had "an extreme need to have every perception validated. When this need was not met, she could not allow herself even to hear what the analyst said. If the analyst did not seem to agree with her every perception, then either she or the analyst had to be 'crazy.'" Interestingly, the first interpretation that seemed to help the patient move away from her angry insistence that the analyst agree with her in every way was the "analyst's (oft-expressed) statement that she (Miss T.) felt the analyst failed to understand her in a fundamental way" (Seelig & Person, 1991, p. 947). This was the first time in the analysis that the analyst seemed to encourage the client to express her perception of how the therapy was actually progressing. However, what the analyst gave, she also took away, as she continued to interpret to Miss T. that she was secretly gratified by her feeling of being misunderstood.

If the analyst had viewed Miss T.'s rageful behavior as tied to her failure to make her feelings clear in a more moderated fashion because she did not feel entitled to them, she might have helped Miss T. to articulate her confusions in something like the following manner:

> I feel overwhelmed and confused by your interpretations. What you say sounds crazy to me. I go back and forth between believing maybe you are right and I am as screwed up as you are telling me that I am, which is upsetting to think about, and believing you are completely wrong, which is also upsetting because it means you do not understand me, perhaps no one can understand me, and my situation might be hopeless. (Wile, 1984, p. 361)

"An Underlying Normality"

The therapist who sees clients as deprived and at an impasse will necessarily approach treatment of a client differently than will one who perceives the client as resistant and overgratified by her symptoms. The "borderline" woman who feels unentitled to her emotions and responses has not, over time, developed the ability to articulate and verbalize them; she has great difficulty making her feelings known, achieving any control in relationships or situations, and getting her needs met. "Tantrum" behaviors may well result when individuals fear their own anger and attempt to avoid anger completely. Whatever secondary gain the individual derives from her symptoms is minor in comparison with the intensity of her frustration and sense of deprivation (Wile, 1984).

Self-accusatory in the extreme, then, these women already disqualify their own responses; they hardly need others to assist them in doing so. As Linehan (1993) maintains:

> Blaming the victim has certain important iatrogenic effects. First, it invalidates an individual's experience of her own problems. What the individual experiences as attempts to end pain are mislabeled as attempts to maintain the pain, to resist improving, or to do something else that the individual is not aware of. Thus, the individual learns to mistrust her own experience of herself. After some time, it is not unusual for the person to learn the point of view of the therapist, both because she does not trust her own self-observations and because doing so leads to more reinforcing outcomes. (p. 64)

The therapist must draw the client's attention to the existence of the self-critical voice and its effects. We ask psychotic individuals what their "voices" tell them, so that they and we may better understand what forces shape their behavior. We must do the same with clients whose "voice" is a self-denigrating one. These clients need to understand the origins of their sensitivities in the past in order not only to comprehend how that voice was shaped but also to understand what triggers their reactivity in the present so that they can avail themselves of other behavioral options. They must likewise understand the roots of their lack of entitlement—what they responded to in context of their past that has foreclosed the possibilities for a direct response and a sense of entitlement to it. Therapists can assist clients in perceiving their responses, not as deviant and abnormal, but as more intense and dramatic versions of common human tendencies, such as, in the case of Miss T., the tendency to hold feelings in and then suddenly burst out with them (Wile, 1984). The BPD diagnosis has been tailored to fit individuals—typically female—who enter treatment struggling with extreme difficulties of an interpersonal nature that derive, in part, from an overwhelming sense of pressure to satisfy strong, previously unmet, legitimate dependency needs in the absence of any learned, appropriate means of so doing. The medical profession has chosen to lump together a diverse population with diverse and often diffuse symptoms. How far have we come from the time when Charcot concluded that hysteria was "caused by the effect of violent emotions, protracted sorrows, family conflicts, and frustrated love, upon predisposed and hypersensitive persons" (Charcot, quoted in Ellenberger, 1970, p. 142)?

Epilogue

What do Charlotte Perkins Gilman, Alice James, Anne Sexton, and the woman sitting in my office have in common? All have experienced multiple and confusing symptoms, all have suffered acute distress, and all have at times disturbed, baffled, saddened, and angered themselves and those around them. The medical professionals of their day have attempted to categorize their afflictions. Despite their differences, these women might all qualify for a borderline diagnosis, given the amplitude and vagueness of the category. However, since the borderline personality disorder, as it is currently conceptualized, is not a unitary diagnostic entity, the rendering of the diagnosis would offer the clinician little help in treatment planning.

What would contribute substantially toward improved treatment of women called "borderline" would be the increasing ability of clinicians to understand the relationship between "borderline" symptoms and female socialization and to accept the "underlying normality" (Wile, 1984, p. 361) of the affliction. So-called borderline women are more like us than they are different, and attempts by the psychiatric establishment to the contrary, we must attend to context, both interpersonal and historical.

The *DSM-IV*'s "Borderline Personality Disorder" is a categorical diagnosis; the borderline syndrome, however, should be conceptualized as a dimensional variable, with individuals varying to the extent to which they manifest borderline symptomatology (Trull, Widiger, & Guthrie, 1990).[11] In a dimensional approach to diagnosis, the clinician uses a scale to rate the client on several enduring aspects of personality. Cloninger (1987) has isolated three such dimensions that he believes to be universal: novelty-seeking (impulsivity), harm avoidance (fearfulness, anxiety), and reward dependence (warmth, need for emotional support). For example, if Miss T., of our earlier acquaintance, were rated +3 (severely high, the highest rating possible) on the dimension of novelty-seeking, it would be said that she "consistently seeks thrilling adventures and exploration; [is] disorderly and unpredictable; [is] intolerant of structure and monotony regardless of consequences; [makes] decisions and opinions based on vague global impressions and intuitions; consistently plays roles for dramatic effect so that real feelings and beliefs are uncertain" (p. 576). Miss T. would also be rated on the remaining two dimensions. Her therapist would not be forced to determine whether she did or did not have a specific disease.

The dimensional approach to diagnosing personality disorders holds out the possibility of tailoring personality evaluation to the individual without recourse to the use of labels. Dimensional ratings offer a large quantity of useful information (Trull, Widiger, & Guthrie, 1990), appear to be more reliable than categorical ones for the personality disorders (Heumann & Morey, 1990), and eliminate the dilemma of overlap among the personality disorders. Instead of substituting a new label for "Borderline Personality Disorder," as was attempted with the proposed substitution of "Self-Defeating Personality Disorder" (*DSM-III-R*, 1987) for "Masochistic Personality Disorder" (*DSM-III*, 1980), the clinician could substitute an accurate description of an individual's personality. However, since new incarnations of the categorical system of classification seem destined to spring forth like dragon's teeth from the soil of psychiatric speculation, we may need to find other ways to combat the prejudices inherent in the borderline diagnosis. The means at hand involve humanizing rather than medicalizing disorder, and this we can do regardless of whether our current system of classification endures. Women can only benefit from the attempt to represent their experience with both accuracy and compassion.

Notes

Prologue

1. These are generally the *DSM-III* or *DSM-III-R* criteria, or they may be criteria derived from the diagnostic interview for borderline patients. See Gunderson, Kolb, & Austin (1981).

2. See Abend, Porder, & Willick (1983); Waldinger & Gunderson (1987), in which one out of every five case study examples was male and no mention was made of gender issues; and Kroll (1988), in which seventeen women were used as case examples, as against five men.

3. Quoted in Ussher (1992, p. 13).

4. See Nolen-Hoeksema (1990) for a comprehensive discussion of these differences.

5. In a random sample of 2,500 patients in the Michigan public mental health system, Mowbray, Herman, & Hazel (1992) did a cluster analysis and found women overrepresented in the Suicidal/Aggressive and the Demoralized/Depressed clusters, whereas men were overrepresented in the clusters of Mentally Ill Substance Abuser and Psychotic.

6. Another proposed category, "Late Luteal Phase Dysphoric Disorder," which is not a personality disorder, can only occur in the female population. It would seem, by the *DSM-III-R*'s definition, to be premenstrual syndrome writ large as mental illness.

7. Separation and divorce rates were also lower in the BPD group than in the larger community.

Chapter One

1. I refer throughout this section to chapter 3 of Ussher (1992) as well as to John Demos's book-length study of witchcraft in New England (Demos, 1982). See these works also for a more complete discussion of witchcraft and its modern interpretations.

2. The following discussion of the "domestication of insanity," as she calls it, is derived from Showalter (1985).

3. Psychiatric "alienists" were those who worked in insane asylums. They viewed mental illness as basically untreatable. See Strouse (1980, p. 110).

4. In this discussion of the life of Charlotte Perkins Gilman, I am heavily indebted to Ann J. Lane's excellent psychologically oriented biography (1990).

5. See Strouse (1980, pp. 23–28) for further discussion of Mary James.

6. For the biographical material in this section, I relied upon Strouse's excellent biography of Alice James (Strouse, 1980); extracts from Alice's letters in James (1981); her published diary (James, 1964); and Westkott's discussion of the sexualization of Alice—particularly by her brother William (Westkott, 1986, pp. 101–104).

7. See Westkott (1986, pp. 101–107) for a discussion of Alice's and William's relationship and Horney's ideas about compulsive masculinity.

8. Although *DSM-IV* has added transient psychotic symptoms as one of the criteria for the disorder (*DSM III-R* had no such criterion), an individual can qualify for the diagnosis in the absence of such symptoms.

9. Cf. the similar thesis in Wood (1973).

10. See Cauwels (1992, p. 285), for a brief review of the literature on treatment termination among borderline patients.

11. This discussion owes its substance to the exhaustive history of psychoanalysis in the United States by Hale (1971, 1995).

12. The debate was entitled, "Resolved: The Etiology of Borderline Personality Disorder Is Predominantly Biological," 143rd annual meeting of the American Psychiatric Association, New York, 16 May 1990.

Chapter Two

1. For the following discussion of stress and differences between male and female deviance, see Cloward & Piven (1979).

2. This discussion of the history of the *DSM* and its relationship to psychiatry is based on a more extended description in Wylie (1995).

3. A relatively recent replication of McKee and Sheriffs's 1957 exploration of sex-role conceptions has shown the remarkable stability of those conceptions over a nearly thirty-year period. See Werner & La Russa, 1985.

4. Kaplan (1983) refers to the personality disorders as they were presented in the *DSM-III* (1980).

5. Kaplan sees both the histrionic and dependent personality disorders as stereotypes rather than caricatures.

6. Landrine drew these conclusions from a study she performed in which respondents read descriptions of a number of personality disorders and were asked to indicate the social class, gender, and marital status of the group that most often received the label.

7. See Franks (1986) for a discussion.

8. See references to Seiden's argument in Fernbach, Winstead, & Derlega (1989).

9. This summary of the most significant forms of sex bias was composed by Robert F. Bornstein from discussions of Widiger & Spitzer (1991) and others and presented in Bornstein (1996).

10. See p. 1528 of Henry & Cohen (1983). The characteristics that were more frequently reported by men included: impulsive gambling, excessive use of drugs and alcohol, one-night stands, intense and unstable relationships, superficial relationships, numerous manifestations of identity disturbance, marked shifts from normal mood to irritability, depressed feelings when alone, involvement in physical fights, and frequent feelings of emptiness.

11. The DIS/Borderline Index used in the ECA study included the following symptoms: anxiety attacks, anxious a month or more, tense or jumpy, irritable or edgy, three or more depressive symptoms, sleeping too much, worthlessness, thoughts of death, wanted to die, thoughts of suicide, suicide attempt, hopelessness, spending sprees, increased libido, distractibility, hit partner in a fight, lied a lot as an adult, used a weapon in a fight, fear of being alone, amnestic periods, unusual spells, had to give up work owing to somatic symptoms. The list composed by Henry and Cohen included: impulsive spending, impulsive shoplifting, impulsive gambling, excessive use of drugs or alcohol, "one-night stands," intense and unstable relationships, superficial relationships, feelings of anger, loss of temper, symptoms of identity disturbance, marked shifts from normal mood to anxiousness, marked shifts from normal mood to depression, marked shifts from normal mood to irritability, intolerance of being alone, physically self-damaging acts (includes suicidal gestures and involvement in physical fights), feelings of emptiness and boredom.

12. The final adjusted response rate was over 45 percent of that number.

13. In actuality, three "male" and three "female" versions of the case study were sent, each identical in their symptomatic features but different along other dimensions—age, living situation, and so on. That was done to ensure that no single element would unduly influence subjects in their assessment of the case. Upon analysis, no significant differences were found among the three versions in each group, and the versions were collapsed into one "male" and one "female" version.

14. Dysthymia, intermittent explosive disorder, posttraumatic stress disorder, schizophrenia (paranoid type), generalized anxiety disorder, delusional disorder (jealous type), and adjustment disorder with mixed emotional features.

15. Narcissistic, schizoid, dependent, histrionic, antisocial, borderline, and self-defeating personality disorders.

Chapter Three

1. See introduction and chap. 1 in Fine (1989) and chaps. 3 and 4 in Cauwels (1992) for a more extended discussion of the history of the borderline concept and diagnosis.

2. See Fine (1989, p. 8) for a list of these elements.

3. Kernberg distinguishes splitting as a defensive operation from repression.

4. There is (considerable) evidence, however, that the so-called borderline defenses are not unique to borderline patients. See Bond (1990).

5. For the following developmental arguments, refer to Stern (1985, chap. 10).

6. See Cauwels (1992, pp. 200–201) for an extended discussion by Gunderson of his formulation of splitting.

7. See the Prologue for complete list of criteria.

8. In a chart review of 180 inpatient cases, Fryer, Frances, Sullivan, Hurt, & Clarkin (1988a) found that most of the BPD patients met the criteria for at least one other psychiatric diagnosis.

9. Others have likewise pointed out the substantial overlap between the BPD, other personality disorder diagnoses, and the histrionic personality disorder diagnosis. See Nurnberg, Hurt, Feldman, & Suh (1988); Kernberg (1984); and Oldham et al. (1992).

10. Clarkin, Widiger, Frances, Hurt, & Gilmore (1983), in comparing two groups of Axis II patients (a group with BPD and those with various other personality disorders), found unstable or intense relationships and chronic boredom/emptiness to be sensitive and specific indicators for BPD. They did not find intolerance of being alone to be a specific marker. Gruenrich (1992) found unstable interpersonal relationships and self-injurious acts to be the symptoms most specific to BPD. McGlashan's (1987) comparison of two groups of inpatients diagnosed as having either BPD or schizotypal personality disorder found discriminating symptoms for BPD to be unstable relationships, impulsivity, and self-damaging acts. The least differentiating of the criteria were inappropriate anger and intolerance of aloneness. Zanarini, Gunderson, Frankenburg, & Chauncey (1990) compared 50 BPD outpatients, 55 patients with other personality disorders, 46 "normal" control subjects, and 32 schizophrenic patients, and found quasi-psychotic thought to be "a highly discriminating clinical feature" (p. 61) of BPD. BPD patients were the only personality disorder patients for whom this was significantly true. Nurnberg et al. (1988) compared a small group of BPD patients to normal controls and found several combinations of five criteria to be sensitive, specific, and have predictive power. However, the small sample size and the fact that the only comparison group consisted of "normals" may have accounted for the broad findings.

11. Researchers used the DIS/Borderline Index to make the BPD diagnosis. Symptoms used in the index are listed in Swartz et al. (1990, p. 270).

Chapter Four

1. See Gunderson & Singer (1975) for a list of symptoms commonly thought to be characteristic of borderline patients.

2. Paul H. Soloff, who was interviewed by Cauwels (1992, p. 223), makes particular mention of the study by Fryer and her colleagues.

3. About three out of ten girls who had been physically abused and four out of ten girls who had been sexually abused had never told anyone of the abuse.

4. Suicide risk was based on assessment of suicidal ideation.

5. Margo & McClees's 1991 study of thirty-eight female inpatients showed that those who reported histories of physical or sexual abuse (76 percent of the sample did report some abuse prior to age sixteen) rated higher on measures of psychopathology and symptomatology.

6. In Brown & Anderson's (1991) large study, the group of patients who had suffered childhood physical and/or sexual abuse was diagnosed as having personality disorders significantly more often than other groups, and the proportion of diagnosed BPD increased significantly as severity of reported abuse increased. Briere & Zaidi (1989) found similar results in a study of women who sought psychiatric emergency room treatment. Those women who had a sexual abuse history were significantly more likely than the nonabused control group to have been given a diagnosis of personality disorder or traits and five times as likely to have been diagnosed as having *borderline* personality disorder. BPD was the only diagnosis that reliably differentiated the two groups. The researchers noted that given the relatively small size of their sample and the corresponding reduction in statistical power to detect significant differences, these findings were all the more robust.

7. In this study, BPD patients were compared with two other groups: those who were diagnosed as having antisocial personality disorder and those who carried a diagnosis of dysthymia combined with one other personality disorder.

8. Briere & Runtz's 1987 study of 277 female undergraduates found relationships between psychological abuse and low self-esteem; sexual abuse and dysfunctional sexual behavior; and physical abuse and problems with anger and aggression.

9. Literature review performed by Hart, Germain, & Brassard (1987).

10. Scurfield (1985) critiqued early studies for failing to look at both clinical and nonclinical populations and for employing unsophisticated instruments—methodological problems that call the reliability and validity of the *DSM-III* (1980) criteria for PTSD into question.

11. The discussion that follows is a recapitulation of the central arguments in Green et al. (1985).

12. This paragraph and much of the section to follow makes frequent reference to Stern (1985).

13. This notion of representation as interaction contrasts sharply with the concept of separate representations of self and other that forms the basis of Kernberg's idea of splitting.

14. It is important to remember that, in Stern's view, this new sense of an intersubjective self exists alongside the core sense of self and that the two domains continue to affect each other throughout the life span.

15. See Adler & Buie (1979), who makes prominent reference to Selma Fraiberg's concept of evocative memory—an elaboration of Piaget's concept of object permanence. Perry et al. (1990) make extensive reference to Adler and Buie's work in their article.

Chapter Five

1. Jean Piaget, the eminent Swiss psychologist, identifies the period of "formal operations" as a shift in cognitive development that occurs when the adolescent becomes capable of higher-level abstract thinking.

2. This hypothesis, quite popular in the 1970s, was that women who had a masculine/feminine mix in their sex role identity were better adjusted than women who were strictly "feminine."

3. For example, in their speech, women employ more linguistic categories connoting uncertainty than do men. Cf. McMillan, Clifton, McGrath, & Gale (1977).

4. The codependency literature offers particularly egregious examples of the latter.

5. Nowhere in the article, however, does Benedict say that she is talking only about boys and men; one is led to believe that she means her conclusions to apply to children and adults of both sexes.

6. For a more complete description of cultural expectations for middle-class women from the turn of the century through the 1920s, see Westkott (1986, chap. 1, pp. 20–52).

7. For further elaboration of the ideas in this section, see Westkott (1986, chap. 3, pp. 66–87).

Chapter Six

1. Researchers using Gunderson's Diagnostic Interview of Borderlines (cf. Gunderson, Kolb, & Austin, 1981) interviewed more than 100 female adolescents.

2. This discussion of the core dependent personality is, in large part, based on Westkott (1986, chap. 6).

3. See Wile's (1993) excellent discussions of self-blame and of accusation of the other in his most recent book on marriage.

4. Let me make it clear here that I am not doubting the part that temperamental (biological) vulnerability plays in predisposing many individuals to develop "borderline symptoms"; I am suggesting that this is not the only pathway to the development of such symptoms.

5. Kroll (1993, p. 21) cites six studies that support this finding.

6. The diathesis/stress model often used to conceptualize the development of schizophrenia has utility in discussions about the development of borderline psychopathology if we consider the "diathesis" a contextually based vulnerability rather than a genetic one.

Chapter Seven

1. At different times, her impulsivity took the form of suicide attempts, promiscuity, and drug and alcohol abuse. See Middlebrook (1992) for an insightful analysis of Sexton's life and work.

2. Paris (1990), having reviewed several studies, concluded that Stone's figure of 9.5 percent most accurately reflects the suicide rate among the entire population of those diagnosed with BPD.

3. Although van der Kolk et al. (1991) believe that these communications are related to trauma, I believe that just as all BPD patients have not been physically or sexually abused, not all suicidal communications are specifically related to trauma.

4. My personal recommendations for clinical books on treatment of BPD include Linehan's previously cited (1993) book and workbook, Kroll's (1988) book on PTSD/borderlines, Herman's (1992) book on trauma and recovery, and Briere's (1992) book on treatment of sexual abuse.

5. Patients were defined borderline either because they met *DSM-III* criteria for BPD or because they satisfied Kernberg's criteria for borderline personality organization.

6. The researchers explained that the other two (smaller) groups dropped out because (1) the therapist failed to engage families in treatment (this was true for adolescents particularly), and (2) the clients were antisocial and were unmotivated from the outset.

7. Lindberg & Distad (1985) found that the average period between the last incest experience and treatment was seventeen years.

8. For a discussion of Jane Eyre's journey as a metaphor for the journey from the imprisonment of childhood toward mature autonomy, see Gilbert & Gubar (1979).

9. Over half of these patients were diagnosed with antisocial personality disorder.

10. The following discussion of the nature of psychodynamic interpretation and its effects is based on Wile's (1984) provocative article, "Kohut, Kernberg, and Accusatory Interpretations."

11. Trull and his colleagues used a sophisticated statistical technique (MAXCOV) to analyze charts of 409 psychiatric inpatients in order to determine whether the borderline construct is categorical or dimensional. See Trull, Widiger, & Guthrie (1990, pp. 42–43), for a description of their technique.

References

Abend, S. M., Porder, M. S., & Willick, M. S. (1983). *Borderline patients: Psychoanalytic perspectives.* New York: International Universities Press.

Abramowitz, S. I., Abramowitz, C. V., Roback, H. B., Corney, R., & McKee, E. (1976). Sex-role countertransference in psychotherapy. *Archives of General Psychiatry, 33,* 71–73.

Adams, C. H., & Sherer, M. (1985). Sex-role orientation and psychological adjustment: Implications for the masculinity model. *Sex Roles, 12* (11/12), 1211–1218.

Adinolfi, A. A. (1971). Relevance of person perception research to clinical psychology. *Journal of Consulting and Clinical Psychology, 37,* 167–176.

Adler, D. A., Drake, R. E., & Teague, G. B. (1990). Clinicians' practices in personality assessment: Does gender influence the use of DSM-III Axis II? *Comprehensive Psychiatry, 31* (2), 125–133.

Adler, G., & Buie, D. H. (1979). Aloneness and borderline psychopathology: The possible relevance of child development issues. *International Journal of Psychoanalysis, 60,* 83–93.

Akhtar, S., Byrne, J. P., & Doghramji, K. (1986). The demographic profile of borderline personality disorder. *Journal of Clinical Psychiatry, 47* (4), 196–198.

Akiskal, H. S., Chen, S. E., Davis, G. C., Puzantian, V. R., Kashgarian, M., & Bolinger, J. M. (1985). Borderline: An adjective in search of a noun. *Journal of Clinical Psychiatry, 46* (2), 41–48.

Al-Issa, I. (1980). *The psychopathology of women.* Englewood Cliffs, NJ: Prentice Hall.

Allport, G. W. (1954). *The nature of prejudice.* Reading, MA: Addison Wesley.

American Psychiatric Association. (1980). *Diagnostic and statistical manual of mental disorders.* Washington, DC: Author.

American Psychiatric Association. (1987). *Diagnostic and statistical manual of mental disorders.* (3rd ed., rev.). Washington, DC: Author.

American Psychiatric Association. (1994). *Diagnostic and statistical manual of mental disorders.* (4th ed.). Washington, DC: Author.

Antill, J. K., & Cunningham, J. D. (1979). Self-esteem as a function of masculinity in both sexes. *Journal of Consulting and Clinical Psychology, 47* (4), 783–785.

Armsworth, M. W. (1984). Post traumatic stress responses in women who experienced incest as children and adolescents. *Dissertation Abstracts International, 46* (5-B), 1674.

Armsworth, M. W. (1989). Therapy of incest survivors: Abuse or support? *Child Abuse and Neglect, 13* (4), 549–562.

Aronson, T. A. (1985). Historical perspectives on the borderline concept: A review and critique. *Psychiatry, 48,* 209–222.

Ashmore, R. D., & Del Boca, F. K. (1979). Sex stereotypes and implicit personality theory: Toward a cognitive-social psychological conceptualization. *Sex Roles, 5,* 219–248.

Bakan, D. (1966). *The duality of human existence: An essay on psychology and religion.* Chicago: Rand McNally.

Barnard, C. P., & Hirsch, C. (1985). Borderline personality and victims of incest. *Psychological Reports, 57,* 715–718.

Becker, D., & Lamb, S. (1994). Sex bias in the diagnosis of borderline personality disorder and posttraumatic stress disorder. *Professional Psychology: Research and Practice, 25* (1), 55–61.

Belenky, M. F., Clinchy, B. M., Goldberger, N. R., & Tarule, J. M. (1986). *Women's ways of knowing: The development of self, voice, and mind.* New York: Basic Books.

Belle, D. (1980). Who uses mental health facilities? In M. Guttentag, S. Salasin, & D. Belle (Eds.), *The mental health of women* (pp. 21–30). New York: Academic Press.

Bem, S. L. (1974). The measurement of psychological androgyny. *Journal of Consulting and Clinical Psychology, 42,* 155–162.

Benedict, R. (1938/1955). Continuities and discontinuities in cultural conditioning—1938. In M. Mead & M. Wolfenstein (Eds.), *Childhood in contemporary cultures* (pp. 21–30). Chicago: University of Chicago Press. (Originally published as article, 1938.)

Berger, J. (1972). *Ways of seeing.* Harmondsworth: Penguin.

Bernardez, T. (1991). Adolescent resistance and the maladies of women: Notes from the underground. In C. Gilligan, A. G. Rogers, & D. L. Tolman (Eds.), *Women, girls, and psychotherapy: Reframing resistance* (pp. 213–222). New York: Harrington Park Press.

Blazer, D. G., Hughes, D., George, L. K., Swartz, M., & Boyer, R. (1991). Generalized anxiety disorder. In L. N. Robins & D. A. Regier (Eds.), *Psychiatric disorders in America: The epidemiologic catchment area study* (pp. 180–203). New York: Free Press.

Block, J. H. (1976). Conceptions of sex role: Some cross-cultural and longitudinal perspectives. In A. G. Kaplan & J. P. Bean (Eds.), *Beyond sex-role stereotypes: Readings toward a psychology of androgyny* (pp. 64–78). Boston: Little, Brown. (Reprinted from *American Psychologist,* 1973, *28* [6], 512–526.)

Block, J. H. (1983). Differential premises arising from differential socialization of the sexes: Some conjectures. *Child Development, 54,* 1335–1354.

Block, M. J., Westen, D., Ludolph, P., Wixom, J., & Jackson, A. (1991). Distinguishing female borderline adolescents from normal and other disturbed female adolescents. *Psychiatry, 54,* 89–103.

Bond, M. (1990). Are "borderline defenses" specific for borderline personality disorders? *Journal of Personality Disorders, 4* (3), 251–256.

Bornstein, R. F. (1996). Sex differences in dependent personality disorder prevalence rates. *Clinical Psychology: Science and Practice, 3,* 1–12.

Brehony, K. A. (1983). Women and agoraphobia: A case for the etiological significance of the feminine sex-role stereotype. In V. Franks & E. D. Rothblum (Eds.), *The stereotyping of women* (pp. 112–128). New York: Springer.

Breslau, N., Davis, G. C., Andreski, P., & Petersen, E. (1991). Traumatic events and posttraumatic stress disorder in an urban population of young adults. *Archives of General Psychiatry, 48,* 216–222.

Briere, J., Evans, D., Runtz, M., & Wall, T. (1988). Symptomatology in men who were molested as children: A comparison study. *American Journal of Orthopsychiatry, 58* (3), 457–461.

Briere, J., & Runtz, M. (1987). Post sexual abuse trauma, data and implications for clinical practice. *Journal of Interpersonal Violence, 2,* 367–379.

Briere, J., & Zaidi, L. Y. (1989). Sexual abuse histories and sequelae in female psychiatric emergency room patients. *American Journal of Psychiatry, 146,* 1602-1606.

Briere, J. N. (1992). *Child abuse trauma: Theory and treatment of the lasting effects.* Newbury Park, CA: Sage.

Brodsky, A. M., & Hare-Mustin, R. T. (1980). *Women and psychotherapy: An assessment of research and practice.* New York: Guilford.

Broverman, I. K., Broverman, D. M., Clarkson, F. E., Rosenkrantz, P. S., & Vogel, S. R. (1970). Sex role stereotypes and clinical judgments of mental health. *Journal of Consulting and Clinical Psychology, 34* (1), 1–7.

Broverman, I. K., Broverman, D. M., Clarkson, F. E., Rosenkrantz, P. S., & Vogel, S. R. (1972). Sex role stereotypes: A critical appraisal. *Journal of Social Issues, 28* (2), 59–78.

Brown, G. R., & Anderson, B. (1991). Psychiatric morbidity in adult inpatients with childhood histories of sexual and physical abuse. *American Journal of Psychiatry, 148* (1), 55–61.

Browne, A., & Finkelhor, D. (1986). Impact of child sexual abuse: A review of the literature. *Psychological Bulletin, 99,* 66–77.

Brumberg, J. J. (1992). From psychiatric syndrome to "communicable" disease: The case of Anorexia nervosa. In C. E. Rosenberg & J. Golden (Eds.), *Framing disease: Studies in cultural history* (pp. 134–154). New Brunswick, NJ: Rutgers University Press.

Bryer, J. B., Nelson, B. A., Miller, J. B., & Krol, P. A. (1987). Childhood sexual and physical abuse as factors in adult psychiatric illness. *American Journal of Psychiatry, 144*, 1426–1430.

Calef, V., & Wenshel, E. M. (1989). The new psychoanalysis and psychoanalytic revisionism: Book review essay on *Borderline conditions and pathological narcissism*. In R. Fine (Ed.), *Current and historical perspectives on the borderline patient* (pp. 222–241). New York: Brunner/Mazel. (Reprinted from *Psychoanalytic Quarterly*, 1979, *48*, 470–491.)

Caplan, N., & Nelson, S. D. (1973). On being useful: The nature and consequences of psychological research on social problems. *American Psychologist, 28* (3), 199–211.

Caplan, P. J. (1985). *The myth of women's masochism*. New York: Dutton.

Caplan, P. J. (1988). The name game: Psychiatry, misogyny, and taxonomy. In M. Braude (Ed.), *Women, power, and therapy* (pp. 187–202). New York: Harrington Park Press.

Carmen, E. H., Rieker, P. R., & Mills, T. (1984). Victims of violence and psychiatric illness. *American Journal of Psychiatry, 141* (3), 378–383.

Carmen, E. H., Russo, N. F., & Miller, J. B. (1981). Inequality and women's mental health: An overview. *American Journal of Psychiatry, 138* (10), 1319–1330.

Castaneda, R., & Franco, H. (1985). Sex and ethnic distribution of borderline personality disorder in an inpatient sample. *American Journal of Psychiatry, 142* (2), 1202–1203.

Cauwels, J. M. (1992). *Imbroglio: Rising to the challenges of borderline personality disorder*. New York: Norton.

Chesler, P. (1972). *Women and madness*. New York: Avon Books.

Chess, S., & Thomas, A. *Temperament in clinical practice*. New York: Guilford.

Chodoff, P. (1982). Hysteria and women. *American Journal of Psychiatry, 139* (5), 545–551.

Chodorow, N. (1978). *The reproduction of mothering*. Berkeley: University of California Press.

Chodorow, N., & Contratto, S. (1992). The fantasy of the perfect mother. In B. Thorne & M. Yalom (Eds.), *Rethinking the family: Some feminist questions* (pp. 191–214). Boston: Northeastern University Press.

Chu, J. A., & Dill, D. L. (1990). Dissociative symptoms in relation to childhood physical and sexual abuse. *American Journal of Psychiatry, 147* (7), 887–892.

Clarkin, J. F., Widiger, T. A., Frances, A., Hurt, S. W., & Gilmore, M. (1983). Prototypic typology and the borderline personality disorder. *Journal of Abnormal Psychology, 92* (3), 263–275.

Cloninger, C. R. (1987). A systematic method for clinical description and classification of personality variants. *Archives of General Psychiatry, 44*, 573–588.

Cloward, R. A., & Piven, F. F. (1979). Hidden protest: The channeling of female innovation and protest. *Signs: Journal of Women in Culture and Society, 4* (4), 651–669.

Coie, J. D., Pennington, B. F., & Buckley, H. H. (1974). Effects of situational stress and sex roles on the attribution of psychological disorder. *Journal of Consulting and Clinical Psychology, 42* (4), 559–568.

Condry, J. C., & Condry, S. (1976). Sex differences: A study of the eye of the beholder. *Child Development, 47,* 812–819.

Conrad, P., & Schneider, J. W. (1992). *Deviance and medicalization: From badness to sickness.* Philadelphia: Temple University Press.

Constantinople, A. (1973). Masculinity-femininity: An exception to a famous dictum? *Psychological Bulletin, 80* (5), 389–407.

Cooley, C. H. (1902). *Human nature and the social order.* New York: Charles Scribner.

Coons, P. M., Bowman, E., Pellow, T. A., & Schneider, P. (1989). Post-traumatic aspects of the treatment of victims of sexual abuse and incest. *Psychiatric Clinics of North America, 12* (2), 325–335.

Costrich, N., Feinstein, J., Kidder, L., Marecek, J., & Pascale, L. (1975). When stereotypes hurt: Three studies of penalties for sex-role reversals. *Journal of Experimental Social Psychology, 11,* 520–530.

Cotroneo, M. (1986). Families and abuse: A contextual approach. In M. A. Karpel (Ed.), *Family Resources* (pp. 413–437). New York: Guilford Press.

Courtois, C. A. (1988). *Healing the incest wound: Adult survivors in therapy.* New York: Norton.

Coward, R. (1984). *Female desire: Women's sexuality today.* London: Paladin.

Craine, L. S., Henson, C. E., Colliver, J. A., & MacLean, D. G. (1988). Prevalence of a history of sexual abuse among female psychiatric patients in a state hospital system. *Hospital and Community Psychiatry, 39* (3), 300–304.

Deaux, K. (1984). From individual differences to social categories: Analysis of a decade's research on gender. *American Psychologist, 39,* 105–116.

Deaux, K., & Major, B. (1987). Putting gender into context: An interactive model of gender-related behavior. *Psychological Review, 94,* 369–389.

Demos, J. P. (1982). *Entertaining Satan: Witchcraft and the culture of early New England.* New York: Oxford University Press.

Doane, M. A. (1986). The clinical eye: Medical discourses in the "Women's film" of the 1940s. In S. R. Suleiman (Ed.), *The female body in Western culture: Contemporary perspectives* (pp. 152–174). Cambridge, MA: Harvard University Press.

Dohrenwend, B. P., & Dohrenwend, B. S. (1976). Sex differences and psychiatric disorders. *American Journal of Sociology, 81* (6), 1447–1454.

Dohrenwend, B. S. (1973). Social status and stressful life events. *Journal of Personality and Social Psychology, 28* (2), 225–235.

Donaldson, M. A., & Gardner, R. (1985). Diagnosis and treatment of traumatic stress among women after childhood incest. In C. R. Figley (Ed.), *Trauma and its wake: The study and treatment of post-traumatic stress disorder* (pp. 356–377). New York: Brunner/Mazel.

DSM-III. (1980). See American Psychiatric Association. (1980).

DSM-III-R. (1987). See American Psychiatric Association. (1987).

DSM-IV. (1994). See American Psychiatric Association. (1994).

Earl, W. L. (1991). Perceived trauma: Its etiology and treatment. *Adolescence, 26* (101), 97–104.

Easser, B. R., & Lesser, S. R. (1965). Hysterical personality: A reevaluation. *Psycho-analytic Quarterly, 34,* 390–405.

Eaton, W. W., Dryman, A., & Weissman, M. M. (1991). Panic and phobia. In L. N. Robins & D. A. Regier (Eds.), *Psychiatric disorders in America: The epidemio-logic catchment area study* (pp. 155–179). New York: Free Press.

Ebata, A. T., Petersen, A. C., & Conger, J. J. (1990). The development of psy-chopathology in adolescence. In J. E. Rolf, A. S. Masten, D. Cicchetti, K. H. Nuechterlein, & S. Weintraub (Eds.), *Risk and protective factors in the develop-ment of psychopathology* (pp. 308–333). New York: Cambridge University Press.

Edwards, P. W., & Donaldson, M. A. (1989). Assessment of symptoms in adult sur-vivors of incest: A factor analytic study of the responses to childhood incest ques-tionnaire. *Child Abuse and Neglect, 13* (1), 101–110.

Eherenreich, B., & English, D. (1978). *For her own good: 150 years of the experts' ad-vice to women.* Garden City, NY: Anchor Press/Doubleday.

Ellenberger, H. F. (1970). *The discovery of the unconscious.* New York: Basic Books.

Eme, R. F. (1980). Sex differences in childhood psychopathology: A review. *Annual Progress in Child Psychiatry and Child Development,* 436–469. (Reprinted from *Psychological Bulletin,* 1979, *86* [3], 574–595.)

Emslie, G. J., & Rosenfeld, A. (1983). Incest reported by children and adolescents hospitalized for severe psychiatric problems. *American Journal of Psychiatry, 140* (6), 708–711.

Erikson, E. H. (1950). *Childhood and Society.* New York: Norton.

Eth, S., & Pynoos, R. S. (1985). Developmental perspective on psychic trauma in childhood. In C. R. Figley (Ed.), *Trauma and its wake: The study and treatment of post-traumatic stress disorder* (pp. 36–52). New York: Brunner/Mazel.

Fagot, B. (1978). The influence of sex of child on parental reactions to toddler chil-dren. *Child Development, 49,* 459–465.

Fagot, B. I., & Hagan, R. (1985). Aggression in toddlers: Responses to the assertive acts of boys and girls. *Sex Roles, 12* (3/4), 341–351.

Famularo, R., Kinscherff, R., & Fenton, T. (1991). Posttraumatic stress disorder among children clinically diagnosed as borderline personality disorder. *Journal of Nervous and Mental Disease, 179* (7), 428–431.

Favazza, A. R. (1987). *Bodies under siege.* Baltimore: Johns Hopkins University Press.

Fernbach, B. E., Winstead, B. A., & Derlega, V. J. (1989). Sex differences in diag-nosis and treatment recommendations for antisocial personality disorder and somatization disorders. *Journal of Social and Clinical Psychology, 8* (3), 238–255.

Fidell, L. S. (1981). Sex differences in psychotropic drug use. *Professional Psychol-ogy, 12* (1), 156–162.

Fine, R. (1989). *Current and historical perspectives on the borderline patient.* New York: Brunner/Mazel.

Finkelhor, D. (1978). Psychological, cultural and family factors in incest and family sexual abuse. *Journal of Marriage and Family Counseling, 4* (4), 41–49.

Finkelhor, D. (1979). *Sexually victimized children.* New York: Free Press.

Finkelhor, D. (1984). *Child sexual abuse: New theory and research.* New York: Free Press.

Finkelhor, D., & Browne, A. (1985). The traumatic impact of child sexual abuse: A conceptualization. *American Journal of Orthopsychiatry, 55* (4), 530–541.

Finkelhor, D., Hotaling, G., Lewis, I. A., & Smith, C. (1990). Sexual abuse in a national survey of adult men and women: Prevalence, characteristics, and risk factors. *Child Abuse and Neglect, 14* (1), 19–28.

Fisher, W. A., & Barak, A. (1989). Bias and fairness in the diagnosis of Primary Orgasmic Dysfunction in women. *American Psychologist, 44* (7), 1080–1081.

Ford, M., & Widiger, T. A. (1989). Sex bias in the diagnosis of histrionic and antisocial personality disorders. *Journal of Consulting and Clinical Psychology, 57* (2), 301–305.

Foucault, M. (1965). *Madness and civilization.* New York: Pantheon.

Frances, A., & Widiger, T. A. (1987). A critical review of four DSM-III personality disorders: Borderline, avoidant, dependent and passive-aggressive. In G. L. Tischler (Ed.), *Diagnosis and classification in psychiatry: A critical appraisal of DSM-III* (pp. 269–289). New York: Cambridge University Press.

Frank, J. D., & Frank, J. B. (1991). *Persuasion and healing: A comparative study of psychotherapy.* Baltimore: Johns Hopkins University Press.

Franks, V. (1986). Sex stereotyping and the diagnosis of psychopathology. *Women and Therapy, 5* (2/3), 219–232.

Franks, V., & Rothblum, E. D. (Eds.). (1983). *The stereotyping of women: Its effects on mental health.* New York: Springer.

Frenken, J., & Van Stolk, B. (1990). Incest victims: Inadequate help by professionals. *Child Abuse and Neglect, 14* (2), 253–263.

Freud, S. (1939). Moses and monotheism. In J. Strachey (Ed.), Standard Edition, vol. 23. London: Hogarth Press, 1964.

Fryer, M. R., Frances, A. J., Sullivan, T., Hurt, S. W., & Clarkin, J. (1988a). Comorbidity of borderline personality disorder. *Archives of General Psychiatry, 45,* 348–355.

Fryer, M. R., Frances, A. J., Sullivan, T., Hurt, S. W., & Clarkin, J. (1988b). Suicide attempts in patients with borderline personality disorder. *American Journal of Psychiatry, 145* (6), 737–739.

Fuller, A. K., & Blashfield, R. K. (1989). Masochistic personality disorder. A prototype analysis of diagnosis and sex bias. *Journal of Nervous and Mental Disease, 177* (3), 168–172.

Gabarino, J., & Vondra, J. (1987). Psychological maltreatment: Issues and perspectives. In M. R. Brassard, R. Germain, & S. N. Hart (Eds.), *Psychological maltreatment of children and youth* (pp. 25–44). New York: Pergamon.

Gallop, R., Lancee, W. J., & Garfinkel, P. (1989). How nursing staff respond to the label "Borderline Personality Disorder." *Hospital and Community Psychiatry, 40* (8), 815–819.

Gannon, L. (1982). The role of power in psychotherapy. *Women and Therapy, 5* (2/3). 219–232.

Gelinas, D. J. (1983). The persisting negative effects of incest. *Psychiatry, 46* (4), 313–332.

Geller, J. L., & Munetz, M. R. (1988). The iatrogenic creation of psychiatric chronicity in women. In L. L. Barchrach & C. C. Nadelson (Eds.), *Treating chronically mentally ill women* (pp. 141–178). Washington, DC: American Psychiatric Association Press.

Gibson, D. (1990). Borderline personality disorder: Issues of etiology and gender. *Occupational Therapy in Mental Health, 10* (4), 63–77.

Gil, E. (1988). *Treatment of adult survivors of childhood abuse.* Walnut Creek, CA: Launch Press.

Gilbert, L. A. (1981). Toward mental health: The benefits of psychological androgyny. *Professional Psychology, 12* (1), 29–36.

Gilbert, S. M., & Gubar, S. (1979). *The madwoman in the attic: The woman writer and the nineteenth century literary imagination.* New Haven: Yale University Press.

Gilbertson, A. D., McGraw, L. K., & Brown, N. E. (1986). A different empirical perspective on sex bias in the diagnosis of DSM-III Axis II disorders. *Psychiatric Quarterly, 58* (2), 144–147.

Gilligan, C. (1982). *In a different voice.* Cambridge, MA: Harvard University Press.

Gilligan, C. (1991). Women's psychological development: Implications for psychotherapy. In C. Gilligan, A. G. Rogers, & D. L. Tolman (Eds.), *Women, girls and psychotherapy: Reframing resistance* (pp. 5–31). New York: Harrington Park Press.

Gilman, S. L. (1988). *Disease and representation: Images of illness from madness to AIDS.* Ithaca: Cornell University Press.

Goldberg, S., & Lewis, M. (1969). Play behavior in the year old infant: Early sex differences. *Child Development, 40,* 21–31.

Goldman, N., & Ravid, R. (1980). Community surveys: Sex differences in mental illness. In M. Guttentag, S. Salasin, & D. Belle (Eds.), *The Mental Health of Women* (pp. 31–55). New York: Academic Press.

Gomberg, E. S. (1981). Women, sex roles, and alcohol problems. *Professional Psychology, 12* (1), 146–154.

Goodwin, D. W., & Guze, S. B. (1989). *Psychiatric diagnosis.* New York: Oxford University Press.

Gove, W. R. (1980). Mental illness and psychiatric treatment among women. *Psychology of Women Quarterly, 4* (3), 345–362.

Gove, W. R., & Tudor, J. F. (1973). Adult sex roles and mental illness. *American Journal of Sociology, 78* (4), 812–835.

Green, B. L., Lindy, J. D., & Grace, M. C. (1985). Posttraumatic stress disorder: Toward DSM-IV. *Journal of Nervous and Mental Disease, 173* (7), 406–411.

Greenwald, E., Leitenberg, H., Cado, S., & Tarran, M. J. (1990). Childhood sexual abuse: Long-term effects on psychological and sexual functions in a nonclinical and nonstudent sample of adult women. *Child Abuse and Neglect, 14* (4), 503–513.

Grimm. (1989). *Household stories from the collection of the Bros. Grimm.* L. Crane, translator. New York: Dover. (Originally published 1886.)

Grinker, R., Sr., Werble, B., & Drye, R. (1968). *The borderline syndrome.* New York: Basic Books.

Gruenrich, R. (1992). The borderline personality disorder diagnosis: Reliability, diagnostic efficiency, and covariation with other personality disorder diagnoses. *Journal of Personality Disorders, 6* (3), 197–212.

Gunderson, J. G. (1984). *Borderline personality disorder.* Washington, DC: American Psychiatric Press.

Gunderson, J. G., & Elliott, G. R. (1985). The interface between borderline personality disorder and affective disorder. *American Journal of Psychiatry, 142* (3), 277–288.

Gunderson, J. G., Frank, A. F., Ronningstam, E. F., Wachter, S., Lynch, V. J., & Wolf, P. J. (1989). Early discontinuance of borderline patients from psychotherapy. *Journal of Nervous and Mental Disease, 177,* 38–42.

Gunderson, J. G., Kerr, J., & Englund, D. W. (1980). The families of borderlines: A comparative study. *Archives of General Psychiatry, 132* (1), 1–10.

Gunderson, J. G., Kolb, J., & Austin, V. (1981). The diagnostic interview for borderline patients. *American Journal of Psychiatry, 138,* 896–903.

Gunderson, J. G., Links, P. S., & Reich, J. H. (1991). Competing models of personality disorders. *Journal of Personality Disorders, 5* (1), 60–68.

Gunderson, J. G., & Sabo, A. N. (1993). The phenomenological and conceptual interface between borderline personality disorder and PTSD. *American Journal of Psychiatry, 150* (1), 19–27.

Gunderson, J. G., & Singer, M. T. (1975). Defining borderline patients. *American Journal of Psychiatry, 132,* 1–10.

Haan, N., & Livson, N. (1973). Sex differences in the eyes of expert personality assessors: Blind spots? *Journal of Personality Assessment, 37,* 492–496.

Hale, N. G., Jr. (1971). *Freud and the Americans: The beginnings of psychoanalysis in the United States, 1876–1917.* New York: Oxford University Press.

Hale, N. G., Jr. (1995). *The rise and crisis of psychoanalysis in the United States: Freud and the Americans,* vol. 2. New York: Oxford University Press.

Hamilton, S., Rothbart, M., & Dawes, R. M. (1986). Sex bias, diagnosis, and DSM-III. *Sex Roles, 15* (5/6), 269–274.

Hare-Mustin, R. T. (1983). An appraisal of the relationship between women and psycho-therapy: Eighty years after the case of Dora. *American Psychologist, 38,* 593–601.

Hare-Mustin, R. T., & Marecek, J. (1988). The meaning of difference: Gender theory, postmodernism, and psychology. *American Psychologist, 43,* 455–464.

Harris, L. Blum, R. W., & Resnick, M. (1991). Teen females in Minnesota: A portrait of quiet disturbance. In C. Gilligan, A. G. Rogers, & D. L. Tolman (Eds.), *Women, girls, and psychotherapy: Reframing resistance* (pp. 119–135). New York: Harrington Park Press.

Hart, S. N., Germain, R. B., & Brassard, M. R. (1987). The challenge: To better understand and combat psychological maltreatment of children and youth. In M. R. Brassard, R. Germain, & S. N. Hart (Eds.), *Psychological maltreatment of children and youth* (pp. 3–24). New York: Pergamon.

Harter, S. (1990). Self and identity development. In S. S. Feldman & G. R. Elliott (Eds.), *At the threshold: The developing adolescent* (pp. 352–387). Cambridge, MA: Harvard University Press.

Haugaard, J. J., & Emery, R. E. (1989). Methodological issues in child sexual abuse research. *Child Abuse and Neglect, 13* (1), 89–100.

Helzer, J. E., Robins, L. N., McEvoy, L. (1987). Post-traumatic stress disorder in the general population: Findings of the Epidemiologic Catchment Area Survey. *New England Journal of Medicine, 317* (26), 1630–1634.

Henry, K. A., & Cohen, C. I. (1983). The role of labeling processes in diagnosing borderline personality disorder. *American Journal of Psychiatry, 140* (11), 1527–1529.

Herman, J. (1981). *Father-daughter incest.* Cambridge, MA: Harvard University Press.

Herman, J., & Hirschmann, L. (1977). Father-daughter incest. *Signs: Journal of Women in Culture and Society, 2,* 735–756.

Herman, J., Russell, D., & Trocki, K. (1986). Long-term effects of incestuous abuse in childhood. *American Journal of Psychiatry, 143* (10), 1293–1296.

Herman, J., & van der Kolk, B. (1987). Traumatic antecedents of borderline personality disorder. In B. van der Kolk (Ed.), *Psychological trauma.* Washington, DC: American Psychiatric Press.

Herman, J. L. (1986). Histories of violence in an outpatient population: An exploratory study. *American Journal of Orthopsychiatry, 56* (1), 137–141.

Herman, J. L. (1992). *Trauma and recovery.* New York: Basic Books.

Herman, J. L., Perry, J. C., & van der Kolk, B. A. (1989). Childhood trauma in borderline personality disorder. *American Journal of Psychiatry, 146* (4), 460–465.

Heumann, K. A., Morey, L. C. (1990). Reliability of categorical and dimensional judgments of personality disorder. *American Journal of Psychiatry, 147* (4), 498–500.

Higonnet, Margaret. (1986). Speaking silences: Women's suicide. In S. R. Suleiman (Ed.), *The female body in Western culture: Contemporary perspectives* (pp. 68–83). Cambridge, MA: Harvard University Press.

Horney, K. (1937). *The neurotic personality of our time.* New York: W. W. Norton.

Horney, K. (1942). *Self analysis.* New York: W. W. Norton.

Horney, K. (1950). *Neurosis and human growth.* New York: W. W. Norton.

Horowitz, M. (1976). *Stress response syndromes.* New York: Jason Aronson.

Horwitz, A. V. (1982). Sex role expectations, power, and psychological distress. *Sex Roles, 8* (6), 607–623.

Howard, J. A. (1984). Societal influences of attribution: Blaming some victims more than others. *Journal of Personality and Social Psychology, 47,* 494–505.

Husain, A., & Chapel, J. L. (1983). History of incest in girls admitted to a psychiatric hospital. *American Journal of Psychiatry, 140* (5), 591–593.

Huston, A. (1983). Sex typing. In E. M. Hetherington (Ed.), *Handbook of child psychiatry,* vol. 4 (pp. 388–467). New York: John Wiley.

Hyler, S. E., Rieder, R. O., Williams, J. B. W., Spitzer, R. L., Lyons, M., & Hendler, J. (1989). A comparison of clinical and self-report diagnoses of DSM-III personality disorders in 552 patients. *Comprehensive Psychiatry, 30* (2), 170–178.

Israel, A. C., Raskin, P. A., Libow, J. A., & Pravder, M. D. (1978). Gender and sex-role appropriateness: Bias in the judgment of disturbed behavior. *Sex Roles, 4* (3), 399–413.

Jack, D. C. (1991). *Silencing the self: Women and depression.* Cambridge, MA: Harvard University Press.

Jack, R. (1992). *Women and attempted suicide.* Hillsdale, NJ: Lawrence Erlbaum.

Jacobson, A., & Richardson, B. (1987). Assault experiences of 100 psychiatric inpatients: Evidence of the need for routine inquiry. *American Journal of Psychiatry, 144* (7), 908–913.

James, A. (1964). *The diary of Alice James.* L. Edel (Ed.). New York: Dodd, Mead.

James, A. (1981). *The death and letters of Alice James: Selected correspondence.* R. B. Yeazell (Ed.). Berkeley: University of California Press.

James, W. (1977). What pragmatism means. In J. M. McDermott (Ed.), *The writings of William James.* Chicago: University of Chicago Press.

Janoff-Bulman, R. (1979). Characterological versus behavioral self-blame: Inquiries into depression and rape. *Journal of Personality and Social Psychology, 37,* 1798–1809.

Janoff-Bulman, R. (1985). The aftermath of victimization: Rebuilding shattered assumptions. In C. R. Figley (Ed.), *Trauma and its wake: The study and treatment of post-traumatic stress disorder* (pp. 15–35). New York: Brunner/Mazel.

Jones, W. H., Chernovetz, M. E., & Hansson, R. O. (1978). The enigma of androgyny: Differential implications for males and females? *Journal of Consulting and Clinical Psychology, 46* (2), 298–313.

Jordan, J. (1991). Empathy and self boundaries. In J. V. Jordan, A. G. Kaplan, J. B. Miller, I. P. Stiver, & J. L. Surrey (Eds.), *Women's growth in connection* (pp. 67–80). New York: Guilford.

Jordan, J., Surrey, J. L., & Kaplan, A. G. (1991). Women and empathy: Implications for psychological development and psychotherapy. In J. V. Jordan, A. G. Kaplan, J. B. Miller, I. P. Stiver, & J. L. Surrey (Eds.), *Women's growth in connection* (pp. 27–50). New York: Guilford.

Kaplan, M. (1983). A woman's view of the DSM-III. *American Psychologist, 38,* 786–792.

Kaplan, M. J., Winget, C., & Free, N. (1990). Psychiatrists' beliefs about gender-appropriate behavior. *American Journal of Psychiatry, 147* (7), 910–912.

Kaysen, S. (1993). *Girl, Interrupted.* New York: Turtle Bay.

Kegan, R. (1982). *The evolving self: Problem and process in human development.* Cambridge, MA: Harvard University Press.

Kemper, S. (1984). When to speak like a lady. *Sex Roles, 10* (5/6), 435–443.

Kernberg, O. (1967). Borderline personality organization. *Journal of the American Psychoanalytic Association, 15,* 641–685.

Kernberg, O. (1975). *Borderline conditions and pathological narcissism.* New York: Jason Aronson.

Kernberg, O. (1977). The structural diagnosis of borderline personality organization. In P. Hartocollis (Ed.), *Borderline personality disorders* (pp. 87–121). New York: International Universities Press.

Kernberg, O. (1980). *Internal world and external reality: Object relations theory applied.* New York: Jason Aronson.

Kernberg, O. (1984). *Severe personality disorders: Psychotherapeutic strategies.* New Haven: Yale University Press.

Kernberg, O. (1989). Theoretical perspectives. In R. Fine (Ed.), *Current and historical perspectives* on the borderline patient (pp. 123–148). New York: Brunner/Mazel. (Reprinted from *Borderline conditions and pathological narcissism,* chap. 5, by O. Kernberg, New York: Jason Aronson, 1975.)

Kessler, R. C., Brown, R., & Broman, C. (1981). Sex differences in psychiatric help-seeking: Evidence from four large-scale surveys. *Journal of Health and Social Behavior, 20,* 2–16.

Kirshner, L. A., & Johnston, L. (1983). Effects of gender on inpatient psychiatric hospitalization. *Journal of Nervous and Mental Disease, 171* (11), 651–657.

Kleinman, A. (1988). *Rethinking psychiatry: From cultural category to personal experience.* New York: Free Press.

Knight, R. (1953). Borderline states. *Bulletin of the Menninger Clinic, 17,* 1–12.

Kroll, J. (1993). *PTSD/borderlines in therapy: Finding the balance.* New York: Norton.

Kroll, J., Sines, L., Martin, K., Lari, S., Pyle, R., Zander, J. (1981). Borderline personality disorder: Construct validity of the concept. *Archives of General Psychiatry, 38,* 1021–1026.

Kroll, J. K. (1988). *The challenge of the borderline patient: Competency in diagnosis and treatment.* New York: W. W. Norton.

Landrine, H. (1989). The politics of personality disorder. *Psychology of Women Quarterly, 13,* 325–339.

Lane, A. J. (1990). *To Herland and beyond: The life and work of Charlotte Perkins Gilman.* New York: Pantheon.

Langer, E. J., & Abelson, R. P. (1974). A patient by any other name . . . : Clinician group difference in labeling bias. *Journal of Consulting and Clinical Psychology, 42* (1), 4–9.

Lasch, C. (1977). *Haven in a heartless world: The family besieged.* New York: Basic Books.

Lerner, H. G. (1974). The hysterical personality: A woman's disease. *Comprehensive Psychiatry, 15* (2), 157–164.

Lerner, H. G. (1983). Female dependency in context: Some theoretical and technical considerations. *American Journal of Orthopsychiatry, 53,* 697–705.

Lerner, H. G. (1988a). Internal prohibitions against female anger. In H. G. Lerner, *Women in therapy* (pp. 59–75). Northvale, NJ: Jason Aronson. (Reprinted from *American Journal of Psychoanalysis,* 1980, *40* [2], 137–148.)

Lerner, H. G. (1988b). Origins of envy and devaluation of women. In H. G. Lerner, *Women in therapy* (pp. 3–24). Northvale, NJ: Jason Aronson. (Reprinted from *Bulletin of the Menninger Clinic,* 1974, *38* [6], 538–553.)

Lilienfeld, S., Van Valkenburg, C., Larntz, K., Akiskal, H. (1986). The relationship of histrionic personality disorder to antisocial personality and somatization disorders. *American Journal of Psychiatry, 143,* 718–722.

Lindberg, F. H., & Distad, L. J. (1985). Post-traumatic stress disorders in women who experienced childhood incest. *Child Abuse and Neglect, 9* (3), 329–334.

Linehan, M. M. (1973). Suicide and attempted suicide: Study of perceived sex differences. *Perceptual and Motor Skills, 37,* 31–34.

Linehan, M. M. (1987). Dialectical behavior therapy for borderline personality disorder. *Bulletin of the Menninger Clinic, 51* (3), 261–276.

Linehan, M. M. (1993). *Cognitive-behavioral treatment of borderline personality disorder.* New York: Guilford.

Lipshitz, S. (1978). Women and psychiatry. In J. Chetwynd & O. Hartnett (Eds.), *The sex role system* (pp. 93–108). London: Routledge & Kegan Paul.

Livesley, W. J. (1986). Trait and behavioral prototypes of personality disorder. *American Journal of Psychiatry, 143* (6), 728–732.

Lofgren, D. P., Bemporad, J., King, J., Lindem, K., & O'Driscoll, G. (1991). A prospective follow-up study of so-called borderline children. *American Journal of Psychiatry, 148* (1), 1541–1547.

Loranger, A. W., Oldham, J. M., & Tulis, E. H. (1982). Familial transmission of DSM-III borderline personality disorder. *Archives of General Psychiatry, 39,* 795–799.

Loring, M., & Powell, B. (1988). Gender, race, and DSM-III: A study of the objectivity of psychiatric diagnostic behavior. *Journal of Health and Social Behavior, 29* (1), 1–22.

Ludolph, P. S., Westen, D., Misle, B., Jackson, A., Wixom, J., & Wiss, F. C. (1990). The borderline diagnosis in adolescents: Symptoms and developmental history. *American Journal of Psychiatry, 147* (4), 470–476.

Luthar, S. S., & Zigler, E. (1991). Vulnerability and competence: A review of research on resilience in childhood. *American Journal of Orthopsychiatry, 61,* 6–22.

Lykowski, J. C., & Tsuang, M. T. (1980). Precautions in treating DSM-III personality disorder. *American Journal of Psychiatry, 137,* 110–111.

Macaulay, J. (1985). Adding gender to aggression research: Incremental or revolutionary change? In V. E. O'Leary, R. K. Unger, & B.S. Wallston (Eds.), *Women, gender, and social psychology* (pp. 191–224). Hillsdale, NJ: Lawrence Erlbaum.

Maccoby, E. E. (1988). Gender as a social category. *Developmental Psychology, 24* (6), 755–765.

Maccoby, E. E., & Jacklin, C. N. (1974). *The psychology of sex differences.* Stanford: Stanford University Press.

Maccoby, E. E., & Jacklin, C. N. (1980). Sex differences in aggression: A rejoinder and reprise. *Child Development, 51,* 964–980.

Madonna, P. G., Van Scoyk, S., & Jones, D. P. H. (1991). Family interactions within incest and nonincest families. *American Journal of Psychiatry, 148* (1), 46–49.

Maffeo, P. A. (1979). Thoughts on Stricker's "Implications of research for psychotherapeutic treatment of women." *American Psychologist, 34,* 690–695.

Mahler, M. (1971). A study of the separation-individuation process and its possible application to borderline phenomena in the psychoanalytic situation. In M. S. Mahler (Ed.), *The selected papers of Margaret S. Mahler, M.D.,* vol. 2 (pp. 169–187). New York: Jason Aronson.

Mahler, M. S., & Kaplan, L. K. (1977). Developmental aspects in the assessment of narcissistic and so-called borderline personalities. In P. Hartocollis (Ed.), *Borderline personality disorders: The concept, the syndrome, the patient* (pp. 71–85). New York: International Universities Press.

Mahler, M. S., Pine, F., & Bergman, A. (1975). *The psychological birth of the human infant: Symbiosis and individuation.* New York: Basic Books.

Margo, G. M., & McClees, E. M. (1991). Further evidence for the significance of a childhood abuse history in psychiatric inpatients. *Comprehensive Psychiatry, 32,* 362–366.

Marsella, A. J. (1984). An interactional model of psychopathology. In B. Lubin & W. Connors (Eds.), *Ecological models in clinical and community psychiatry* (pp. 232–250). New York: Wiley.

Masterson, J. F. (1972). *Treatment of the borderline adolescent: A developmental approach.* New York: Wiley.

Masterson, J. F. (1976). *Psychotherapy of the borderline adult: A developmental approach.* New York: Brunner/Mazel.

Masterson, J. F. (Ed.). (1978). *New perspectives on the psychotherapy of the borderline adult.* New York: Brunner/Mazel.

Masterson, J. F. (1981). *The narcissistic and borderline disorders: An integrated developmental approach.* New York: Brunner/Mazel.

Masterson, J. F., & Rinsley, D. B. (1975). The borderline syndrome: The role of the mother in the genesis and psychic structure of the borderline personality. *International Journal of Psycho-Analysis, 56,* 163–178.

Maudsley, H. (1873). *Body and mind.* London: Macmillan.

McCullers, C. (1946). *The member of the wedding.* Boston: Houghton Mifflin.

McGlashan, T. H. (1987). Testing DSM-III symptom criteria for schizotypal and borderline personality disorders. *Archives of General Psychiatry, 44,* 143–148.

McKee, J. P., & Sheriffs, H. C. (1957). The differential evaluations of males and females. *Journal of Personality, 25,* 356–371.

McMillan, J. R., Clifton, A. K., McGrath, D., & Gale, W. S. (1977). Woman's language: Uncertainty or interpersonal sensitivity and emotionality? *Sex Roles, 3,* 545–559.

Meissner, W. W. (1989). Theoretical perspectives. In R. Fine (Ed.), *Current and historical perspectives on the borderline patient.* New York: Brunner/Mazel. (Reprinted from *The borderline spectrum: Differential diagnoses and developmental issues,* chap. 2, by W. W. Meissner, New York: Jason Aronson, 1984.)

Middlebrook, D. W. (1992). *Anne Sexton: A biography.* New York: Vintage Books.

Miller, J. B. (1976). *Toward a new psychology of women.* Boston: Beacon Press.

Miller, J. B. (1991a). The development of women's sense of self. In J. V. Jordan, A. G. Kaplan, J. B. Miller, I. P. Stiver, & J. L. Surrey (Eds.), *Women's growth in connection* (pp. 11–26). New York: Guilford.

Miller, J. B. (1991b). The construction of anger in women and men. In J. V. Jordan, A. G. Kaplan, J. B. Miller, I. P. Stiver, & J. L. Surrey (Eds.), *Women's growth in connection* (pp. 181–196). New York: Guilford.

Millon, T. (1987). On the genesis and prevalence of the borderline personality disorders: A social learning thesis. *Journal of Personality Disorders, 1,* 354–372.

Mitchell, S. A. (1988). *Relational concepts in psychoanalysis: An integration.* Cambridge, MA: Harvard University Press.

Mowbray, C. T., & Chamberlain, P. (1986). Sex differences among the long-term mentally disabled. *Psychology of Women Quarterly, 10,* 383–392.

Mowbray, C. T., Herman, S. E., & Hazel, K. L. (1992). Gender and serious mental illness. *Psychology of Women Quarterly, 16,* 107–126.

Murdock, N. L. (1988). Category-based effects in clinical judgment. *Counselling Psychology Quarterly, 1* (4), 341–355.

Nawas, M. M. (1971). Change in efficiency of ego functioning and complexity from adolescence to young adulthood. *Developmental Psychology, 4,* 412–415.

Newcomb, T. M. (1961). *The acquaintance process.* New York: Holt, Rinehart, & Winston.

Newson, J., Newson, E., Richardson, D., & Scaife, J. (1978). Perspectives in sex-role stereotyping. In J. Chetwynd & O. Hartnett (Eds.), *The sex role system* (pp. 29–49). London: Routledge & Kegan Paul.

Nigg, J. T., Silk, K. R., Westen, D., Lohr, N., Gold, L. J., Goodrich, S., & Ogata, S. (1991). Object representations in early memories of sexually abused borderline patients. *American Journal of Psychiatry, 148,* 864–869.

Nolen-Hoeksema, S. (1990). *Sex differences in depression.* Stanford: Stanford University Press.

Nowacki, C. M., & Poe, C. A. (1973). The concept of mental health as related to sex of person perceived. *Journal of Consulting and Clinical Psychology, 40* (1), 160.

Nurnberg, H. G., Hurt, S. W., Feldman, A., & Suh, R. (1988). Evaluation of diagnostic criteria for borderline personality disorder. *American Journal of Psychiatry, 145* (10), 1280–1283.

Nurnberg, H. G., Raskin, M., Levine, P. E., Pollack, S., Siegel, O., & Prince, R. (1991). The comorbidity of borderline personality disorder and other DSM-III-R Axis II personality disorders. *American Journal of Psychiatry, 148* (10), 1371-1377.

Ogata, S. N., Silk, K. R., Goodrich, S., Lohr, N. E., Westen, D., & Hill, E. M. (1990). Childhood sexual and physical abuse in adult patients with borderline personality disorder. *American Journal of Psychiatry, 147* (8), 1008–1013.

Oldham, J. M., Skodol, A. E., Kellman, H. D., Hyler, S. E., Rosnick, L., & Davies, M. (1992). Diagnosis of DSM-III-R personality disorders by two structured interviews: Patterns of comorbidity. *American Journal of Psychiatry, 149,* 213–220.

O'Leary, K. M., Cowdry, R. W., Gardner, D. L., Leibenluft, E., Lucas, P. B., & de Jong-Meyer, R. (1991). Dysfunctional attitudes in borderline personality disorder. *Journal of Personality Disorder, 5* (3), 233–242.

Orlinsky, D. E., & Howard, K. I. (1980). Gender and psychotherapeutic outcome. In A. Brodsky & R. T. Hare-Mustin (Eds.), *Women and psychotherapy* (pp. 3–34). New York: Guilford.

Palumbo, J. (1989). Critical review of the concept of the borderline child. In R. Fine (Ed.), *Current and historical perspectives on the borderline patient* (pp. 263–281). New York: Brunner/Mazel. (Reprinted from *Clinical Social Work,* 1982, *10* (4), 246–264.)

Paris, J. (1990). Completed suicide in borderline personality disorder. *Psychiatric Annals, 20* (1), 19–21.

Paris, J., Brown, R., Nowlis, D. (1987). Long-term follow up of borderline patients in a general hospital. *Comprehensive Psychiatry, 28,* 530–535.

Parsons, T., & Bales, R. (1955). *Family, socialization, and interaction process.* Glencoe, IL: Free Press.

Perry, J. C., & Cooper, S. H. (1986). A preliminary report on defenses and conflicts in borderline personality disorder. *Journal of the American Psychoanalytic Association, 34,* 863–893.

Perry, J. C., Herman, J. L., van der Kolk, B., & Hoke, L. A. (1990). Psychotherapy and psychological trauma in borderline personality disorder. *Psychiatric Annals, 20* (1), 33–43.

Phillips, D., & Segal, B. E. (1969). Sexual status and psychiatric symptoms. *American Sociological Review, 34* (1), 58–72.

Phillips, R. D., & Gilroy, F. D. (1985). Sex-role stereotypes and clinical judgments of mental health: The Brovermans' findings reexamined. *Sex Roles, 12* (1/2), 179–193.

Piliavin, J. A., & Unger, R. K. (1985). The helpful but helpless female: Myth or reality? In V. E. O'Leary, R. K. Unger, & B. S. Wallston (Eds.), *Women, gender, and social psychology* (pp. 149–189). Hillsdale, NJ: Lawrence Erlbaum.

Plath, S. (1981). *Collected poems.* T. Hughes (Ed.). New York: Harper & Row.

Plath, S. (1982). *The journals of Sylvia Plath.* T. Hughes & F. McCullough (Eds.). New York: Dial Press.

Pope, H. G., Jonas, J., Hudson, J., Cohen, B., Gunderson, J. (1983). The validity of DSM-III borderline personality disorder. *Archives of General Psychiatry, 40,* 23–30.

Reich, J. (1987). Sex distribution of DSM-III personality disorders in psychiatric outpatients. *American Journal of Psychiatry, 144,* 485–488.

Reis, H. T., & Wright, S. (1982). Knowledge of sex-role stereotypes in children aged 3 to 5. *Sex Roles, 8* (8), 1049–1056.

Reiser, D. E., & Levenson, H. (1984). Abuses of the borderline diagnosis: A clinical problem with teaching opportunities. *American Journal of Psychiatry, 141,* 1528–1532.

Richardson, M. S., & Johnson, M. (1984). Counseling women. In S. D. Brown & R. W. Lent (Eds.), *Handbook of counseling psychology* (pp. 832–877). New York: Wiley.

Rickles, N. K. (1971). The angry woman syndrome. *Archives of General Psychiatry, 24,* 91–94.

Rieker, P., & Carmen, E. (1986). The victim-to-patient process: The disconfirmation and transformation of abuse. *American Journal of Orthopsychiatry, 56* (3), 360–370.

Rinsley, D. (1977). An object-relations view of borderline personality. In P. Hartocollis (Ed.), *Borderline personality disorders* (pp. 47–70). New York: International Universities Press.

Robins, L. N., Helzer, J. E., Weissman, M. M., Orvaschel, H., Gruenberg, E., Burke, J. D., Jr., Regier, D. A. (1984). Lifetime prevalence of specific psychiatric disorders in three sites. *Archives of General Psychiatry, 41,* 949–959.

Robins, L. N., Locke, B. Z., & Regier, D. A. (1991). An overview of psychiatric disorders in America. In L. N. Robins & D. A. Regier (Eds.), *Psychiatric disorders in America: The epidemiologic catchment area study* (pp. 328–366). New York: Free Press.

Robins, L. N., & Regier, A. (Eds.). (1991). *Psychiatric disorders in America: The Epidemiologic Catchment Area study.* New York: Free Press.

Rosenberg, F. R., & Simmons, R. G. (1975). Sex differences in the self-concept in adolescence. *Sex Roles, 1* (2), 147–159.

Rosenfeld, A. A. (1979). Incidence of a history of incest among 18 female psychiatric patients. *American Journal of Psychiatry, 136,* 791–795.

Rosenkrantz, P. S., Vogel, S. R., Bee, H., Broverman, I. K., & Broverman, D. M. (1968). Sex-role stereotypes and self-concepts in college students. *Journal of Consulting and Clinical Psychology, 32* (3), 287–295.

Rosewater, L. B. (1988, Fall). Women who love too much: Victimizing the victim. *aWP Newsletter,* p. 11.

Rothbart, M. K., & Rothbart, M. (1976). Birth order, sex of child, and maternal help-giving. *Sex Roles, 2* (1), 39–46.

Rothblum, E. D. (1983). Sex role stereotypes and depression in women. In V. Franks & E. D. Rothblum (Eds.), *The stereotyping of women: Its effects on mental health* (pp. 83–111). New York: Springer.

Rothblum, E. D., & Franks, V. (1983). Introduction: Warning: Sex-role stereotypes may be hazardous to your health. In V. Franks & E. D. Rothblum (Eds.), *The stereotyping of women: Its effects on mental health* (pp. 3–10). New York: Springer.

Rubin, J. Z., Provenzano, F. J., & Luria, Z. (1976). The eye of the beholder: Parents' views on sex of newborns. In A. G. Kaplan & J. P. Bean (Eds.), *Beyond sex-role stereotypes: Readings toward a psychology of androgyny* (pp. 179–186). Boston: Little, Brown. (Reprinted from *American Journal of Orthopsychiatry,* 1974, *44* [4], 512–519.)

Ruddick, S. (1980). Maternal thinking. *Feminist Studies, 6,* 342–367.

Russ, M. J. (1992). Self-injurious behavior in patients with borderline personality disorder: Biological perspectives. *Journal of Personality Disorders, 6* (1), 64–81.

Russell, D. (1985). Psychiatric diagnosis and the oppression of women. *International Journal of Social Psychiatry, 31* (4), 298–305.

Russo, N. F., & Sobel, S. B. (1981). Sex differences in the utilization of mental health facilities. *Professional Psychology, 12* (1), 7–19.

Rutter, M. (1990). Psychosocial resilience and protective mechanisms. In J. E. Rolf, A. S. Masten, D. Cicchetti, K. H. Neuchterlein, & S. Weintraub (Eds.), *Risk and protective factors in the development of psychopathology* (pp. 181–214). New York: Cambridge University Press.

Rutter, M., & Garmezy, N. (1983). Developmental psychopathology. In E. M. Hetherington (Ed.), *Handbook of child psychology,* vol. 4 (pp. 776–911). New York: Wiley.

Ryan, W. (1976). *Blaming the victim.* New York: Vintage Books.

Saunders, E. A., & Arnold, F. (1991). Borderline personality disorder and childhood abuse: Revisions in clinical thinking and treatment approach. *Work in progress,* Working Paper series, No. 51. Wellesley Press: Stone Center for Developmental Services and Studies, Wellesley College.

Schafer, R. (1974). Problems in Freud's psychology of women. *Journal of the American Psychoanalytic Association, 22,* 459–485.

Schafer, R. (1984). The pursuit of failure and idealization of unhappiness. *American Psychologist, 39* (4), 398–405.

Scheff, T. J. (1984). *Being mentally ill: A sociological theory.* New York: Aldine.

Scull, A. (1989). *Social order/Mental disorder.* Berkeley: University of California Press.

Scull, A. (1993). *The most solitary of afflictions: Madness and society in Britain, 1700–1900.* New Haven: Yale University Press.

Scurfield, R. M. (1985). Post-trauma stress assessment and treatment: Overview and formulations. In C. R. Figley (Ed.), *Trauma and its wake: The study and treatment of post-traumatic stress disorder* (pp. 219–256). New York: Brunner/Mazel.

Seelig, B. J., & Person, E. S. (1991). A sadomasochistic transference: Its relation to distortions in the rapprochement subphase. *Journal of the American Psychoanalytic Association, 39,* 939–965.

Seiden, A. M. (1979). Gender differences in psychophysiological illnesses. In E. S. Gomberg & V. F. Franks (Eds.), *Gender and disordered behavior.* New York: Brunner/Mazel.

Serbin, L. A., O'Leary, K. D., Kent, R. N., & Tonick, I. J. (1973). A comparison of teacher response to the preacademic and problem behavior of boys and girls. *Child Development, 44,* 796–804.

Sexton, A. (1988). *Selected poems.* D. W. Middlebrook & D. H. George (Eds.). Boston: Houghton Mifflin.

Shapiro, D. (1981). *Autonomy and rigid character.* New York: Basic Books.

Shearer, S. L., Peters, C. P., Quaytman, M. S., & Ogden, R. L. (1990). Frequency and correlates of childhood sexual and physical abuse histories in adult female borderline inpatients. *American Journal of Psychiatry, 147* (2), 214–216.

Shearer, S. L., Peters, C. P., Quaytman, M. S., & Wadman, B. E. (1988). Intent and lethality of suicide attempts among female borderline inpatients. *American Journal of Psychiatry, 145* (11), 1424–1427.

Sheehy, M., Goldsmith, L., & Charles, E. (1980). A comparative study of borderline patients in a psychiatric outpatient clinic. *American Journal of Psychiatry, 137* (11), 1374–1379.

Sherif, C. W. (1979). Bias in psychology. In J. A. Sherman & E. T. Beck (Eds.), *The prism of sex* (pp. 93–133). Madison: University of Wisconsin Press.

Sherman, J. A. (1980). Therapist attitudes and sex-role stereotyping in psychotherapy with women. In A. M. Brodsky & R. T. Hare-Mustin (Eds.), *Women and psychotherapy* (pp. 35–66). New York: Guilford.

Showalter, E. (1985). *The female malady.* New York: Pantheon.

Sicherman, B. (1977). The uses of a diagnosis: Doctors, patients, and neurasthenia. *Journal of the History of Medicine, 32,* 33–54.

Skrypnek, B. J., & Snyder, M. (1982). On the self-perpetuating nature of stereotypes about women and men. *Journal of Experimental Social Psychology, 18,* 277–291.

Skultans, V. (1975). *Madness and morals: Ideas on insanity in the nineteenth century.* London: Routledge & Kegan Paul.

Smith, M. L. (1980). Sex bias in counseling and psychotherapy. *Psychological Bulletin, 87,* 392–407.

Smith-Rosenberg, C. (1972). The hysterical woman: Sex roles in nineteenth century America. *Social Research, 39,* 652–678.

Spence, J. T., Helmreich, R., & Stapp, J. (1975). Ratings of self and peers on sex role attributes and their relation to self-esteem and conceptions of masculinity and femininity. *Journal of Personality and Social Psychology, 32* (1), 29–39.

Spence, J. T., & Sawin, L. L. (1985). Images of masculinity and femininity: A reconceptualization. In V. E. O'Leary, R. K. Unger, & B. S. Wallston, *Women, gender, and social psychology* (pp. 35–66). Hillsdale, NJ: Lawrence Erlbaum.

Sroufe, L. A., & Fleeson, J. (1986). Attachment and the construction of relationships. In W. Hartup & Z. Rubin (Eds.), *Relationships and development.* Hillsdale, NJ: Lawrence Erlbaum.

Sroufe, L. A., & Rutter, M. (1984). The domain of developmental psychopathology. *Child Development, 55,* 17–29.

Stake, J. E. (1992). Gender differences and similarities in self-concept within everyday life contexts. *Psychology of Women Quarterly, 16,* 349–363.

Stangl, D., Pfohl, B., Zimmerman, M., Bowers, W., & Corenthal, C. (1985). A structured interview for the DSM-III personality disorders. *Archives of General Psychiatry, 42,* 591–596.

Stern, D. N. (1985). *The interpersonal world of the infant: A view from psychoanalysis and developmental psychology.* New York: Basic Books.

Stern, L. (1991). Disavowing the self in female adolescence. In C. Gilligan, A. G. Rogers, & D. L. Tolman (Eds.), *Women, girls, and psychotherapy: Reframing resistance* (pp. 105–117). New York: Harrington Park Press.

Stiver, I. P. (1991a). The meanings of "dependency" in female-male relationships. In J. V. Jordan, A. G. Kaplan, J. B. Miller, I. P. Stiver, & J. L. Surrey (Eds.), *Women's growth in connection* (pp. 143–161). New York: Guilford.

Stiver, I. P. (1991b). The meaning of care: Reframing treatment models. In J. V. Jordan, A. G. Kaplan, J. B. Miller, I. P. Stiver, & J. L. Surrey (Eds.), *Women's growth in connection* (pp. 250–267). New York: Guilford.

Stone, M. H. (1980). *The borderline syndromes: Constitution, personality and adaptation.* New York: McGraw-Hill.

Stone, M. H. (1990). Toward a comprehensive typology of personality. *Journal of Personality Disorders, 4,* 416–421.

Stone, M. H., Unwin, A., Beacham, B., & Swenson, C. (1988). Incest in female borderlines: Its frequency and impact. *International Journal of Family Psychiatry, 9* (3), 277–293.

Storr, A. (1960). *The integrity of the personality.* London: Routledge & Kegan Paul.

Stricker, G. (1977). Implications of research for psychotherapeutic treatment of women. *American Psychologist, 32,* 14–22.

Strouse, J. (1980). *Alice James: A biography.* New York: Bantam Books.

Surrey, J., Swett, C., Michaels, A., & Levin, S. (1990). Reported history of physical and sexual abuse and severity of symptomatology in women psychiatric outpatients. *American Journal of Orthopsychiatry, 60* (3), 412–417.

Swartz, M., Blazer, D., George, L., & Winfield, I. (1990). Estimating the prevalence of borderline personality disorder in the community. *Journal of Personality Disorders, 4* (3), 257–272.

Swett, C., Surrey, J., & Cohen, C. (1990). Sexual and physical abuse histories and psychiatric symptoms among male psychiatric patients. *American Journal of Psychiatry, 147* (5), 632–636.

Szasz, T. S. (1961). *The myth of mental illness.* New York: Hoeber-Harper.

Taylor, E. (1984). *William James on exceptional mental states: The 1896 Lowell Lectures.* Amherst: University of Massachusetts Press.

Taylor, S. (1982). *Durkheim and the study of suicide.* London: Macmillan.

Tellegen, A., & Lubinski, D. (1983). Some methodological comments on labels, traits, interaction, and types in the study of "femininity" and "masculinity": Reply to Spence. *Journal of Personality and Social Psychology, 44* (2), 447–455.

Temerlin, M. K. (1968). Suggestion effects in psychiatric diagnosis. *Journal of Nervous and Mental Disease, 147,* 349–353.

Teri, L. (1982). Effects of sex and sex-role style on clinical judgment. *Sex Roles, 8* (6), 639–649.

Terr, L. C. (1991). Childhood traumas: An outline and overview. *American Journal of Psychiatry, 148* (1), 10–29.

Tevlin, H. E., & Leiblum, S. R. (1983). Sex-role stereotypes and female sexual dysfunction. In V. Franks & E. D. Rothblum (Eds.), *The stereotyping of women* (pp. 129–150). New York: Springer.

Trimble, M. R. (1985). Post-traumatic stress disorder: History of a concept. In C. R. Figley (Ed.), *Trauma and its wake: The study and treatment of post-traumatic stress disorder* (pp. 5–14). New York: Brunner/Mazel.

Trull, T. J., Widiger, T. A., & Guthrie, P. Categorical versus dimensional status of borderline personality disorder. *Journal of Abnormal Psychology, 99* (1), 40–48.

Unger, R. K. (1978). The politics of gender: A review of relevant literature. In J. Sherman & F. Denmark (Eds.), *The psychology of women: Future directions of research* (pp. 459–518). New York: Psychological Dimensions.

Unger, R. K. (1979). Toward a redefinition of sex and gender. *American Psychologist, 34,* 1085–1094.

Ussher, J. (1992). *Women's madness: Misogyny or mental illness?* Amherst: University of Massachusetts Press.

van der Kolk, B. A. (1984). *Post-traumatic stress disorders: Psychological and biological sequelae.* Washington, DC: American Psychiatric Press.

van der Kolk, B. A., Perry, J. C., & Herman, J. L. (1991). Childhood origins of self-destructive behavior. *American Journal of Psychiatry, 148,* 1665–1671.

Waites, Elizabeth. (1993). *Trauma and survival: Post-traumatic and dissociative disorders in women.* New York: Norton.

Wakefield, J. C. (1987). Sex bias in the diagnosis of primary orgasmic dysfunction. *American Psychologist, 42* (5), 464–471.

Waldinger, R. J., & Gunderson, J. G. (1984). Completed psychotherapies with borderline patients. *American Journal of Psychotherapy, 38,* 190–201.

Waldinger, R. J., & Gunderson, J. G. (1987). *Effective psychotherapy with borderline patients.* New York: Macmillan.

Walker, L. E. (1981). Battered women: Sex roles and clinical issues. *Professional Psychology: Research and Practice, 12* (1), 81–91.

Walkerdine, V. (1990). *School girl fictions.* London: Virago.

Wallace, E. R. (1988). What is "truth"? Some philosophical contributions to psychiatric issues. *American Journal of Psychiatry, 145* (2), 137–147.

Wallston, B. S., & Grady, K. E. (1985). Integrating the feminist critique and the crisis in social psychology: Another look at research methods. In V. E. O'Leary, R. K. Unger, & B. S. Wallston (Eds.), *Women, gender, and social psychology* (pp. 7–33). Hillsdale, NJ: Lawrence Erlbaum.

Walsh, F. (1977). Family study 1976: Fourteen new borderline cases. In R. R. Grinker & B. C. Werble (Eds.), *The borderline patient* (pp. 121–126). New York: Jason Aronson.

Warner, R. (1978). The diagnosis of antisocial and hysterical personality disorders: An example of sex bias. *Journal of Nervous and Mental Disease, 166* (12), 839–845.

Warner, R. (1979). Racial and sexual bias in psychiatric diagnosis. *Journal of Nervous and Mental Disease, 167* (5), 303–310.

Wasserman, G. A., & Lewis, M. (1985). Infant sex differences: Ecological effects. *Sex Roles, 12* (5/6), 665–675.

Weissman, M., & Klerman, G. (1977). Sex differences in the epidemiology of depression. *Archives of General Psychiatry, 34,* 98–111.

Weissman, M. M., Bruce, M. L., Leaf, P. J., Florio, L. P., & Holser III, C. (1991). Affective disorders. In L. N. Robins & D. A. Regier (Eds.), *Psychiatric disorders in America: The Epidemiologic Catchment Area study* (pp. 53–80). New York: Free Press.

Werner, E. E. (1989). High-risk children in young adulthood: A longitudinal study from birth to 32 years. *American Journal of Orthopsychiatry, 59,* 72–81.

Werner, P. D., & La Russa, G. W. (1985). Persistence and change in sex-role stereotypes. *Sex Roles, 12* (9/10), 1089–1100.

Westen, D., Ludolph, P., Misle, B., Ruffins, S., & Block, J. (1990). Physical and sexual abuse in adolescent girls with borderline personality disorder. *American Journal of Orthopsychiatry, 60* (1), 55–66.

Westkott, M. (1986). *The feminist legacy of Karen Horney.* New Haven: Yale University Press.

Wheeler, B. R., & Walton, E. (1987). Personality disturbances of adult incest victims. *Social Casework, 68,* 597–602.

Whitely, B. E. (1979). Sex roles and psychopathology: A current appraisal. *Psychological Bulletin, 86,* 1309–1321.

Whitely, B. E. (1983). Sex role orientation and self-esteem: A critical meta-analytic review. *Journal of Personality and Social Psychology, 44,* 765–778.

Widiger, T. A., & Frances, A. J. (1989). Epidemiology, diagnosis, and comorbidity of borderline personality disorder. In A. Tasman, R. E. Hales, & A. J. Frances (Eds.), *Review of psychiatry,* vol. 8, Washington, DC: American Psychiatric Press.

Widiger, T. A., Frances, A., Spitzer, R. L., & Williams, J. B. W. (1988). The DSM-III-R personality disorders: An overview. *American Journal of Psychiatry, 145* (7), 786–795.

Widiger, T. A., & Rogers, J. H. (1989). Prevalence and comorbidity of personality disorders. *Psychiatric Annals, 19,* 132–136.

Widiger, T. A., & Settle, S. A. (1987). Broverman et al. revisited: An artifactual sex bias. *Journal of Personality and Social Psychology, 53* (3), 463–469.

Widiger, T. A., & Spitzer, R. L. (1991). Sex bias in the diagnosis of personality disorders: Conceptual and methodological issues. *Clinical Psychology Review, 11,* 1–22.

Widiger, T. A., Trull, T. J., Hurt, S. W., Clarkin, J., & Frances, A. (1987). A multidimensional scaling of the DSM-III personality disorders. *Archives of General Psychiatry, 44,* 557–563.

Wile, D. B. (1984). Kohut, Kernberg, and accusatory interpretations. *Psychotherapy, 21* (3), 353–364.

Wile, D. B. (1993). *After the fight: A night in the life of a couple.* New York: Guilford.

Williams, J. B. W., & Spitzer, R. L. (1983). The issue of sex bias in *DSM-III:* A critique of "A Woman's View of *DSM-III*" by Marcie Kaplan. *American Psychologist, 38,* 793–798.

Williams, J. E., & Bennett, S. M. (1975). The definition of sex stereotypes via the adjective check list. *Sex Roles, 1* (4), 327–337.

Wilson, J. P., Smith, W. K., & Johnson, S. K. (1985). A comparative analysis of PTSD among various survivor groups. In C. R. Figley (Ed.), *Trauma and its wake: The study and treatment of post-traumatic stress disorder* (pp. 142–172). New York: Brunner/Mazel.

Wolfe, D. A. (1987). *Child abuse: Implications for child development and psychopathology.* Newbury Park, CA: Sage.

Wood, A. D. (1973). "The fashionable diseases": Women's complaints and their treatment in nineteenth-century America. *Journal of Interdisciplinary History, 4* (1), 25–52.

Wylie, M. S. (1995). DSM and the medical model. *Family Therapy Networker,* May/June, p. 27.

Zanarini, M. C., Gunderson, J. G., & Frankenburg, F. R. (1990). Cognitive features of borderline personality disorder. *American Journal of Psychiatry, 147* (1), 57–63.

Zanarini, M. C., Gunderson, J. G., Frankenburg, F. R., & Chauncey, D. L. (1990). Discriminating borderline personality disorders from other Axis II disorders. *American Journal of Psychiatry, 147* (2), 161–167.

Zanarini, M. C., Gunderson, J. G., Frankenburg, F. R., Chauncey, D. L., & Glutting, J. H. (1991). The face validity of the DSM-III and DSM-III criteria sets for borderline personality disorder. *American Journal of Psychiatry, 148* (7), 870–874.

Zanarini, M. C., Gunderson, J. G., Marino, M. F., Schwartz, E. O., Frankenburg, F. R. (1989). Childhood experiences of borderline patients. *Comprehensive Psychiatry, 30* (1), 18–25.

Zanna, M. P., & Pack, S. J. (1975). On the self-fulfilling nature of apparent sex differences in behavior. *Journal of Experimental Social Psychology, 11,* 583–591.

Zeldow, P. B. (1978). Sex differences in psychiatric evaluation and treatment: An empirical review. *Archives of General Psychiatry, 35,* 89–93.

Zigler, E., & Glick, M. (1986). The influence of gender and socioeconomic status on psychopathology. In E. Zigler & M. Glick (Eds.), *A developmental approach to adult psychopathology* (pp. 239–258). New York: Wiley.

Zigler, E., & Phillips, L. (1961). Psychiatric diagnosis: A critique. *Journal of Abnormal and Social Psychology, 63* (3), 607–618.

About the Book and Author

To what extent is borderline personality disorder (BPD) a truly "female" affliction? This question and others are addressed within the context of traditional ideas about women and madness and the psychiatric profession's views of women.

In a refreshing look at the reasons why a preponderance of women are diagnosed with BPD, Dana Becker provides evidence that the struggles of "borderline" women are extreme versions of the day-to-day struggles many women face. Examining the relationship between gender, psychological distress, and the classification of BPD as a psychiatric disorder, the author offers a new emphasis on elements of female socialization as keys to understanding the development of borderline symptoms.

The book offers insight to psychologists, psychiatrists, social workers, and other mental health professionals in addition to graduate students in these disciplines. It will also be valuable to those involved in the fields of women's studies, psychology of women, sociology, and the history of medicine.

Dana Becker, Ph.D., is clinical supervisor of family therapy at the Center for Research on Adolescent Drug Abuse at Temple University. She maintains a private practice in both Philadelphia and Rosemont, Pennsylvania, specializing in the treatment of women and families.

Index